365 Recipes

That will make you

THINK POSITIVE

Alan Cohen

PUSTAK MAHAL®

Delhi • Bangalore • Mumbai • Patna • Hyderabad • London

Published in India in arrangement with Hay House Publications, USA

Publishers
Pustak Mahal®, Delhi

J-3/16 , Daryaganj, New Delhi-110002
☎ 23276539, 23272783, 23272784 • *Fax:* 011-23260518
E-mail: info@pustakmahal.com • *Website:* www.pustakmahal.com

Sales Centre
10-B, Netaji Subhash Marg, Daryaganj, New Delhi-110002
☎ 23268292, 23268293, 23279900 • *Fax:* 011-23280567
E-mail: rapidexdelhi@indiatimes.com

Branch Offices
Bangalore: ☎ 22234025 • *Telefax:* 22240209
E-mail: pmblr@sancharnet.in • pustak@sancharnet.in
Mumbai: ☎ 22010941
E-mail: rapidex@bom5.vsnl.net.in
Patna: ☎ 3294193 • *Telefax:* 0612-2302719
E-mail: rapidexptn@rediffmail.com
Hyderabad: *Telefax:* 040-24737290
E-mail: pustakmahalhyd@yahoo.co.in

This book was earlier published with the title
"365 Gems for Holistic Living"

Edited by: Jill Kramer
Designed by: Highpoint, Inc., Claremont, CA

ISBN 978-81-223-0860-0

Printed at : Param Offsetters, Okhla, New Delhi-110020

Introduction

The journey through a year of life is a wondrous and sacred adventure. Each day brings fresh opportunities to surpass limits and step into our highest identity. Every new moment invites us to release fear and choose love as our guide.

The path can be difficult if we attempt to walk it alone; even while we are whole, we must reach out for support and be open to receive help to weather the challenging times. Indeed, we are not asked to do it all by ourselves; the Great Spirit would not leave us feeling abandoned, and we are sent many friends and supporters to uphold us as we master our lessons.

Consider this book a hand to hold as you scale the mountain of your destiny. In just a few minutes each day, you can step back from your worldly activity and draw in a deep breath of spiritual renewal. You might like to savor each message in the morning to start your day on a positive keynote, and/or review your day in the light of the principles.

Each day's message includes a theme, a quote of wisdom, a parable or real-life anecdote, a prayer, and an affirmation. After reading the day's message, close your eyes for a few moments, and be with the prayer and affirmation. Take these powerful ideas into your subconscious, and allow the truth to shine away any darkness. The spirit within you will expand miraculously as you nourish your inner being.

There is no limit to the healing, inspiration, and positive changes you can enjoy though applying the principles contained between these covers. March on to the high calling of your heart, and your life will be a testament to the magnificence that is you.

— *Alan Cohen*

Contents

1

Clean Slate

Grand adventures await those who
are willing to turn the corner.
— Chinese fortune cookie

In the film *Clean Slate*, Dana Carvey portrays a man named Pogue who has an unusual type of amnesia—when he goes to sleep each night, he forgets everything that happened to him before that time. A woman who had once manipulated Pogue asks him, "Can you ever forgive me for what I did to you last week?"

In an utterly childlike way, Pogue shrugs his shoulders and answers, "Sure!" Of course he can—he doesn't have the slightest clue what she did to him! As far as he is concerned, nothing ever happened; his relationship with her is as new as the current day.

As you enter this new year, nothing in the past has any power to affect what you do now. You are an entirely new person, different from the person you were. This year has never been lived before, and you have never had the consciousness you now have. You are setting sail on a great adventure determined only by how grand you are willing to think. This year, think big thoughts to create miraculous results.

I pray to start over. No matter what has happened,
I am willing to let today be new.
Thank you for the chance to begin again.

Today I begin anew.
I see through the eyes of innocence.

2

Act Now

There are two fatal errors that keep
great projects from coming to life:
1. Not finishing
2. Not starting

— Buddha

While living at a farming community, our group planned to erect a new house. For many months, we discussed the plans, and because we did not fully agree, nothing was done. Then one day, one man went out to the building site with a plumb line and began to hammer stakes into the ground. It wasn't long before the house was built.

You can think and talk about a project for a long time, but only action will manifest it. If you wait until you're ready, you'll never get anything done. Don't wait until all the conditions are perfect for you to begin. Beginning makes the conditions perfect.

Work through my hands to bring about the things that will serve You.

I step forward with the trust that Spirit is moving through me to create good.

3

Grow with the Flow

I said to a man who stood at the gate of the year:
"Give me a light that I may tread safely into the unknown."
And he replied, "Go out into the darkness and
put your hand in the hand of God. That shall be to you
better than a light and safer than a known way."
— Quoted by King George VI of England

Two men were walking beside a river on their way to a town downstream when a storm broke, and a flash flood washed both men into the river. One man panicked, tried to fight his way back to shore, and drowned. The other man realized that the torrent was beyond his control and relaxed to the best of his ability, letting the river carry him. To his happy surprise, the river deposited him on the banks of the town he was headed toward, in a much shorter time than it would have taken him to walk.

When you come up against a situation you cannot control, trust that the universe is working on your behalf. When we fight what is, we lose our power. The sage capitalizes on the energy at hand and makes it work on his behalf.

Help me to remember that You are present in all situations, guiding me home even when I cannot see how.

I am always in the presence of love. Everything that happens to me is a part of the plan for my good.

4

May I Feed You?

Risk! Risk anything! Care no more for the opinion of others, for those voices.
Do the hardest thing on earth for you.
Act for yourself. Face the truth.

— Katherine Mansfield

Waiting for the airplane to take off, I was happy to get a seat by myself. Just then, a flight attendant approached me and asked, "Would you mind changing your seat? A couple would like to sit together." The only other available seat was next to a woman with both arms in casts, a black-and-blue face, and a gloomy aura. No way am I going to sit there, was my immediate thought. But then a deeper, quieter voice spoke, *"Opportunity."* I took my new seat and discovered that Kathy had been in an auto collision, and she was on her way for therapy.

When the snack of nuts and juice arrived, it did not take me long to realize that Kathy would not be able to feed herself. I considered offering to feed her but resisted, as it seemed too intimate a service to offer to a stranger. But then I decided that Kathy's need was more important than my discomfort. I offered to help her eat, and although she too was uncomfortable about accepting, she did. The experience was exhilarating, and she and I grew close in a short period of time. By the end of the five-hour trip, my heart was fully alive, and the time was infinitely better spent than if I had just sat by myself.

I was very glad I had reached beyond my comfort zone to sit next to Kathy and feed her. Love always flows beyond human borders and dissolves the fears that keep us separate. When we stretch to serve another, we grow to live in a larger, more rewarding world.

Help me move beyond the small self so I can connect with the hearts of others.

When I give love to another, I feed my own soul.

5

Be Firm

If you come to a fork in the road, take it.

— Yogi Berra

I was struck by an unusual ad in the classified section of the local newspaper: *"Dodge truck for sale. $5,000 firm or best offer."* Was the price firm, or was the seller willing to negotiate? Apparently he couldn't make up his mind.

Life will support us in our decisions, but we have to make a decision around which the universe can gather. Often it is better to make a wrong decision than no decision. If you make an error, you can either correct it or learn from it; in either case you will move ahead. If you make no decision, you will likely remain just where you are.

A friend of mine had an inspiring bumper sticker on her washing machine: *Sin Boldly.* I loved it! The message, as I understood it, was an advisory to live life with conviction and a whole heart. Be fully whatever you are. The Bible tells us that God "spews the lukewarm out of His mouth." If you are in life, then be fully in life. Don't sit around wondering what you might do until it is too late to do anything. Will Rogers said, "You might be on the right track, but if you are sitting on it, you are going to get run over."

Live by choice, not self-protection. Be active rather than reactive. Make a stand for your truth, and your truth will make a stand for you.

Support me to walk my talk.

My power comes from being what I am.

6

Limitbusters

Do the thing you fear, and the death of fear is certain.
— Ralph Waldo Emerson

"May I speak to you for a moment?" the older woman asked the young hunk on the beach.

"Well, I was hoping to have some quiet time," he replied.

"I won't bother you—I just need to tell you something."

"Okay."

She pulled her beach towel next to his. "I need to talk to you because I am afraid to," Beverly confessed. "I feel too shy to speak to good-looking men who are younger than I am. When I saw you today, I wanted to talk to you, but I felt anxious. So I had to do this to break my sense of 'I can't.'"

The man thanked Beverly for her honesty, and the two engaged in pleasant conversation. Then she excused herself and walked away, stronger than she was when she approached him.

Fear tells us that we are small, powerless, and separate. Love affirms that we are great, creative, and connected. Which voice do you choose to be your guide?

The way to dissolve a limit is to step right up to it and look it in the eye. When we shine the light on the darkness, we see that the thing we ran from had power over us only as long as we kept it at a distance. When we face what frightens us, we discover that we are bigger than it is. We can do anything we choose; we were not born to live in fear, but in love.

I am free as God created me.

I am bigger than fear.
I step forward and live in the light.

7

Finally Made Something

What should it profit a man if he gains the world but loses his soul?

— Jesus Christ

As a boy, my idol was baseball star Mickey Mantle. Along with millions of other kids, I dreamed of playing centerfield for the Yankees, slamming home runs over the fence to the tune of a huge crowd's roar of adoration, and winning the Most Valuable Player Award. Several years ago, I saw an interview with Mickey Mantle after he had come out of the Betty Ford Clinic. I was stunned to learn that my hero had succumbed to a long and grisly bout with alcoholism. The interviewer asked the former star, nearing death due to liver damage, "How would you like people to remember Mickey Mantle?"

With great humility, he answered, "I would like people to think that I finally made something of myself."

Finally? I couldn't believe my ears! If anybody had ever made anything of himself, I thought, it was Mickey Mantle, the most loved and respected athlete of an entire generation. The Mick was the king. Yet, through his eyes, all his stardom was for naught in the face of his losses to drink. To Mickey Mantle, overcoming his alcoholism was a far greater achievement than all the home runs he'd ever hit.

All worldly glory pales in comparison to spiritual awakening. Mickey Mantle mastered his lesson of a lifetime when he graduated from the Betty Ford Clinic. No matter what accolades we achieve in the outer world, it is our inner life we need to come to terms with. Although he had all the laurels a man could dream of, Mickey Mantle found peace only when he found himself.

Should you be tempted to trade inner peace for worldly glory, remember the Mick. It's what's inside that counts.

Help me remember where my true peace lies.

**I am a spiritual being.
I nourish my spirit and I am fed.**

8

From the Rooftops

If only you could love, you would be the most powerful being in the world.

— Emmet Fox

I walked off the airplane along with hundreds of passengers at 11:00 P.M., drenched in weariness after five hours of air travel. Just then I noticed a young man striding down the jetway wearing a huge wooden sign in the shape of a heart, painted with red letters: *"Pam, will you marry me?"*

I looked ahead to see an attractive young woman waiting for him at the door. This is going to be rich, I thought, as I positioned myself to view this historic proposal. Sure enough, the fellow got down on one knee and asked for her hand in marriage. Although Pam was terribly embarrassed, she uttered a definite "yes," echoed by a round of applause from the crowd that had gathered. All the tired travelers came to life in the presence of this bold expression of love, and we walked lightheartedly together to the escalator, laughing and talking buoyantly.

Can you imagine how the world would be different if we all made such a stand to manifest our dreams? *A Course in Miracles*[1] tells us that all acts are expressions of love, either as skillful statements or calls for love in disguised forms. Love is the power that moves the universe, and it is the aching need of our world. If only we stood for love as we have for fear!

Practice expressing your love courageously. My friend Jeffrey has devoted his life to giving love. Whenever he sees me, he showers caring upon me through word, hug, and energy. He is one of the happiest people I know. He is a love giver rather than a love seeker. In giving what he wants, he has gotten it all.

Give me the courage to express my true caring without fear or reservation.

I stand for love, and love stands for me.

9

Your Point of Power

Don't play for safety. It's the most dangerous thing in the world.

— Hugh Walpole

When popular singer Bobby McFerrin got bored with his performances, he faced a crossroad in his career. After the smash success of his 1988 song, "Don't Worry, Be Happy," he set out on a long and grueling concert tour—but then the joy fell out. "I wasn't being fair to my audiences or myself," McFerrin confessed. "I wasn't present. I wasn't scared anymore." McFerrin dropped out for two years, spent quality time with his family, and explored novel musical forms. He came back fresh and imaginative, established the groundbreaking ensemble, Synchestra, performed duets with premier cellist Yo Yo Ma, and went into classical conducting.

I attended a most innovative Bobby McFerrin concert, during which I and the rest of the audience waited the entire evening for Bobby to sing "Don't Worry, Be Happy." He didn't.

I have a formula for knowing if a next step is the right one for you: If you feel both excited and scared, that is it. If you're just excited and not afraid, there is no challenge, no stretching, no initiation; you are still in your safe zone, and growth is unavailable. If you're just afraid, there is no positive motivation. Why walk though a fear unless there is something you are walking toward? But if you are simultaneously turned on and frightened, do it and watch your growth skyrocket.

You owe it to yourself, your loved ones, and your clients to stay on your cutting edge. If your career or relationship is a bore, step back and ask yourself what it would take to make it exciting. Then ask yourself what it would take to make it scary. The intersection of the two answers is your point of power.

I pray to follow my spirit and walk past fear to make my dreams come true.

**Powered by enthusiasm,
I step forward to greater things.**

10

One Frog Per Hand

Never try to catch two frogs with one hand.

— Country wisdom

I remember a television entertainer who balanced spinning plates on thin wooden sticks. At first his act looked easy as he added one plate at a time to the array. Then his job became tense and hilarious as he tried to keep all the teetering plates spinning without letting them fall and crash.

Many of us try to do so many things at once that we don't get any of them done well. Instead of expanding with creative joy, we succumb to "Management by Emergency." We say yes to more than we can handle and then spend most of our time putting out fires. We take on so many projects that we cannot give any of them the attention they deserve, and we leave ourselves overworked, exhausted, ineffective, and sometimes ill.

When my mother was in the hospital awaiting surgery, she was very unhappy. Her biggest complaint was that no doctor would give her quality time; her physicians would rush in and out and treat her like an item on an assembly line. The day before her surgery, I went to visit her, and she was beaming. "I saw the nicest doctor today!" she exclaimed. "He sat down with me, drew me a diagram of what he was going to do, and answered all my questions patiently. Now I feel peaceful."

To be a true healer, teacher, minister, parent, or business person, you will gain more in the long run by giving your clients quality attention. To be successful, no matter what your vocation, you must be fully present with whatever you're doing. Life is best lived one wholehearted moment at a time.

I want to live a quality life. Let me say yes to what belongs to me and let all else go.

My presence is the present.
I give my whole heart, and I find true reward.

11

Big Love, Big Fear

True love calls forth everything unlike itself.
— A Course in Miracles

In my seminars, I often notice a point where most people get a little crazy. Usually around the second or third day of a week-long program, participants start to feel afraid, angry, jealous, small, withdrawn, or lustful. I find this fascinating, since the purpose of the program is to increase the experience of love in our lives; so why should everything *unlike* love come up?

Fear arises because it can be healed in such an environment. Every person on the planet carries a hidden pool of pain and grief. As young children, we were taught very methodically to stuff our pain and sadness to accommodate those around us who could not deal with it. We went on with our lives being unhappy, but not knowing exactly why. Then when we enter into an intimate relationship, open up to a trustworthy counselor, or attend a quality seminar, the buried sewage comes rushing to the surface. *This is wonderful.* The soul knows that for the first time in a very long time it is safe to look at these issues, process them, and heal them so we can get on with enjoying the love that is available.

Dr. Barry Vissell and his wife, Joyce Vissell[2], who offer relationship workshops, described the process this way: "Our method is simple. We just turn up the love light as bright as we can. In that environment, everything unlike love shows up really clearly."

Singer Kenny Loggins explains the phenomenon this way: "Big love calls forth big fear." If you love someone a great deal, you will bump up against the blocks to love you have erected to protect yourself. But don't stop there. The fence has been shown to you not to imprison you; you have already been imprisoned. Now it is time to dismantle it and be free.

Show me where I have protected myself from love,
that I may step forward and live in the light.

I open my heart to all the love there is.

12

Unbeatable

Poor is the man whose pleasures depend on the permission of another.

— Madonna

One of my favorite movie characters is played by Gene Wilder in *Stir Crazy*. Harry is a man who is perpetually happy, and nothing that anyone says or does can remove his joy. Thrown in prison for a crime he did not commit, Harry is the object of the prison officials' campaign to break him into the mold. After the guards hang Harry by his wrists for several days, they return to find him with a big smile on his face. "Thank you!" he exclaims. "You've finally solved my back problem!"

Next, the officials toss Harry into the hot box, a tiny tin enclosure in the sweltering sun. When they extract him, he begs, "Oh, please, could you give me just one more day—I was just starting to get into myself." Finally, they throw Harry into a cell with Grossburger, a 300-pound crazed murderer who even the most hardened criminals avoid like the plague. When the guards return, they find Harry and Grossburger on the floor laughing over a game of cards. Harry just chose joy, and let all else revolve around his choice.

No one can take away your happiness unless you give it to them. People may say all manner of things about you or try to hurt you, but unless you choose to be hurt, they cannot rob you of your good. They are making choices that determine their happiness, just as you are choosing yours. When we feel hurt by another, we are only hurting ourselves. It is said that "offense is something you can only take but never give."

Experiment with finding blessings wherever you go. Quickly you will discover that using a vision of perfection is far more empowering than one of loss. In love you are unbeatable.

I pray to see life through Your eyes, that I may fully reap the gifts of love.

My happiness depends on me.
I choose joy now.

13

Time to Be Free

Lovers make a fool of time.

— Anonymous

When one of Albert Einstein's students asked him to explain his abstruse theory of relativity in a way that anyone could understand, he answered, "A day spent with a beautiful woman seems like a moment; an hour at a job you hate feels like an eternity." Einstein was teaching that our experience of time is determined by the consciousness we are in. Since time is an illusion invented by the human intellect, it is entirely pliable, expanding or contracting to reflect the thoughts we are holding at the time.

We always have enough time to do what needs to be done. Thoughts of "not enough time" are born of fear and a consciousness of lack. The ego fabricates the belief in lack of time as a sleight of hand to move us away from peace. If we make peace our first priority, all things that need to be taken care of in time will be handled.

We are always free in this moment. It is only when we haul the past or future into the now that we feel bound. Practice surfing on the energy of the now. If you become seduced by past or future thoughts, remind yourself that all is well right now. Handle whatever is before you, and leave the rest for another time or another way.

When we live in love, miracles happen that defy the laws of time. Ultimately, time becomes irrelevant, and, as Jesus stated, "The kingdom of heaven is at hand." Prisoners are colloquially described as "doing time." If you are a servant of time rather than letting time serve you, you are a prisoner. Break free of your watch, and bask in the glory of the present moment. Bring more activities that you love into your world, and you will be a millionaire of time.

Help me to move beyond time and celebrate the glory of the present moment.

I live in the timeless kingdom of love.

14

Forge a New Destiny

The future belongs to those who believe in the beauty of their dreams.

— Eleanor Roosevelt

At a restaurant, I noticed a couple enjoying what looked like some very tasty garlic toast. When I asked the waitress for an order of the same, she answered, "I'm sorry, sir, the garlic toast comes only with the dinner."

"Would it be possible to order some as a side order?" I persisted.

She looked puzzled. "I don't know if that's ever been done, sir."

"Then perhaps this is our opportunity to change history and create a new destiny," I suggested. She smiled, went into the kitchen, and soon returned with a dish of piping hot garlic toast—an historic day for the Grosvenor restaurant!

We can transform our lives by changing the way we think about possibilities. We are prone to picture our future as an extension of our past. But we have no guarantee at all that our future will be anything like our past. The nature of a consciousness shift is the release of an old belief system, replacing it with a new and grander one. Just when you think you know it all, life comes along and says, "Here, let me show you a bigger universe!" Thank God we do not know it all; if we did, we would be in big trouble, for most of what we know has made us small. Be grateful that the universe is willing to take away your impotence and replace it with magnitude.

Lead me to a destiny that outshines my history.
I am willing to release my expectations based on the past, and know a better future.

I open my mind to the new and the better.
I live in a universe far grander than I can imagine.

Great Spirits

Great spirits have always encountered violent opposition from mediocre minds.

— Albert Einstein

I saw a film of a meeting held by civil rights workers who were planning to go into the South in the early 1960s. A leader informed the group that three of their colleagues had just been killed by racists. He warned them that their lives would be in danger should they choose to continue their mission. "If any of you wish to change your mind, I will understand," he calmly informed them. After a long moment, one woman in the back of the room stood and began to sing a Negro spiritual. Soon everyone in the room rose and sang with her. All of the workers went to the South.

Dr. Martin Luther King, Jr., is one of my heroes. I respect him because he relied on the power of God, truth, and love rather than falling back on base instincts. Even more important, he walked his talk. Rather than sending other men off to war, he marched in front of his troops. Rather than making a particular person or group the enemy, he singled out fear and prejudice as the enemies to be overcome. He went to jail rather than compromise his integrity. He lived his vision and died with great courage. He didn't just talk about world transformation. He lived it.

Although you and I may not take upon ourselves the breadth of his mission, the same challenge calls to us. We must live what we believe and not give in to fear. We must act on our principles rather than simply talk about them. And we must find ways to join, not separate from, our brothers and sisters.

It is fitting that our country honors a man such as Dr. King. As we live our own ideals, we honor the cause for which he lived and died.

Give me the strength to walk with integrity; help me to live what I believe.

I am here for a mighty purpose.
I change the world by following my truth.

16

Don't Shoot the Screen

It's hard to defeat an enemy who has an outpost in your own head.

— Sally Compton

When motion pictures became popular, a group of cowboys went into a Montana town to watch their first movie. Upon viewing a scene in which a band of Indians was kidnaping a young pioneer woman, a cowboy in the back of the theater stood up and furiously fired a barrel of bullets at the screen. The film stopped, the lights came on, and the audience laughed to behold a blank screen with six bullet holes in it.

We are equally fooled if we attack the movie of our life playing on the screen of our mind. If you fight, hurt, or retaliate against those who do not support or agree with you, you are wasting bullets. Your efforts to prove yourself to others are as useless as shooting the screen.

We "hire" everyone we meet to represent something we believe about ourselves or our world. We can thank those who challenge us, for they help us discover the self-diminutive beliefs lodged below the surface of our conscious awareness. The way to transform our world is not to struggle to manipulate people or events, but to upgrade our thoughts and our consciousness so we attract people and events that demonstrate love rather than fear.

If you know your worth, you do not need anyone else to confirm it, and if you do not recognize your value, you will not gain it by getting others to approve. If you don't like the movie you are watching, don't bother shooting the screen; instead, change the movie—or better yet, turn on the light.

Help me remember that my inner world is where real change occurs. Show me the truth about myself, that I may manifest love in my relationships.

My world reflects the true beauty within me.

17

The Eye of the Beholder

Two men looked out through prison bars;
one saw mud, the other, stars.

— James Allen

One morning while driving through a rural area, I approached a curve where a peahen was leading a queue of babies across the road. I stopped and enjoyed the beauty of the striking deep blue-green color of the chicks, reflected in the morning light. I took a deep breath and thanked God for the opportunity to start my day with this magnificent display.

On the other side of the birds, another car was stopped in the opposite direction. The driver of that car was not so pleased with the display. Obviously in a hurry, she was making scowling expressions as she waited for the animals to cross. As soon as the birds reached the other side of the road, the woman floored the gas pedal and screeched off.

Both of us came upon the same scene and interpreted it in entirely different ways. I viewed it as a gift from God, and she saw it as a nuisance. Behold the power we invoke when we filter our experience through perceptual screens. No occurrence has any absolute reality; everyone who observes it will call it something different. We see the world not as it is, but as we are. No event is intrinsically good or bad; it is the eyes through which we see that make it one or the other.

Experiment with finding the good in every experience. Even if an event seems to be a threat or a problem, adopt a vision through which it can empower you. When you behold life through the eyes of love, you will find the beauty of God everywhere.

I choose to use Your vision today.

Help me to see the good in all people and experiences.

18

For Whom?

To have, give all to all.
— A Course in Miracles

Several years ago, I presented a seminar at which attendance was low. Although we had planned for a huge turnout, only a fraction of those expected showed up. Disappointed, I complained to my musician friend Michael, "It's a drag that we only have this number; I'll just force myself to get through the evening."

"The same thing happened to me once," Michael answered. "Then I asked myself, 'Who are you going to give the program for—the people who showed up, or those who didn't?'" Michael had a point. Why concentrate on the empty seats instead of the full ones? The people who attended believed in me and expected to receive something wonderful. I could not penalize them because others had not met my expectations.

At another sparsely attended program, I was preceded by a musical duo who dashed on stage and gave a fabulous, dynamic performance. You would have thought they were performing for 5,000 people in Las Vegas! They did not compromise their presentation because of the numbers; *they* determined their energy level, not the audience. From them I learned that I need to give 100 percent; what I give to the audience I give to myself. If I give less than all, I steal from myself.

It is not the numbers that make a life; it is the content. It is more valuable to touch a small number of people in a quality way than to amass fame or fortune. Give your full presence and integrity to everyone you meet, and your heart will be full.

I pray to place quality before quantity. Let me live and act for essence before form.

I give all to all, and receive all as I give it.

19

Shoes

Live as if your life depends on it.
— Werner Erhard

The Hawaiian people practice the Eastern custom of removing their shoes before entering a home. At a party I attended, a tai chi student told me, "My master said that you can always tell the level of a person's consciousness by the way they leave their shoes at the door." When I left the party, I surveyed the long line of shoes outside the door. Most of them were lined up neatly next to one another. Then there were mine, criss-crossed and strewn out of line. Oops!

Heaven is gained or lost not just by dramatic deeds, but by the little acts of daily living. A Zen maxim states: "If you can serve a cup of tea correctly, you can do anything," meaning that we can use any mundane act as a meditation to create harmony and beauty. The Japanese have an elaborate ancient tea ceremony in which the server must be very present and conscious of every minute act that comprises the ritual.

I heard a talk by a man who knew Suzuki Roshi, a master who popularized Zen in the West. "Everything Roshi did was a meditation," the man recounted. "Once I watched him eat an apple. By the time he had gotten to the core, the apple was clean and sculpted. All sides were perfectly balanced, and there was no waste. It was a piece of art."

We can make our life a work of art by paying attention to the details of daily living. Let everything be a dance in which we create poise and grace. It's the highest game there is.

*I pray to remain conscious throughout my day
and bring poetic mastery to all I do.*

**I use my life to remember and glorify
the presence of Spirit.**

20

Rethinking Hell

Get off the cross—somebody needs the wood.
— Dolly Parton in *Straight Talk*

In a *Time* magazine interview, evangelist Billy Graham admitted he was rethinking hell. "Hell may not be an eternal dispensation," Rev. Graham noted. "It may just be a sense of separation from God."

The word *hell* is an old English real estate term meaning "border" or "fence." If you wanted to keep a cow or pig in captivity, you would "hell" the critter in a stockade. Then the animal is "helled," or, in its derivative form, "held" in. While many religions present hell as an eternal dispensation, it is not. Hell is a temporary experience that we undergo when we let our heart be ruled by fear. We have all gone through hell in our lives and have come out on the other side. (It is said that religion is for people who are afraid of hell, and spirituality is for those who have already been there.)

There is a purpose for hell, and it has nothing to do with guilt or punishment. Hell is a wake-up call, a corrective device. If you begin to stray from your nature as a loving being, you will have a hellish experience to put you back on track. The only value of hell is educational. Once the lesson is complete, you are done with it, and you can get on with enjoying living in paradise, where you truly belong.

To fear hell is to be in it already, for love is heaven and fear is hell. To punish yourself is to put yourself in hell for no reason. To love yourself and everyone and everything in your life is to give yourself heaven right now and ensure your place there for eternity.

Help me to live in heaven now.
Help me to find innocence and forgiveness for
myself and all persons and things.

I claim my right to live in peace now.
I enter heaven by living with
an open heart.

21

I'm Off to Be the Wizard

If you do not get it from yourself,
where will you go for it?

— Buddha

In the film *Willow,* a young man in medieval times seeks to become an apprentice to the village shaman. Along with two other hopefuls, Willow is tested before an assembled crowd. "If you can answer this question correctly," the wizard informs the three, "I will teach you the ancient magic." The elder extends his hand and asks, "In which finger does the power lie?" Each of the first two applicants chooses a finger, and to the groans of the crowd, the wizard shakes his head. Finally, Willow makes his choice and he, too, is rejected.

Willow goes off to live a life of adventure and romance; he joins an army, weathers a war, and grows through many fascinating encounters. After a long time, Willow returns to the village, where the wizard asks him, "What did you want to answer when I gave you the test?"

"I wanted to say, 'The power lies in my own hand.'"

"That was the correct answer," the wizard affirms. "Why did you not say it?"

"I guess I just didn't believe in myself enough," Willow admits.

The illusion of the world is that other people have the power to make us into something we are not. The truth is that we are already everything, and no one outside of ourselves has the power to add to, or diminish, our wholeness. In spite of this fundamental reality, many of us have spent a great deal of time chasing illusions that the power rests somewhere other than in our own hearts and minds.

Beware of any individuals, organizations, or religions that assert that they have the power to save you or crucify you. People may have worldly power, but that is not the same as spiritual power. In the long run, only spiritual power has any meaning or worth—and you have all of it.

Help me remember that the God I seek lives
within me, as me.

I am the way, the truth, and the life.

22

Fear No Evil

F.E.A.R. is False Evidence Appearing Real
— Anonymous

While horseback riding, I gained a profound insight about fear. Occasionally during the ride, the horse would approach the edge of a cliff or negotiate a steep or rocky part of the trail, and I would have a moment of fear. On that day, I was feeling particularly relaxed, and I noticed that in my generally calm state, the fear would arise and depart in a moment. On previous rides when I had felt more uptight, I would have the moment of fear, followed by many moments of worry: "What if this happens again?"

I realized that what most people call "fear" is really worry. When we obsess about something bad that may happen, the thing we fear is always in the future, and it is generated by something in the past. Examined closely, fear has nothing to do with the now. On my horseback ride, I could see that even my moment of "fear" was actually just a call to pay close attention at that moment. Thus, I realized that fear is not real; it is but a trick of the mind.

Cats are masterful teachers of ease. You have probably observed a cat sleeping underneath a parked car when the driver starts the car. In an instant, the cat springs out from under the car and moves a few feet way. Within seconds, the cat is stretched out and relaxed again, not missing a step in the dance.

When confronted with fear, ask yourself this question: *Am I all right at this moment?* If you are honest, you will see that you are almost always all right in this moment. If not, ask yourself what you need to do *in this moment* to get all right. By peeling away the onion skins of fear in this way, you will find that when you arrive at the center, there is nothing to fear.

A Course in Miracles reminds us, "I could see peace instead of this." Stay in the present moment, and the doors to peace will open.

I pray to be released from anxious worry.
Help me to feel safe in Your love and comforted
in Your Presence.

I am always safe in God.

23

A Few Kind Words

Be kind—remember everyone you meet is fighting a battle—everybody's lonesome.

— Marion Parker

Sandra was born with a physical deformity known as a harelip, and she developed a great deal of self-consciousness about it. Sandra's self-esteem was low, and she constantly feared others making fun of her or rejecting her. Fifth grade was one of Sandra's hardest years, and when the time came for the teacher's end-of-the-year evaluation, Sandra was petrified. She even had nightmares as the dreaded day approached. Finally, the day arrived, and Sandra nervously forced herself to walk up to the teacher's desk and receive Mrs. Harrison's comments about her. When she opened up the envelope, Sandra found but one sentence: *"I wish you were my little girl."* Years later, Sandra recounted, "That was the beginning of the end of my self-esteem problem. Someone I respected loved me."

In a world shrouded with fear, guilt, and separateness, it takes but a little kindness to make someone's day and perhaps change their life. Once I found myself in a strange city at the foot of a huge flight of post office steps, with three boxes I needed to mail and a plane to catch soon after. A man on his way out of the post office took a look at my dilemma and asked, "Would you like some help?" He carried one of the boxes all the way up the stairs and around several corridors with me. The fellow didn't have to do that, but he did. It took him only a few minutes, but it made a huge difference in my day. I was then inspired to pass some extra kindness along to others.

Love only expands when we give it. The fearful mind shrieks that we will lose love if we give too much of it, but we can never love too much; true love only multiplies and returns to bless us many times over.

I pray to move beyond any fear of giving love.
Help me bless the lives of those I touch.

I give life with my love,
and receive more myself.

24

Gotta Serve Somebody

Bury not your faculties in the sepulcher of idleness.
— George Shelley

After traveling extensively for many years, I had several months at home without teaching. At first I found my free time quite refreshing. After a while, however, I became very self-involved. Spending a lot of time alone, I began to focus on my problems and get caught up in small thinking. Although I did not realize it, I was drifting away from the high consciousness I usually enjoy while teaching. Then one evening I presented a seminar, and I was amazed by how much better I felt. I was empowered, uplifted, and back on track. Through that turnaround, I realized I need to give. I need to stay in the presence of God, which I remember through presenting seminars and counseling. As much as students need to take my seminars, I need to give them.

The chemistry of life requires that we give in order to receive. We are not "paid" for giving by receiving later; in the action of giving, we enjoy the benefits of all we are offering. Right livelihood is like making love—as we are serving and blessing the other person, we receive pleasure and healing. In loving, we feel loved.

The prayer of St. Francis affirms the importance of regular service:

In giving we receive;
In pardoning we are pardoned;
And in surrendering we are born to eternal life.

If you feel bottled up, depressed, or self-involved, find someone to love. There is no lack of people and groups needing love, and as you extend service to them, you will find your own healing.

Lift me out of self-involvement, that I may know the joy of true service.

I find peace by giving love.

Tuck in That Ball

Give not that which is holy unto the dogs, neither cast ye your pearls before swine.

— Jesus Christ

In the 1993 Super Bowl, a strange and astounding play occurred. Late in the game, a Dallas Cowboys lineman intercepted a pass. Such a play is a freak, since linemen are essentially blockers and hardly ever touch the football. Seeing no tacklers, the 300-pound fellow went into ecstasy as he ran like mad in pursuit of the only touchdown he would probably ever make. Yards from the goal line, he raised the football triumphantly—but just a little too soon. The lineman did not see a tackler approaching from behind, and soon he was sprawled on the three-yard line, the football bounding away from him. When he looked up, he saw that the football had been recovered by the opposing team.

In the early stages of a project, it is wise to keep our thoughts and energies contained, not waving in the air. If we expose our intimate visions to negative influences, we may be knocked down or lose momentum. Jesus advised us, "Do not cast pearls before swine." He was not referring to people as swine, but the ravaging effects of judgmental or doubtful thinking. No one in the outer world has power over us, but if our own vision has not yet gelled, we must nourish it before sending it out into the world. When a farmer plants a tree in a field, he builds a fence to protect it from being trampled by cattle. After the tree has grown strong and firm, the fence is removed, and the cattle can scratch their backs against it and rest in its shade.

Honor your tender thoughts and dreams by surrounding them with a protective womb. Then when they are born, they will bless everyone.

Great Spirit, help me to hold my visions
like an unborn child.
Help me protect my child so it will emerge in
full strength, health, and vitality.

I honor my tender thoughts,
feelings, and visions.
I surround myself with people, energies,
and influences for success.

Accept the Grace

By Grace I live. By Grace I am released.
— A Course in Miracles

A doctor, lawyer, and engineer were lined up to be executed by guillotine. "Do you wish to face the blade, or look away?" the henchman asked the doctor.

"I'll face the blade!" the physician replied, and placed his neck on the guillotine. The executioner released the blade, which fell to a point just inches above the doctor's neck and stopped.

The assembled crowd buzzed excitedly. "This is obviously a sign from God," announced the king. "You are pardoned." Joyfully, the doctor arose and went on his way.

The lawyer, next in line, also chose to face the blade. Down it fell, and once more it stopped inches from the man's naked throat. Again the throng tittered, and the king informed the prisoner that divine intervention had obviously been issued, and he, too, was free. Happily, he departed.

The final prisoner was the engineer who, like his predecessors, chose to face the blade. He fitted his neck into the crook of the guillotine and looked up at the apparatus above him. The executioner was about to pull the cord when the engineer pointed to the pulley system and called out, "Wait a minute!—I think I see the problem!"

Within us resides an overworking engineer who is more concerned with analyzing the problem than accepting the solution. Many of us have become so resigned to receiving the short end of the stick that if we were offered the long end, we would doubt its authenticity and refuse it. Often we do better to enjoy our good rather than analyze it.

I pray to be open to the good that is offered me.
Help me go beyond my old ideas of
punishment and accept love.

I choose my freedom, and I live in a forgiven world.

27

Money Love

The closed fist locks up heaven, but the open hand is the key of mercy.

— Hindu proverb

Milton Petrie was a wealthy entrepreneur who knew what to do with his money. Each morning, Milton and his wife would read the newspaper to see who had been the victim of a crime or disaster, and then the Petries would help them. One morning, the couple read about a beautiful model who had been viciously assaulted by several men who gashed her face many times, leaving her with huge, gaping scars and ruining her budding career. I saw a heart-rending photo of this young woman with a Frankenstein-like face. Milton Petrie called her to his office and promised her $20,000 a year for the rest of her life. She used her gift to restore her skin to its former beauty and renew her career.

The purpose of money is to extend love, celebrate abundance, and support each other. The more we try to hoard, protect, or withhold money, the more it slips away from us and becomes a source of pain and contention. The more we use money to make each other happy, the greater our own flow of joy becomes.

We do not have to be millionaires to enjoy the blessings of giving love through money. Leaving a larger-than-usual tip at a restaurant, sending an "I love you" greeting card, or simply not arguing over money matters are ways we can use money to enhance our experience of love. In the long run, it will not be our bank accounts that we remember, but the kindness we gave and received.

Abundant God, help me use money to serve love's purpose.

Every dollar I spend expands love and returns to me multiplied.

Boomerang Efforts

That the yielding is more powerful than the rigid, is a fact known by all and practiced by none.

— Lao Tse

"I've been smoking pot nearly every day for six years," Bonnie confessed. "I've tried to quit many times, and every time I fall back. No matter how hard I try, I fail. I need help."

"Then quit trying," I suggested.

"You mean I should just keep smoking?"

"No, just quit fighting it. Your struggle against smoking is keeping it strong in your mind. Rather than battling what you don't want, cultivate what you do want. Meditate, pray, read uplifting books, keep supportive company, walk in nature, listen to joyful music—all the things that make you happy. Don't let the pot smoking be a major issue. If you smoke, love yourself anyway. If the habit is not in your best interests, it will fall away in the presence of the light you are generating."

Six months later, I saw Bonnie and asked her how she was doing. "I haven't smoked in three months," she excitedly proclaimed. "It worked just like you said. I didn't make smoking a big deal; I concentrated on what I wanted instead of what I didn't want, and I am done with it."

Fighting against something only gives it more power over our life. Those who fight Satan reinforce the thought that Satan is real and stronger than we are. The most direct way to dispel satanic thoughts is to focus on the light. In the presence of light, all darkness must vanish. If you lift up a log in the woods, you will find a host of bugs and worms living underneath it. The moment they are exposed to the light, they scatter. So it is with the illusion of evil. Place love where you once found evil, and you will prove that there is only love.

I place all my problems in Your care and trust You to do for me what I cannot do for myself.

God is the only power. Love is the only reality. Nothing in the outer world can have power over me because God is in me.

29

The Search for Myself

All the music I write is a search for myself.
— Bruce Hornsby

While writing my first book, I came upon a Buddhist text in which the author confessed, "I have no pretension that I am writing this book for any purpose other than my own awakening." His candor struck a chord deep within me as I realized that I, too, write primarily for the healing of my own mind and spirit. Since then, I have spoken to countless creative artists who agree that even if no one else ever read their books, saw their paintings, or listened to their music, all of their efforts would be worth the sheer joy of producing the work.

For whom are your creative efforts directed? Do you write, sing, or dance for worldly approval, or are you hearkening to the inner writer, singer, or dancer calling to express and celebrate?

We teach what we need to learn. Sometimes teachers are reluctant to admit that they need to study what they are teaching, but that is the very reason we are in a particular position. In college, I learned a famous relaxation technique developed by a renowned psychologist. My friend met the man and described him as "one of the most uptight people I have ever met." Was he a hypocrite? Not necessarily. If you teach what you have mastered, even while you're learning more, you are in integrity. The technique this man developed for his own healing helped many people who applied it.

Your right place is the one in which you are receiving the most edification. The fact that other people receive a benefit is the icing on the cake. Do what is healing to your spirit, and without effort you will offer the world healing in return.

Direct me to the work that will feed my soul,
that I may feed others.

I do what I love, and the world loves what I do.

30

Moving Targets

All men should strive to learn before they die,
What they are running from, and to, and why.
— James Thurber

I met a woman who changed residences every six months. In a candid conversation, she admitted that she harbored major fears about opening up to an intimate relationship. "You can't hit a moving target," she confessed, as a description of her protection strategy.

When we are excessively busy, we are running from ourselves. Workaholics, busyholics, and planaholics are terrified to be with themselves, dominated by the fear that they will be consumed by the loneliness or pain they have denied—the empty feelings that well up in quiet moments.

Several years ago, I noticed that I had slipped into a pattern of obsessive doingness. At the time, I was ending a relationship, and I felt terrified at the prospect of being with myself at home alone. But I recognized that this was something I had to do, and ultimately the experience turned out to be one of the greatest blessings of my life. I had time to be with myself and face myself. I looked squarely at the fears and old patterns that kept me on the run, and I made conscious choices to use my alone time as a healing, nurturing, and meditative experience. Now I can be with myself or be with people, and enjoy either experience.

A Course in Miracles explains that the fear to look within is not a fear of the darkness, but a fear of the light. If we stopped running, we would have to confront the things that frighten us—and that is wonderful, for on the other side of the shadow is the light. If you look yourself squarely in the eye, you will not find a demon, but a god.

Help me slow down enough to know Your presence.
I will be still and touch the Peace You give.

In quiet I find the God within me.

In-Your-Face Productions

If you do not change direction, you may end up where you are headed.

— Oriental proverb

"That's loud!" I remarked to the massage therapist as a tight muscle on my back popped audibly while she worked it.

"Yes," she answered, "resistance is loud."

When we fight the flow of life, the universe lets us know in a big way. Drama, emergencies, hefty surprises, health or relationship crises, changes beyond our control, and physical and emotional pain all serve to get our attention. When we are asleep to what is happening in or around us, *In-Your-Face Productions* will arrange a wake-up call to get us out of a rut and back on track. Usually, such attention-getters are not gentle or pleasant, and they bring a fair amount of discomfort. The good news is that a temporary period of pain or inconvenience is a small price to pay compared to a lifetime of unconscious self-defeating behavior.

We can minimize or avoid the angst of *In-Your-Face Productions* in two ways. First, we can develop our intuition so that we become aware of our lessons in their early stages rather than waiting until they mount to a huge crisis. If you pay attention to the little red *"brakes"* warning light on your car dashboard, you can avoid full-out brake failure. Spirit usually whispers to us before a potential crash. Through prayer and meditation, you can sensitize yourself to hear important messages before they are played out in the physical world.

The second way to lighten the brunt of wake-up calls is to bless them when they happen. Rather than fight life or adopt a victim position, look for the gift in the experience. Imagine that the universe is conspiring not to hurt you, but to free you. An attitude of appreciation, rather than resentment, will soften and transform otherwise difficult lessons.

We do not have to live by emergency; as we become more attuned to the voice of love, we can glide, not stumble, through life.

Help me hear Your voice at the subtlest level and act on my inner wisdom.

I hear the guidance of love and proceed from the truth that keeps me whole.

Choice Words

Only in the sacredness of inward silence does the soul truly meet the secret, hiding God.

— Frederick William Robertson

A friend of mine conducts retreats in Assisi, Italy, the birthplace and home of St. Francis. Much of the retreat time is spent in silent meditation. The program has a rule: *Do not speak unless what you have to say is more powerful than the silence.*

The Quakers understood this principle and incorporated it into their prayer services. The Quakers sit silently, and no one speaks unless he or she is moved by Spirit to do so. One must not speak until he or she is literally exploding, or *quaking*. That is the sign that God, and not the ego, is moving through the person.

In my seminars, I've noticed a wide range of energies that issue forth when various people speak. When someone speaks from her heart, she may say but a few words and the entire room is riveted; that is how compelling sincere expression can be. Others may go on for a long time and say nothing; the room goes dead, for the speaker is proceeding from their head or ego.

Try practicing periods of silence. Take a morning or a day regularly and go into the quiet chamber of the heart. You will be amazed at the wealth of aliveness you find behind your words, and you will discover that words often detract from truth. When you speak again, your words will be chosen, powerful, and healing. Make every word you speak count, and you will co-create with God.

Lord, make my words an instrument of Your peace.

I use the power of the word to create good, success, and healing.

I Had No Idea

There is more to heaven and earth than meets the eye.
— William Shakespeare

I heard about a man who lived in Kansas all of his life and had never traveled more than a few hundred miles from his home. When Joseph was 85 years old, he took a trip to Oregon and saw the ocean for the first time. Joseph stood on the rugged, windswept beach for a long time, breathing deeply and contemplating its majesty. Then he walked back to his friend and told him, "I had no idea it would be this beautiful. I had to see it to know it."

Many of us have lived for a long time in a world much smaller than the one that is available to us. We tread the familiar path, settle into routine relationships, and find security in the known. But to settle for what has been is to miss out on what could be. Imagine that there is an entire unexplored world available to you if you were to reach even a little bit beyond the familiar. If you open your consciousness, the universe will rush to show you what is truly there.

When I first stepped onto the beach in Hawaii, I was moved to tears. The rugged green mountains towered over the azure sea as the warm waters lapped over my bare feet and washed away years of East Coast insanity. Everything I beheld spoke of beauty, aliveness, and abundance. I had no idea that such riches existed on the planet. Egotistically, I believed that I had seen most of what there was to see and knew what was available. But I didn't. What I thought was available was only a small portion of the good that awaited.

There is an entire unseen ocean waiting for you to explore.

Show me the life that is available to me, and let me live it.
I am willing to be wrong about what I thought
were my limits.

I step out beyond the known to claim the riches of my true potential.

34

Will Power

There is no try; only do.
— Yoda (in *The Empire Strikes Back*)

"I have been going out with this guy for a while, and he is really nice to me," Terri explained, "but I don't feel a lot for him. When I told my girlfriend I would try to make the relationship work, she asked me, 'Why would you want to be in a relationship that you had to *try* to make work? Either you are motivated or you aren't. Trying doesn't create juice.'"

If you experience strain, it is because you are moving against God's will. God's will is the easiest and most effortless thing to do in the world, and it is the most effective. We are empowered when we get out of the way and let God do Its will through us. We are totally disempowered when we try to impose another will over the one that Spirit would effect.

The way that most people approach "will power" is quite self-defeating. The number of broken New Year's resolutions is testimony to the fact that personal will power is paltry. Real will power means hitching your will to God's will and surfing on the strength of what *is*, rather than what you are trying to twist it into. God's will is for health, peace, prosperity, and joy. How much struggle could be required to accomplish what Spirit would give you?

Instead of using your will to fight an uphill battle against a mammoth monster, use it to align with peace. You can be very active and effective in creating world change without bearing the lonely and impossible burden of doing it all yourself. Accept the backing of the home office, and your battle will be transformed into a dance.

I pray to be aligned with Your will. I trust You to do for me what I cannot do for myself.

The will of God is easy and powerful.
I claim it now.

Doctor in the House

Use three physicians still: first, Dr. Quiet.
Next, Dr. Merryman, and Dr. Dyet.
— Regimen Sanitatis Salernitanum (1607)

Health is our natural state, and it is within our ability to main tain good health at all times. Any notion to the contrary is a limited belief system and must be discarded without hesitation. The length and quality of your life is in your hands, and no external force has power over your vitality.

The first prescription, quiet, is essential to well-being. How can you hear the voice of God if you are preoccupied with the outer world? Each day, take time to be with yourself. Meditate, walk in the woods, or lock yourself in the bathroom. God lives not on a distant cloud, but within your heart. Spirit is not playing a hide-and-seek game. To the contrary, God is utterly desirous of being known and enjoyed. If you feel distant from God, who moved? Go to the quiet inner temple regularly, and all outer activity will be more peaceful.

Joy is as vital to good health as air. Every enlightened being I know is filled with happiness and laughter. Do not fall prey to images of God as a somber, mournful entity. God is not a mean old man; She is a joyful child. You do not need to analyze and process every thought and experience; go out and play, laugh, get silly, and cast fear to the wind. You will find truth more quickly through delight than gravity.

Diet is extremely important. Our bodies were constructed to function at a high level of efficiency, flexibility, and well-being. To keep the body healthy, we must feed it in harmony with nature. Eat fresh, live, whole, pure foods, free of artificial ingredients or preservatives. Avoid sugar, fat, salt, and processed food. Make your meals a sacrament; take time to be with your food, thank God for it, and digest it. Give your body love in the form of quality nourishment, and it will respond with robust health.

I pray to be fully healthy and manifest the well-being I deserve.

I am healthy, whole, vital, and happy as I live in harmony with my natural spirit.

Beyond Survivorship

I am not a body. I am free. I am still as God created me.
— A Course in Miracles

At a seminar, I met a woman who had become entirely identified with being a survivor of sexual abuse. When she met others, she would introduce herself, "Hello, my name is Marge. I am a survivor of sexual abuse." Marge had gotten so involved with claiming this identity that she could not conceive of being more than this. While it's important to acknowledge the pain and experience surrounding such a significant trauma, it's also important to remember that there is more to us and our life than being a survivor.

Buddha offered the analogy of traveling across a river on a raft. Once you get to the other side of the waterway, you must leave the raft on the river. It will do you no good to hang the raft on your back and carry it up the mountain. Leave it where you got it, and continue on your journey unimpeded.

All identities serve us temporarily. It is important that we immerse ourselves in an experience as long as it serves us, but then we must grow beyond it. For any affiliation you can identify yourself with, there is a grander one available; we must let go of what we were...to become who we are. Whether you identify yourself as a recovering addict, a student, or even a child of God, there awaits a bigger room to live in.

Ultimately we are simply Spirit. Calling ourselves anything else may help us in the moment, but eventually we must return to what God created us to be.

Help me grow beyond all temporary identities to claim my true nature.

I am Spirit. I am whole.

37

Get Outside

Climb the mountains and get their good tidings. Nature's peace will flow into you as sunshine flows into trees. The winds will blow their own freshness into you, and the storms their energy, while cares will drop away from you like the leaves of Autumn.

— John Muir

One winter day while I was with some friends, I began to feel depressed and anxious. My friend Tom noticed my condition and suggested, "Why don't you take a walk outside?" I continued to stew in my own juices, and later Tom offered again, "I'll bet you'd feel better if you took a little walk." Again I did not heed his suggestion, and my tailspin become worse. Finally, he said, "I know you'd regain your perspective if you just got outside." Then I listened. I went to a little park where I walked around a crystalline ice-covered pond. I breathed the cold air deep into my lungs and felt the blood coursing through my veins. The stark beauty of winter was wondrously invigorating, and I returned to my friends feeling healed and renewed.

Nature is the great healer. Many of the ailments that plague our society stem from the way we have alienated ourselves from nature. We live in little boxes piled high atop one another, breathe fecund air from auto and chimney exhausts, eat food tainted by artificial chemicals, and sit at desks in front of computer monitors for many hours a day. Then we wonder why we do not feel well.

Even small doses of nature will begin to restore our sense of balance, wonder, and aliveness. I love to walk in the mountains, swim in the ocean, and enjoy the warm blessing of the sun. I am a spiritual being, and I honor my body as a friend and vehicle to feel the presence of God.

Choose an aspect of nature that you love, and immerse yourself in the world that God created. Nature will heal you.

Help me return to my source.
Thank you for the beauty of nature, which feeds my soul.

I am healed by the natural world.

38

Buy a Ticket

Pray devoutly, hammer stoutly.

— English proverb

Every day Ralph prayed to God to help him win the lottery. Each week when he didn't win, Ralph became more and more frustrated, and he grew angry at God. Finally, in exasperation, Ralph went to church, stood before the altar, shook his fist, and railed, "If you are a true God, how can you say that prayer works? I have been praying for a long time to win the lottery, and now I have less money than when I started! Why have you not helped me?"

Suddenly, a deep voice from above the altar boomed, "The least you could do, Ralph, is buy a lottery ticket!"

God is delighted to answer our prayers, but we must act in accordance with our intentions. We cannot expect to sit around and do nothing while God dances for us. We must dream with our feet moving. God can do no more for you than It can do *through* you. Manifestation is a co-creative enterprise. You are not expected to do it all yourself (indeed you cannot), but do not expect God to do it all for you. "On earth as it is in heaven" means that we act with the authority of God, even on the physical plane. Vision is the key, but action is that hand that turns it to unlock the door.

I offer you my hands, feet, heart, mind, and voice
to manifest your love on earth.
Together we can do anything.

I act in accordance with my vision, and Spirit manifests blessings through me.

I'll Be Your Rock

A friend may well be reckoned the masterpiece of nature.

— Ralph Waldo Emerson

The acclaimed motion picture *Field of Dreams* touched the hearts of millions and was nominated for an Academy Award as best picture of the year. Actor Kevin Costner accepted the lead role in spite of a deluge of criticism from his advisors, who warned him that he could damage his image and career by making a "Care Bear" film. The sponsoring studio also levied immense pressure against Costner and producer Phil Robinson in an effort to add sex and violence to make the movie more marketable. When Robinson was tempted to buckle, Costner urged him, "Don't give in, Phil—I'll be your rock." Encouraged by Costner's support, Robinson held his ground, and the film went on to be a huge success without exploitative elements.

Is anyone your "rock"? Have you acknowledged this person? Are you a rock for another? What can you do to support someone who is being challenged to hold to their vision?

The support of a friend during a time of adversity can make the difference between success and failure, despair and triumph. Encouragement and confidence are priceless spiritual gifts that can change an entire life.

Give me the strength to be a rock to my friends. Help me sustain the spirit of my loved ones and to be open to receive their support.

Founded in Spirit, I can do all things in the name of love.

40

As Thyself

I have an everyday religion that works for me.
Love yourself first, and everything else falls into line.

— Lucille Ball

"My ex-wife wants me to do one thing, my son wants me to do something else, and my girlfriend has another agenda," Tom complained to me during a seminar.

"What would *you* like to do?" I asked.

Tom looked stunned. "Me? I don't know."

"Think about it," I suggested.

The next day, Tom came on-stage and reported, "Yesterday was a turning point in my life. Alan asked me what *I* wanted to do, and that was the perfect question. I realized that I've spent most of my life trying to please other people. For a moment, I set aside what everyone else was asking me to do and considered what would make *me* happy. I came up with something that not only empowered me but would work for everyone else. I feel like I have my life back!"

Jesus's most often-quoted commandment is: "Love thy neighbor as thyself." Usually we equate this advice with taking good care of our neighbors, but we often overlook the "as thyself" portion. If you are loving your neighbor more than yourself, or at the expense of yourself, you have not fulfilled the commandment. Jesus was suggesting that we love all equally, *including* ourselves. If your vision of service does not include your own happiness, you've left out a very important person.

The universe works on a win-win basis. There is always a way for everyone to be taken care of. Do not stop until you have blessed everyone, including yourself.

Help me find the compassion to honor my own heart, along with others.

I give myself the kindness and forgiveness I would show others.

41

Pass the Salt

Respect the past in the full measure of its desserts, but do not make the mistake of confusing it with the present, or seek in it the ideals of the future.

— Jose Ingenieros

As I unpacked my suitcase at a hotel, I discovered that I had left two of my favorite articles of clothing hanging in a closet at another hotel 2,000 miles away. As I picked up the phone to call the hotel to see if the items had turned up in Lost and Found, I noticed that I was hesitating. I realized I didn't want to call because I didn't really want to retrieve the items. One was a sweatshirt given to me years ago, and another was a casual shirt I have customarily worn on plane flights. Both felt very old, laden with memories and history I no longer wanted to carry with me. I put down the phone and smiled. I was done with the shirts. They did not belong to me now, and I would not call them back to me.

Every time we haul an old, painful memory into the now, we are phoning a distant hotel and asking for our tattered garments to be forwarded to our new abode. Messengers will do so if we ask. Then we wonder why our present looks like our past. But we are under no obligation to replay old scenes; all of life is optional, including reliving ancient pain. Every day we are free to choose anew. If today looks gruesomely like yesterday, and your life is a long replay of *Groundhog Day*, do not blame karma, the environment, or other people. Instead, look at the choices you are making today.

The Bible tells how, as Sodom was being destroyed, God told Lot and his family not to look back. Lot's wife disobeyed, and she was turned into a pillar of salt. The story is a metaphor. When we clutch at the old after it no longer serves us, we become petrified. Salt is a preservative. We cannot preserve the past; we must release it to make way for a fresh new future.

I return my past to You, and allow You to make me new.

I release the past and invite love to meet me in the present.

Priorities

If you greatly desire something, have the guts to stake everything on obtaining it.

— Brendan Francis

"You've got to hear this woman play the violin," my friend Albert elbowed me. "It will bring you to tears." (That wouldn't surprise me, I thought—some of my friends have played the violin for me, and each time I wanted to cry.) When Barbara played at the concert I was attending, however, I was moved to my depths. She wielded the bow with awesome mastery and extracted a tone from her instrument unlike any I have ever heard. Within moments I was enraptured, and I did not want Barbara to stop. When she did, the audience gave her a standing ovation.

After the concert, Albert told me, "The way that Barbara got that violin—a Stradivarius—was as amazing as her performance. She was looking for a new violin in a modest price range, but when she found this violin, she knew it was for her. As you can expect, the price was astronomical. So she sold her house to buy the violin."

I believe that Barbara made the right choice. The breadth of passion, joy, and beauty she brought into the world through playing that violin far exceeded any gifts she might have offered by inviting friends to her house for tea.

It is said that "all healing occurs outside of the safety zone." In the same way, success and extraordinary beauty are born of leaps of faith. When your heart is intent on living your dream, you will gladly let go of everything that is unlike the dream in order to manifest your vision.

Give me the knowledge of my worthiness,
and the courage to invest in myself.

I am willing to give it all to have it all.

43

Sweet Success

Disappointments are the hooks upon which God hangs his victories.

— Anonymous

Let me tell you about a man who was plagued by defeat. In '31 he failed in business and declared bankruptcy. In '32 he lost an election for the legislature. In '34 his business failed again, and he declared bankruptcy a second time. The following year, his fiancée died. The year after that, he suffered a nervous breakdown. Two years later, in '38 he was defeated in another election. In '43 he ran for the U.S. Congress and lost. In '46 he made another bid for a seat in Congress, and he was defeated. In '48 he ran again for Congress, and again he lost. Seven years later, he entered a race for the U.S. Senate, and he was defeated. In '56 his name was placed on the ballot for the Vice Presidency of the United States, and he lost the election. In '58 he ran for the Senate and lost again.

In '60—1860—he was elected President of the United States. His name was Abraham Lincoln. In spite of an incredible string of setbacks, he went on to become one of the greatest statesmen of history. He said, "You cannot fail unless you quit."

The greatest victories are those we must persevere to accomplish. It is rare that great people just show up on the planet shining in glory. Often the most powerful world-change agents grow through experience and adversity. As a young lawyer, Mahatma Gandhi was literally laughed out of court when he became tongue-tied while arguing a ten-dollar case. Later he was thrown off a South African train because his skin was dark. Gandhi went on to become one of the greatest human liberators of the 20th century.

Eat defeat for breakfast. Do not let setbacks put you off; instead, use them as springboards to the success you desire. Only those who are willing to go the distance can taste the sweetness of victory.

Help me to not be put off by setbacks.
Give me the strength to go all the way.

I succeed because I make up my mind to emerge victorious.

44

Still Good

The art of living lies not in eliminating
but in growing with troubles.
— Bernard Baruch

"How's everything going?" my friend Tori asked me as we passed in a restaurant.

"Life is good," I answered readily.

"It sure is," Tori agreed. "Even at its worst, life is still good."

Even when times are tough and we can't see our direction, life is a gift. Sometimes the hardest times are our most productive and growth producing. I visited the home of a very wealthy doctor named John in Bremerton, Washington, where he and his family lived in a magnificent mansion with a heavenly view of the Olympic Mountains. John owned several expensive automobiles, played on a world-class pool table in his den, and enjoyed many comforts and luxuries.

As I chatted with his family over dinner, John reminisced, "When we first got married, we had nothing. We lived in a tiny apartment and watched our pennies. Jan worked hard to help us get by while I was immersed in school; we really didn't know how we were going to make it. As I look back now, that was one of the best times of our life. In a way I enjoyed that period of earnest striving more than being successful and having all this stuff."

Life is always good. It isn't always comfortable, easy, or understandable, but it is good. Sometimes the most difficult moments bring us together in ways that we would miss if we stayed isolated. When I lived in New Jersey, the only time I saw and talked to some of my neighbors was after a snowstorm, when we would help push each other's cars out of the snow. Many families have told me that a health crisis reunited them in a way that never would have happened otherwise.

Life is good, even at its worst. Love is always present.

Thank You for all the blessings You shower on me,
even when I am not aware of them.
Help me to continually celebrate the goodness
of the life You give.

I bless every experience, trusting that God is with me.

Be My Valentine

O, be swift to love! Make haste to be kind.

— Henri F. Amiel

The legend of St. Valentine goes back to the early days of Christianity when Christians were being persecuted by the Romans. One Christian, Valentinus, was tried as a heretic and sentenced to death. In prison, Valentinus befriended a guard who respected his wisdom, and soon the guard brought his seven-year-old blind daughter, Julia, to Valentinus for lessons. Daily, the two talked of important things, and Julia developed a deep love and respect for her mentor. One day Julia asked him, "Valentinus, do you think I will ever be able to see?"

Valentinus thought for a moment and answered, "With love in your heart and belief in God, anything is possible, Julia."

At that moment, Julia was overtaken with a flash of light, and suddenly her eyesight was restored. "Valentinus, I can see!" the child shouted.

"Praise be to God," he humbly answered.

The next day when Julia came to visit Valentinus, he was gone. He had been taken to his execution. Julia found this note:

> *My Dear Julia,*
>
> *Although we shall never see each other again, know that I will always love you. You are very dear to me. I will stay unseen by your side, and I will live in your heart. I believe in you.*
>
> *Your Valentine*

Be a true valentine by reminding your beloved ones that they are unlimited. Inspire them to trust their heart's wisdom, and miracles will occur. And if you are your own valentine, remember that all the love you need is within you, just as you are, right where you are.

I pray to remind my loved ones of their highest possibilities.

I create miracles by using the vision of divine love.

46

Maybe Better Off

Lust brings excitement. Love brings peace.
— Harvey Freeman

When I was 15 years old, I saw a flashy red electric guitar hanging in a music store window. It was shiny, slickly shaped, and looked like the kind of guitar a rock star would play. I ran home and told my father that I absolutely *had* to have that guitar. "Do you know how to play it?" he asked.

"No, but I *swear* I'll learn," I promised.

"Maybe you could take some guitar lessons on a basic model, and then if you still want this one, we can get it then," he reasonably suggested.

"But Dad," I argued, "then this guitar might not be there. I really want to get this one *now*!"

My father looked me squarely in the eye and asked me the most compelling question he ever confronted me with. In Yiddish he asked, *"Voss brendt ba dir?"* which meant, *"What's burning in you?"* Needless to say, I didn't get the guitar. But my father's question still haunts me to this day: *What's burning in you?*

While passion imbued by Spirit can save our life, passion directed by ego can ruin it. The fear-driven mind will tell us that we *must* have what we want, and we *must* have it *now*. The voice of peace, on the other hand, knows that all good things come to us by right of consciousness, and we do not have to fight, sweat, or rush to receive our good.

Looking back now, I realize it was a blessing that I didn't get that guitar; the thing was all flash and no quality, and sooner or later I would have discovered I had made a bad deal. I was better off without it. My father's words, however, have blessed me for a lifetime.

Help me to be patient to receive Your gifts.
I pray to focus on what will truly bring me peace.

All quality things come to me at the right time by the hand of a gracious God.

Don't Stop Now

Before you die, you must allow your genius to walk the wildest unknown way.
— Bryce Courtenay, author of T*he Power of One*

"You will be sleeping in the Ernest Hemingway room," the desk clerk told me. I cast open the wooden door and found a bedroom decorated exactly as Ernest Hemingway's might have been. The wrought-iron bed, hurricane lamp, and wooden treasure chest were accented by several of Hemingway's hardcover texts and some of his actual handwritten correspondence. I peered down the hall to catch glimpses of rooms decorated *a la* Robert Louis Stephenson, Louisa May Alcott, and my favorite, Dr. Seuss. The Sylvia Beach Hotel[3], perched over the rugged beach of Newport, Oregon, is the fruition of a long-time dream by owner Gudrun Cable.

"I yearned to create a space that would honor the great writers and nourish lovers of inspiring words," Gudi told me over tea in the library late one night. "When this old hotel came up for sale, I went through two years and forty rejected loans before I got funding. I told my friends that if they each decorated a room according to the style of their favorite author, I would trade them a week's vacation here for five years. When we were ready to open, I put the tiniest ad in the local classifieds, and I expected a few dozen people for the grand opening. Fourteen hundred people showed up that day, along with a triple rainbow. Since that time, business has been amazing, and I have sat in our library and sipped tea and rich conversation with some of the great authors of our time."

What dream is calling you? Do you believe in your idea enough to let it come true? In retrospect, Gudi's rejections seem like a wispy dream in comparison to the joy and success she has found. I can't wait to get back to Sylvia Beach; perhaps, if my dreams come true, this time I can get the Dr. Seuss room.

Give me the faith to persevere to make my dreams a reality.

I will realize my goals because I believe in myself.

48

Formative Minutes

Thrice blest whose lives are faithful prayers,
whose loves in higher love endures.
— Alfred, Lord Tennyson

A *Wonder Bread* commercial reminded viewers of the importance of "the formative years"—the first five years of life when a child's foundation is established. The ad suggested it was important to feed the child *Wonder Bread,* which "builds strong bodies 12 ways." The premise of the commercial was correct. The early years of life imprint the important programs upon which a life will be built.

Each day is like a life unto itself, and so the first minutes of each day are the formative minutes. We must take special care to sound the keynote that will set the tone for our entire day. How do you begin your day? Do you spend it with God, in peace, in attunement with yourself? Or do you pop out of bed and immediately dive into the busy-ness of the day, postponing your soul's needs in favor of lesser activities?

For many years, I have begun my day with mediation and prayer. Before I speak to anyone, do chores, or even think about work, I sit and commune with Spirit. This practice has empowered my life in such profound ways that I cannot conceive of starting my day in any other way.

Take at least the first 20 minutes of your day to meditate, pray, read an inspiring book, practice yoga or tai chi, walk in the woods, sing, dance, or engage in any practice that links you to a higher power. Establish your center, and the day that follows will reflect clarity, strength, and love. Any time you spend with Spirit will be returned and will multiply many times over. Whenever possible, renew your spirit throughout the day. Even a few seconds of closing your eyes and remembering the presence of love will make a big difference. At the end of your day, be with God before entering sleep. The formative minutes will build the consciousness that makes a productive life.

Be with me today, Spirit.
Hold my hand throughout the day, and never let me forget
that You walk with me.

I start the day with love, fill the day with love, and end the day with love.

Supposed to Stink

You desire to know the art of living, my friend?...
Make use of suffering.

— Henri F. Amiel

As I lifted the lid off my compost container, my nose was assaulted by the acrid aroma of rotting food. "Argh!" I recoiled, "That really stinks!" Then an inner voice reminded me, "It's supposed to stink." Of course it is. If rotten food wasn't repulsive, we might eat it and get sick. The obnoxious smell is nature's way of keeping us away from what would hurt us.

In life, too, nature tries to repulse us from what would hurt us. Whenever we experience pain, conflict, antagonism, or frustration, the universe is, in effect, sending us the message, *"This is not the way you are supposed to be doing it. Try another way."*

Stubborn as we humans can be, we sometimes put up with rotten smells for a long time for all the wrong reasons. Many of us tolerate dysfunctional relationships, addictive behaviors, abusive business situations, and noxious health conditions that undermine us every time we participate in them. We convince ourselves that it is noble to put up with pain, or "one day he will change," or "next week I will talk to my boss." Meanwhile, we deny the message the universe is trying to communicate: *Do it differently so you can be happy and healthy.*

If a rat learns to maneuver through a maze to get to some cheese, and then the cheese is taken away, the rat will go through the maze a few more times, but soon it realizes that there is no further reward in the journey. Unlike the rat, we may go down a dead-end maze many times, still hoping that somehow the cheese will be there. The real cheese lies in honoring ourselves to live in the light. We must tell the truth about our pain so we can extricate ourselves from it. There is a better way. Love yourself enough to claim it.

Speak to me so clearly that I fully recognize the message You are sending.

I claim my right to live in light without pain.

How Big Is Your Basket?

Every good gift and every perfect gift is from above,
and cometh down from the Father of Lights.
— James 1:17

While I was leading a group meditation, I had a mystical vision. Above the group, I saw a vast reservoir of golden light, as if there was no ceiling on the room. I beheld an infinite heaven beaming down a luminous rain of blessings upon the group. Then I saw each person in the room sitting with a basket in their lap, catching the gifts of light from above. Each basket was a different size; some were small, and others were large. Although an infinite volume of blessings was streaming down, each person was able to catch gifts in accordance with the size of their basket. Those with large baskets caught many blessings, while those with small baskets caught only some.

A great reservoir of abundance is offered to each of us; how much we shall enjoy it is determined by how much we are open to receive. The gifts of God are like a vast immeasurable ocean. You can go to the ocean with a thimble, a cup, a bucket, or a tanker, and you will come away with a volume of gifts relative to the size of the vessel you bring.

How big is your basket? Are you allowing all the good that is offered you to be manifested? You may have a huge tank of water with which to water your garden, but if you're standing on the hose, you will see only a small dribble.

Get off the hose by saying "yes" to good when it comes. Find a way to turn negative experiences into gifts, and you will discover that they *are* good. Practice increasing your receptivity, and you will prove that our Source is infinite.

Help me deepen my receptivity to Your love.
I pray to be open to all You give.

I am open to receiving
the fullest abundance that life has to offer.

Homey Don't Play That

It's a funny thing about life; if you accept anything but the very best, you will get it.

— W. Somerset Maugham

The hit television show *In Living Color* featured an endearing clown named Homey who refused to do anything that would make him look silly. When the kids in Homey's audience asked him, "When will your baggy pants fall down?" Homey made a sour face and told them bluntly, "Homey don't play that." When the youngsters beseeched him, "Let's see you slip on the banana peel, Homey!" he tartly declared, "I don't think so."

Homey unknowingly taught a supremely important metaphysical principle: We never need to demean ourselves to be socially acceptable; it is not necessary to give other people pleasure at our expense. When friends, co-workers, or authority figures ask us to violate our integrity or peace, we cannot afford to dishonor our spirit.

Every challenge is an opportunity to choose our identity. If you do not know your worth, you will accept and stay in conditions that deny the light you are and the happiness you deserve. If you remember that you deserve only love, you will accept the good that comes to you and categorically reject all else. The next time you are asked to make yourself small, remember that "Homey Don't Play That."

Help me honor what You created me to be.

Established in peace,
I live to my full potential.

52

Shake Up, Wake Up

We turn to God for help when our foundation is shaking, only to recognize that it is God who is shaking it.

— Charles Weston

In Bali I observed a cremation procession. The body of the deceased was placed on top of a high ornate wooden tower called a "horse." Every few minutes along the way to the cremation ground, the pallbearers broke into shouts of glee and laughter and twirled the horse, with the body fastened to its apex, in circles. When I asked a local fellow about the purpose of this ritual, he explained that the pallbearers spun the bier to confuse the deceased's spirit so it could not find its way back to the body, and thus hasten the soul on its journey to the next life.

From time to time, life shakes us up, twirling or even destroying the foundation we've built. Such an experience can be quite disorienting—and it is supposed to be. The purpose of change beyond our control is to shake us up so we must hasten in a new direction.

Like the soul that has left the body of the deceased, we may not be able to find our way back to our past base. But the past is dead, and there is no reason to return. We are free to move on to discover a new life in a new world. Upheaval is a gift of love. When it comes, ask to see the blessing in what you're being forced to release, to make way for something new and better.

Help me let go gracefully so I can be open to richer blessings.

I accept change as a gift.
I move from good to better to best.

53

Just Be You

Now all that is left is for you to become yourself.

— Sense

The renowned sage Rabbi Zusya wept as he lay on his deathbed. His students, gathered by his side, were astonished. "Rabbi, why do you weep?" one of them asked. "If anyone is assured of a place in heaven, it is you!"

"I'll tell you why," the learned one answered softly. "If, when I approach the gates of heaven, I am asked, 'Why were you not a Moses?' I will answer, 'Because I was not born to do what Moses did.' And if the heavenly host argues, 'You did not perform the miracles that Elijah did,' I shall tell them, 'Those were Elijah's miracles to perform, not mine.' My friends, the only question I fear I shall be unable to answer is: 'Why were you not a Rabbi Zusya?'"

Destiny is a personal adventure. Just as no two snowflakes or fingerprints are alike, every soul comes into this world for a unique purpose. Each of us manifests good according to our own strengths and intentions. Never compare your worth to that of others because you did not accomplish what they did; you were never supposed to be like them.

Your highest purpose in life is to be true to yourself. If you honor your personal gifts, intuition, inclinations, and visions, you will fulfill your destiny and serve many others in the process.

Help me be true to who and what I am.
I trust that the gifts and visions You planted within me are good.
Illuminate my path that I may bless the world.

I am whole as God created me.
I walk the path appointed me with confidence and joy.

54

Ain't No Future in the Past

Don't let the past remind us of what we are not now.
— from the song, "Suite: Judy Blue Eyes," by Stephen Stills

The last time I had seen Cora, she was a weak, heavily medicated chronic asthma patient who labored to walk from her living room to her bathroom. She had literally died in the hospital and been revived. When Cora showed up at my seminar a year later, I was amazed to see that she had lost a great deal of weight, gotten free of her medication, and looked vital and radiant.

When, during the seminar, the attendees were slated to hike up a mountain, I worried that this moderate trek would be too much for Cora, and I suggested she take a more gentle walk. Instead, she began to lead the group up the mountain! She set a dynamic pace, and the rest of the participants had to hustle to keep up with her. Was this the same woman, I wondered, whose family had been advised by doctors to say their good-byes to her?

No, it was not the same woman. The sick woman I remembered had died and been resurrected as healthy. It was only in my thoughts that I maintained a distorted image of an ill Cora. I was trying to stuff a new and expanded being into a tiny box to which I consigned her in my mind.

Cora's transformation offers a profound model of the way we keep each other bound to our past—and can liberate ourselves to be entirely new in the present. We must be open to being new and seeing new; otherwise we freeze our friends and ourselves as we were, and we die to the life and power of the moment. Our only hope to truly live is to release our past in favor of the *now* moment. Ever since I saw Cora master that mountain, I've realized that *anything* is possible—if we let it be.

Help me to see anew today. Exchange everything that was, for everything that could be.

Infinite possibilities are available to me now. I accept the best as reality.

55

So Far So Good

Through many dangers, toils, and snares we have already come;
'Twas grace that brought me safe thus far, and grace will lead me home.
— from the song, "Amazing Grace," by John Newton

When I was in college, I went to a rock festival in Puerto Rico, replete with every drug possible. One night I took a walk along the beach where many rock 'n' rollers were camping, and each person I passed handed me a pill or swig of alcohol. With great foolishness, I ingested every consciousness-altering agent I was given. It is no surprise that I had a bad trip. Every fearful and paranoid thought I ever entertained riled up to literally scare the hell out of me. During the night, I knew that I had really done it this time, and I was going to die.

Yet, somehow I made it through the night, and I remember sitting on a rock overlooking the beach, watching the sunrise. It was the most welcome sight I had ever seen. With the sun came the awareness that I had been forgiven, and my delusional fantasies were untrue. My idea of how I was to be punished was superseded by God's idea of love.

Perhaps you, too, felt that you would never make it through the night or week. Then consider that you are still here. God's law of grace is bigger than our notion of karma. You have a purpose here, and there is a force of love that keeps you going as long as your purpose is yet to be fulfilled. There are angels, guides, and guardians who watch over us to keep us safe and protected. There is an invisible force of good that guides us home, even when we have turned away from it.

Should you become fearful about the future or fall prey to the expectation of punishment, consider that you have been well taken care of thus far. All of your fears have been offset by grace. Could the current situation be an exception to the law of love?

Help me to remember that You are present wherever I am. Thank You for taking such good care of me even when I have not honored myself. Let me learn to love me as You do.

Surely goodness and mercy shall follow me all the days of my life, and I will dwell in the House of the Lord forever.

56

For Your Own Sake, Forgive

Holding resentment is like eating poison and then waiting for the other person to keel over.

— Anonymous

As a massage therapist in a hospital, Irene was assigned to give physical therapy to a cancer patient who, according to the doctors' prognosis, had but a short time to live. While Irene was treating Mrs. Harmon, she asked the elderly woman about the pain in her life. "My greatest sorrow is that I have not spoken to my sister in 20 years," lamented Mrs. Harmon. When Irene encouraged the woman to talk about her long-held resentment, Mrs. Harmon burst into tears, reporting how hard it had been to hold a grudge against her sister, whom she truly loved. The two women embraced, and Mrs. Harmon reported that she felt relieved.

The following week when Irene returned to the hospital, she was surprised to find Mrs. Harmon dressed, wearing makeup, and looking significantly healthier. "Where are you going?" asked Irene.

"Home, darling," Mrs. Harmon answered. "When they took me in for x-rays, they found no sign of cancer."

When we hold on to anger, hurt, or resentment, we only hurt ourselves. By withholding love from another, we deny it to ourselves. If you keep someone in prison with your thoughts, you have to sit at their jail door to keep them from escaping, and thus become a prisoner yourself.

To free another is to free yourself. When you give the gift of release, your spirit is healed.

Lift all negativity, resentment, and sense of victimhood from my heart.
I want to recreate my relationships to reflect only love, honor, and healing.

I give freedom and I am free.

57

Who's the Phony?

Be humble before God, but great in Him.
— A Course in Miracles

An interviewer asked a number of movie executives, "What is your greatest fear?" Over 80 percent of these wealthy, powerful, and successful people answered, "I fear that if people knew who I really am, they would discover I am a phony and that I don't really know what I am doing." The irony of this common fear is that these people are among the most respected in their industry—not for fooling people, but for the real achievements they have engineered. So, indeed, each is a phony—but the phony one is not the successful business person; it is the one who believes, "I am a phony."

To be successful in any endeavor, we must allow Spirit to work through us. There is a higher power that will flow through us if we allow it. Rarely do great artists claim credit for their own achievements. When we are at our best, we become an open channel through which Spirit can express. In the Hindu tradition, Krishna is the incarnation of God who gingerly plays the flute that makes all the maidens swoon. God is the player, and we are the flute.

The belief system of the ego, demonstrated by the movie executives' responses, is the inverse of the truth. We are phony in our unworthiness and genuine in our strength.

Let me not identify with smallness, but the greatness in which You created me.

I cannot fail because Spirit lives in me, through me, as me.

58

Thank You for Everything

The attitude of gratitude brings altitude.

— Anonymous

In *The Gospel According to Jesus*[4], Stephen Mitchell adapts a marvelous Zen parable from Zenkei Shibayama's *A Flower Does Not Talk:*

There lived a woman named Sono, whose devotion and purity of heart were respected far and wide. One day a fellow Buddhist, having made a long trip to see her, asked, "What can I do to put my heart at rest?"

Sono said, "Every morning and every evening, and whenever anything happens to you, keep on saying, 'Thank you for everything. I have no complaint whatsoever.'"

The man did as he was instructed for a whole year, but his heart was still not at peace. He returned to Sono crestfallen. "I've said your prayer over and over, and yet nothing in my life has changed; I'm still the same selfish person as before. What should I do now?"

Sono immediately said, "Thank you for everything. I have no complaint whatsoever." On hearing these words, the man was able to open his spiritual eye, and he returned home with a great joy.

Gratitude is the most powerful meditation of a lifetime. As you focus on gratitude, you will quickly find your way home to God. It is not the things that happen to us that make or break us; it is the way we think about them. It is possible to find something to be grateful for in every situation. The happiest people are those who practice thankfulness.

Appreciation is more of a gift to the giver than to the receiver. Those who constantly appreciate others prime the flow of love through their own hearts. Even if the recipient does not receive the gift, the giver is blessed by giving it. In real estate, when a property appreciates, its value increases. When we give appreciation, the value of our life increases.

Help me to give thanks. As I bless, I am blessed.

Thank you for everything.
I have no complaint whatsoever.

59

Come Home

Keep love in your heart. A life without it is like a sunless garden when the flowers are dead. The consciousness of loving and being loved brings a warmth and richness to life that nothing else can bring.

— Oscar Wilde

In a small town in Spain, a man named Jorge had a bitter argument one morning with his young son, Paco. When he arrived home later that day, Jorge discovered that Paco's room was empty—he had run away from home.

Overcome with remorse, Jorge searched his soul and realized that his son was more important to him than anything else. He wanted to start over. Jorge went to a well-known grocery store in the center of town and posted a large sign that read, *"Paco, come home. I love you. Meet me here tomorrow morning."*

The next morning, Jorge went to the store, where he found no less than seven young boys named Paco who had also run away from home. They were all answering the call for love, hoping it was their dad inviting them home with open arms.

Love is the great need of this world. While we have achieved all manner of material success, human beings on this planet daily cry out—and die—for love. If only we could love, how quickly would our problems dissipate! No matter how old, hardened, or sophisticated we are, there always lives within us a tender child that yearns to give and receive love.

At the age of 35, I went to visit my mother while I was hurting emotionally. She sensed my pain and invited me to sit on her lap. She held me tenderly and caressed me, and in that moment I learned that I will never be too old to receive motherly love, and that a mother will never outgrow her joy in giving it.

Consider the people in your life, including yourself, who are calling out for love. How can you give it? In your answer rests the key to your healing and freedom.

Help me to recognize calls for love, and give me the ability to respond.

My life is about connecting with my brothers and sisters. I live from the heart.

Time for Myself

It's important to run not on the fast track, but on your track. Pretend you have only six months to live. Make three lists: the things you have to do, want to do, and neither have to do nor want to do. Then, for the rest of your life, forget everything in the third category.

— Robert S. Eliot and Dennis L. Breo

One of the reports I hear most frequently from people who have been married and/or parents for a long time is, "It took me a long time to claim my right to take time for myself." Many spouses believe they must fulfill their partner's needs before their own, and they subsequently build up resentment. This need not be the case. If you are honest and diligent about nourishing your own soul as you go along, you will not need to do a lot of catching up later.

Leap Day is a rare moment when we catch our calendar up to the actual number of trips we have taken around the sun. We may consider this day symbolic of our need to catch up with ourselves. Time is an arbitrary invention of the human mind, and as such, we can use it, contract it, or stretch it to meet our needs and fulfill our visions. Energizing your spirit is the best use of time.

After an intensive seminar, Becky, one of the attendees, announced that her theme upon returning home would be, *My turn now.* "I have taken care of so many people for so long that I forgot how to take care of myself. Now I am ready." I was happy to soon receive a letter from Becky informing me that she had won a songwriter's contest.

Giving yourself time is the same as giving yourself love. Start by recognizing that you deserve to operate from a fully charged battery, and then go about the business of charging it.

Help me stay true to my ideals and visions.

I use my time productively and joyfully.
I make meaningful use of my day.

Prototype, Not Exception

Let not the world see fear and sad distrust govern the motion of a kingly eye.
— William Shakespeare

On my birthday, I made up my mind to have a wonderful day. I made plans to be with friends, scheduled a massage, and put worldly matters aside. Then an emergency repair forced me to curtail some of my celebration appointments. As I stood in the rain with the repairman, my mind began to grumble. Then I decided, "No, I will not allow this to ruin my day," and I kept my attitude high. The repair was handled, and I went on with my celebration. At the end of the day, I felt wonderful, and the interruption actually added to my joy, for I gained strength in choosing peace. I remember the love, not the disappointment.

The next morning, I began to feel sad that my day of joy had passed. Then I realized that I have the power to make every day a celebration. Why would a birthday, weekend, or vacation be an exception to life? Happiness is the way of life, and any other kind of day is the exception.

During World War I, the French and German armies held a cease-fire on Christmas. Soldiers from both armies went into local towns, ate dinner, drank wine, and sang together in the same taverns. The next day, they went back to killing each other. It seems to me that if they could agree to not fight for one day, they could agree to not fight for another, and another, and another, and sooner or later they would not fight at all.

Some theologians teach that Jesus was an exception to life—that he was God's only begotten son. But Jesus was not an only child. He had many brothers and sisters, including you and me. We, too, are the sons and daughters of God, holy offspring of a perfect divinity. Jesus was our elder brother who found his way home and showed us the path. He is not a deity to be worshiped, but a model to be emulated and equaled. He said, "Even greater things than I shall you do." He would not have uttered those words if we were lesser or different than he.

The love and the good and the beauty is the truth; anything else is the exception.

Help me to live my potential of love every day.

I am a child of God.
I deserve to live in celebration.

Take the Best and Leave the Rest

Love is the way I walk in gratitude.
— A Course in Miracles

My dog Munchie is quite discerning. He eats only what he likes and rejects everything else. If I offer Munchie a piece of plain bread, he walks away from it. If I give him a slice with peanut butter on it, however, he licks off the peanut butter and leaves the bread.

Take what belongs to you by right of your joy and consciousness, and let the rest go. We are not required to put up with situations we cannot digest. We are required to do what expands and heals us and reject what causes us to contract.

The awakened mind functions as a "blessing extractor." Like a vegetable juicer that grinds up a carrot and spits the pulp out of one chute and sends juice out of another, the blessing extractor takes any experience and draws forth the good from it. It shows you how you can enjoy, learn, or grow from all events and relationships. All else is chaff, which goes back into the field to grow next year's crops.

When looking back on past relationships, we must take the best and leave the rest. Bless the other person, yourself, and the relationship for the gifts you gained and the experience through which you grew. Hold on to your appreciation, and release the regret. It does not belong to you. Recycled properly, the relationship will become fertilizer to grow on.

Similarly, every teacher will offer you wisdom you can use, as well as ideas you do not understand, agree with, or wish to employ. Take the best and leave the rest. There is a nugget of good in every experience. Receive what God wants you to have, and let Spirit take care of the rest.

Show me what is mine, and give me the wisdom and strength to put aside all else.

I open myself to be fed by love in the forms that speak to my heart, and I release everything that does not belong to me.

Beyond the Dark Night

Though I walk through the valley
of the shadow of death, I will fear no evil.
— Psalm 23

At some point, everyone passes through a dark night of the soul. This is a difficult time in which we are moving from an old life to a new one, with no apparent security or help in sight. It appears that the old is being taken away by a hand larger than our own, and there is no solid ground on which to stand. As old friends or supporters fall away, we feel like misfits in a world that does not understand us. The activities and things that once gave us comfort seem empty or unavailable, and sometimes it appears that all is lost. At such a time, we are called upon to search deep within ourselves for faith.

Although the dark night is painful and harrowing, it is an important and productive time. If you are passing though a dark night, take comfort in the truth that there is a bigger picture than the one you are seeing, a larger hand operating behind appearances. The dark is a time to clear away the old to make way for the new and better. Nothing is taken away that is not replaced with something more valuable. The field is being turned over so that old weeds and dead roots can be dissolved and new seeds sown. Spring is not far behind the winter.

When I have gone through such experiences, this message has come to me loud and clear: *Surrender to love.* Do not try to fight the changes, and do not try to understand them. In your anxiety, do not attempt to clutch at the old for security; instead, do your best to release what was, and be open to what is to come. Define all the changes as good, and look for their blessings. The day will come when you will look back at such a time and say, "Thank you."

Hold my hand, God, during a time of shadows.
Though I see You not,
I trust that You are present.

All change is good. I surrender to love.

From Where?

No one reaches love with fear beside him.
— A Course in Miracles

Carla sat down with Brian, her newly hired business manager, and formulated a priority list of jobs that needed to be done. After the list was recorded, Brian handed the paper back to Carla and asked her to make one more distinction among the listed tasks: "Write an 'F' next to those jobs that you think need to be done immediately because you are in fear, and place a 'J' next to those jobs that proceed from joy and creativity."

Fear is never a good reason to do anything. Any action born of fear cannot succeed, except as a lesson that fear does not work. Enthusiasm, delight, and service, on the other hand, are excellent motivations for endeavors, and they will attract tremendous support because you are investing in aliveness rather then self-protection.

We always get more of whatever energy we put out into the universe; our actions are less important than the beliefs and feelings that motivate them. At a world peace conference, an African priest told me, "In my hotel room I saw a big sign warning, *'Be sure to keep your suitcase locked. Protect yourself from thieves.'* As I began to lock my suitcase, something did not feel right. I was not afraid of theft before I saw that sign, so why should I go into anxiety after reading it? It occurred to me that the problem of nuclear weapons stems from people protecting themselves before the bad guys get them. I felt hypocritical being a speaker at a peace conference and buying into paranoia. I would have been contributing to the very energy I am trying to offset."

While you must consult your own intuition about what you lock, the priest illuminated an important principle: When we act out of fear, we add to the sum total of darkness on the planet, and when we act from love, we bring light to the world.

I pray to stay on purpose. I am here to love.

I release fear and embrace trust.

65

Whom Did You Expect?

Experience is the worst teacher. It always gives the test first and the instruction afterward.

— Niklaus Wirth

When I taught adult school, I offered a yoga class followed by a stress-management course that I called "Easing on Down the Road." The first night of the semester, the yoga class ran a few minutes overtime, and I noticed one of the students from the second class standing outside the door, nervously pacing back and forth. The man kept looking in the window, checking his watch, and making an anxious face. When his class began, he fidgeted and squirmed most of the time. He was one of the most uptight students I have ever encountered. During his class, I found myself inwardly complaining, "Why does someone as nervous as he is have to be in my class?" Then another internal voice asked me, "Whom did you expect to take this class—calm and peaceful people?" The voice had a point. I had advertised to teach stress management, and I shouldn't have been surprised to get stressed students. My complaint was as unfounded as a doctor wanting to see only healthy patients.

If you offer a service, welcome challenge from those who come to you to receive it. They are the contingent that will keep you on the cutting edge of your creativity and force you to go deeper into your latent genius. Your difficult clients will motivate you to open to the next level beyond the one that is currently comfortable, and ultimately improve your skills.

You are here to make the world a better place. Staying in the safety zone changes nothing. Stretching into uncharted territory will bring light to places that were dark. Congratulations on signing up to be an angel.

I pray to offer service to those who can be most helped by my unique talents.

I serve on the cutting edge of my destiny.

Masters All

Don't bunt. Aim out of the ball park.
Aim for the company of the immortals.
— David Ogilvy

One of the ways in which we hurt ourselves on the spiritual path is to define ourselves as seekers, students, or addicts. For a time, we are, of course, looking and learning. After that, however, we must acknowledge the truth of our wholeness.

Everyone on the planet is a master of something. The question is not *"Are you a master?"* but *"What are you a master of?"* As godly beings, we have the ability to succeed at whatever we put our mind to. Humanity's challenge is not that we lack the ability to succeed, but that we have applied our skills to things that hurt us.

I once hired a man who I did not know was a drug addict. I loaned him money that he hedged about repaying, and I gave him privileges he abused. When I confronted him, he manufactured some of the most convincing lies I have ever heard. I would go to him with facts that clearly pointed to his lack of integrity, and he would quickly and deftly come up with excuses that I believed. Eventually, he stole a few items and left without notice. In retrospect, I realized I was dealing with a master—a master liar. This fellow was also a master artist. He could have been a great success, but most of his energies went down the drain of his addiction.

Many of us have mastered drama, emergency, lack, worry, and sabotaged relationships. We are able to take a situation with great potential and find a way to undermine it—that is truly mastery! Now we must take the skills we have used to hurt ourselves and apply them to our healing. We must harness the force of intelligent love and build the life we choose rather than the one we fear. We must step forward with the magnificent, innate wisdom we were given and make the planet a heavenly place to live. All of this is clearly within our capacity. Let us manifest our mastery of the divine, which is what we came here to do.

Help me use my gifts to make my life and the world a magnificent place.

God has imbued me with greatness.
I let it shine!

67

God's Law Above All

I am under no laws but God's.
— A Course in Miracles

A woman came to our healing group and requested prayer while she awaited the results of a biopsy. That night in a dream, I saw a photographic negative covered by a large book. When I meditated on the meaning of the dream, I recognized that the negative was a medical x-ray, symbolizing the laws of medicine. The book was *A Course in Miracles,* symbolizing the power of Spirit to heal anything. The message was clear: The laws of God supersede the "laws" of this world. The next day I received a phone call from the woman, telling me that her test results showed that she was healthy.

All of the "laws" to which the world subscribes have no power in the face of divine grace and true love. The "laws" of medicine, economics, government, and social expectations are limited belief systems and cannot provide us with the security that universal principles offer us. To truly be healed, we must go beyond what the world tells us and take refuge in the reality of Spirit.

Let me know without a doubt that only
Your law of peace is constant.

I surrender all beliefs in limited laws.
My power is absolute
universal love.

The Right of Consciousness

Circumstances do not make the man—they reveal him.
— James Allen

When I complimented my friend on her car, she reported, "My husband wants the car as part of our divorce. But because I brought the car into the marriage, I argued with him. Then I realized that it was *my consciousness* that drew the car to me. My husband can take the car, but not my consciousness. I told him he could have the car. I still have my consciousness, and with that I can attract a dozen more cars if I want to."

What we have is not a result of luck or circumstance, but thought and attitude. Some people succeed at everything they do, and others fail consistently. The life we live is not cast upon us like a net; it is magnetized by our attitude. No one can take from you anything you deserve by right of your consciousness, and you cannot keep something you have not earned by virtue of your thoughts.

The most powerful way to improve your circumstances is by upgrading your consciousness. If you try to change your situation without changing your mind, sooner or later you will revert to your former position. When you change your mind, life has no choice but to re-cluster itself according to the new level of vibration at which you are operating.

Help me keep You in my thoughts, that my world may reflect divinity everywhere I look.

My consciousness of good magnetizes ever-increasing blessings to me.

69

Hold Your Ground

If you don't run your own life, someone else will.
— John Atkinson

After the filming of *Field of Dreams* was completed on location in Iowa, one of the farmers who owned the plot of land where the movie was shot, plowed a section of the baseball field. Soon he was faced with such an outcry from neighbors and visitors that he yielded and restored the field. Later he acknowledged, "Well, I guess if it makes people happy to come, that's fine with me."

Don't let anyone plow under your field of dreams. While it may mean little to them, it is precious to you. If you love your project or vision, stand behind it. It needs your energy and caring. If your venture is worthwhile, the world will come around. And even if the world does not stand in acclaim, you cannot afford to abandon the child of your heart.

Give me the strength to uphold what
You would have me do.
I believe in me, and I believe in You.

I bring my visions to life with faith and action.

70

Get Fired

If you aren't fired with enthusiasm,
you will be fired with enthusiasm.

— Vince Lombardi

Andrew was an attorney who hated law but loved computers. It was no surprise, then, that when his firm went bankrupt Andrew researched bankruptcy laws and recorded his notes on his computer. After several months, he realized that he had arranged a wealth of information in a way that no one else had. Andrew took his notes and computer program to some executives at Apple Computers, who were so impressed by what he had done that they offered him a handsome sum of money to develop the program. Now he works with enthusiasm as a legal program consultant for Apple.

The key ingredient for success is enthusiasm. You can have a wealth of skills, but if your heart is not fully present, you will feel unfulfilled, and your work will reflect it. If you have enthusiasm, you will find the energy to acquire the necessary skills and draw to you all the people and support you need to succeed.

We dishonor ourselves and others by staying in positions out of familiarity or obligation. If you tolerate boredom or compromise, the universe will fire you so you can be in your right place where you can really be fired. The word *enthusiasm* comes from the Latin *de Teos,* meaning "from God." Whenever you are enthusiastic about something, no matter what it is, you are in God. When you act without excitement, you have strayed from your source. If it is not a "Hell, yes!," it is a "No." If you practice this principle, you will be in your right place, you will feel fulfilled, and miracles will happen through you.

Give me the courage to live from enthusiasm and not fear.

I do what I love, and the universe fulfills me and everyone I affect.

One Link at a Time

It is a mistake to try to look too far ahead.
The chain of destiny can only be grasped
one link at a time.
— Winston Churchill

Author and Unity minister Eric Butterworth gave a 15-minute radio talk every day for over 30 years, during which he inspired countless millions with illuminating ideas. When someone asked Dr. Butterworth how he was able to come up with a unique address for such a long time, he answered, "I just do one at a time. Sometimes I sit down to write a week's worth of talks, and the prospect seems overwhelming. Then I remember that I just have to write one. So I write what is most alive within me at that moment, and when I am done, I ask myself what is stimulating to me now. Before I know it, they are all done."

I have written a dozen books in 15 years. If at the outset someone had told me I would do that, or asked me to take on such a project, there is no way I would have agreed. But each book showed up in its own time, along with the energy and enthusiasm to make it happen. Somehow they add up.

If you feel overwhelmed with projects or responsibilities, ask yourself, "What do I really need to attend to right now?" Then handle the project at hand as if it is the only one. You will have a lot more fun thinking of it in that way, and you will be amazed at how the bowling pins fall one after another if you focus on what can be done in the moment. God never requires anything of us that is beyond our capacity to perform. The secret is to forge the chain one link at a time.

Show me how to live one day at a time.
I will do what I can with joy and enthusiasm, and trust You
to do what I cannot.

Now is my moment. I do my best and
leave the rest to God.

Rocks or Light?

Your task is not to seek for love, but to find the barriers in yourself that you have built against it.
— A Course in Miracles

The Hawaiian spiritual tradition teaches that every child born into this world is like a "bowl of light" containing the radiance of heaven. If rocks are placed into the bowl, the light of original innocence is hidden. Fear, guilt, and unworthiness are some of the stones that mask our true brilliance. The more rocks in our bowl, the less light we shine. Angry, nasty, or irksome people have lots of rocks in their bowls, while radiant, happy, and joyful people have few.

The game of enlightenment is not about going out and getting something we do not have or becoming something we are not. We are already enlightened; we have simply covered our wisdom. We started out fine; then we got de-fined; now we must be re-fined.

Health, happiness, and success are our birthright, and we carry all we need within us to manifest all the good we seek. But first we must remove everything from our consciousness that works against the full expression of what we are.

What rocks are in your bowl? Begin to note the beliefs and attitudes you hold that stand between you and the light that you are. When you act out of fear or self-doubt, you add more rocks to your bowl. When you let go of one of these impediments, you release your true essence to shine.

Help me to release anything that stands between me and the expression of the light that I am.
I claim my identity and inheritance as a being of splendid light.

I am as God created me.
I am the light of the world.

73

The Way Out

Live for another if you wish to live for yourself.
— Seneca

"I just called to let you know how much I love you," a friendly voice resonated over the telephone.

"Thank you, Cliff—I really appreciate that," I responded.

"I'll tell you why I called now," continued Cliff. "My knee was hurting, and I know the only way I can feel better is to give love."

Just as it is impossible to whistle and chew crackers at the same time, you cannot give love and be depressed. *A Course in Miracles* teaches that there are only two emotions, love and fear; at any moment we are experiencing one or the other. The surest antidote to pain, self-pity, loneliness, or depression is to reach out to give love or help someone. Dr. Gerald Jampolsky, author of *Love Is Letting Go of Fear,* recounts that if he began to feel depressed, he would call someone who was ill or visit a nursing home. I learned the same lesson when teaching. On many occasions I would feel tired, upset, or self-involved when scheduled to teach. If I hadn't been obligated to be there, I probably would have stayed balled up in my own little world. Going to teach and being present for the students always shifted my attitude. By the end of the class, after giving of myself I would feel 100 percent better, and I would wonder how I could have ever felt so troubled.

Studies have shown that people in nursing homes and rehabilitation centers heal more quickly when they have a pet or plants to care for. The act of giving love is nurturing to the soul.

Should you feel separate, make a list of people to whom you could give love through a phone call, visit, or other act of kindness. Simply making this list will lift you immeasurably, and acting on it will change your life.

I pray to reach out beyond my separateness and discover that my healing is joined with service.

Love heals me as I give it.

Becoming

I call on your pride. Remember what you've done,
what you dream of doing,
and rise up. Great Heavens,
consider yourself with more respect!
— Gustave Flaubert's advice to a depressed friend

While waiting at a stoplight, I found myself next to a thrift-store truck transporting donated clothing and household goods. On the side of the truck, a huge sign suggested, *"If It's Not Becoming to You, It Should Be Coming to Us."*

Every person and thing in this world has a purpose and a right place. If you are using and enjoying what you have, then bless it. If it is not working for you or if you don't use it, pass it on—it has more value elsewhere.

I once took a job in a sheltered workshop for retarded people. While the job offered many valuable lessons and rewards, I was not happy there. For months I guilt-tripped myself for wanting to leave, and rationalized all sorts of reasons why I should stay. Egotistically, I believed I was doing a better job than anyone else could, and if I left, these unfortunate retarded people would be bereft. I even made up a story in my mind that I had been retarded in a previous life, and some kind fellow had taken care of me; now I was repaying the karma I owed. Finally, I got sick and realized I would rather leave and take my chances than wither in the position. The moment I gave notice, I felt free, healthy, and alive again. At that point, my career as a writer took off, which has blessed me immeasurably. When I later visited the workshop, I saw that the fellow who replaced me was doing a far better job than I ever did. Out of guilt, I was stealing his job from him and withholding my right work from myself!

Make a vow to participate in only those career and social situations that are becoming to you; if not, let them "be coming" to someone else.

Give me the strength and wisdom to be in my right place.

I claim my right place and support others to be in their right place.

Dolphins Await

Dismiss whatever insults your soul.
— Walt Whitman

One night at a Hawaiian retreat, I had a vivid dream of swimming with dolphins. The next morning I attended a business meeting that I found boring and purposeless. Although I sat and tried to be present, all I could think about was going to the beach. When I recognized I was useless at the meeting, I politely excused myself and made a beeline for the beach. Soon after I arrived, a huge pod of dolphins surfaced in the bay, and I swam out to play with them. For a long time I was surrounded by their delightful presence, and I was thrilled to frolic with them. I was able to look into their eyes, which was like peering into a warm eternity. Was I ever glad I left the meeting!

If your spirit is not present where you are, and you feel intuitively called elsewhere, you must hearken to your inner voice. I am not encouraging you to be irresponsible and run away from things you need to do. I am encouraging you to be responsive to your spirit. It is not responsible to engage in activities that affront your soul.

Years ago I sat in a group with my teacher Hilda[5], watching a video of an old musical. I was tired and wanted to leave, but I felt socially obligated to stay. So I sat there and silently fumed; my body was present, but I was elsewhere. The next day when I told Hilda about my experience, she commented, "So you were the one who was fogging the atmosphere. I felt a disturbance somewhere in the group. You should have gotten up and gone when you wanted to. That would have been a greater service to yourself and everyone."

Honor your soul by being where you belong.

Help me to be attuned to the call of my soul.
Give me the courage to honor my intuition.

Spirit speaks to me through my heart,
and I answer through my deeds.

ILVU4FR

The trick, according to Chiang, was for Jonathan to stop seeing himself as trapped inside a limited body with a forty-two inch wingspan....The trick was to know that his true nature lived, as perfect as an unwritten number, everywhere at once across space and time.

— from *Jonathan Livingston Seagull*, by Richard Bach

Robert signed Janet's senior yearbook in the above personal shorthand, meaning: *"I love you forever."* Shortly after graduation, the two married and bore a beautiful son, Teddy. Robert was offered a good job and flew to New York for an interview, from which he called with the exciting news that he had been hired. Tragically, he never arrived home; he was killed by a drunk driver. Several months later, Janet's funds were dwindling, and her life looked hopeless. Four-year-old Teddy was drawing with crayons one day when he said, matter-of-factly, "Daddy," and wrote "ILVU4FR," followed by "MDTNBK34STBX1142."

Janet took the paper to Robert's business partner and the two decoded: "Midtown Bank on 34th St." Remembering Robert's business trip, Janet dipped into her small savings and flew to New York. There she found Midtown Bank and learned that Robert had taken a safe deposit box, in which she found a life insurance policy for $200,000.

A very thin veil separates the physical world from the world of spirit. While everything on earth seems solid, it is interpenetrated with other dimensions that we can perceive with higher vision. If necessary, we can communicate with those in spirit, and they with us.

Love has the power to span dimensions. If you have a dream or the sensation of departed loved ones, it is likely that they are in your field of consciousness and wish to communicate with you. There is nothing spooky about interdimensional communication; it is as real and natural as two people on different parts of the globe communicating via telephone.

Open your mind and heart to a greater universe, and be blessed by love from all dimensions.

Open my eyes, mind, and heart to the highest communication in spirit.

Everyone I love is always with me.

Move the Spotlight

If someone in your life talked to you the way you talk to yourself, you would have left them long ago.

— Dr. Carla Gordan*

I wondered why I had signed up for this expensive astrology consultation. As the astrologer discussed my chart, I found myself feeling bored and impatient. Finally, he made an assessment that rang my chimes: "You are the kind of person who, if you did a job with 99 percent excellence, would berate yourself for the other one percent." I had never thought about myself that way, but he was correct. The entire reading and fee were worth that insight.

The amount of abusive self-talk we put up with is incredible. We must retrain our mind to spotlight what is working rather than what is not. The rational mind is programmed to search for errors and imperfections. But the nature of the heart is to find what is lovable and expand on that. The habit of fault-finding is learned and, as such, we can re-educate our vision to find perfection. *A Course in Miracles* tells us that we are much too tolerant of mind-wandering. We allow our fearful mind to run in every which way without calling it to return to sanity. We will have as much insanity in our lives as we allow; we can eliminate it entirely if we choose.

In prayer or meditation, ask that you become aware of patterns of thought with which you hurt yourself: *"Poor me," "Never enough,"* and *"Why can't I?"* are trains of thought that will take you over a cliff if you ride them. If you read the destination printed on the train before you step onto it, you can choose another train and replace those negative patterns with *"Blessed me," "Always enough,"* and *"How can I?" A Course in Miracles* asks us to affirm, *"I can elect to change all thoughts that hurt."*

Instead of being a fault-finder, become a perfection-finder, and quickly the world you live in will reflect your vision.

Show me how to think in harmony with Your will.
I want to live in the world You created.

I find the good because I seek it.

The C.C.C.C.

Hands of invisible spirits touch the strings
of that mysterious instrument, the soul,
and play the prelude of our future.
— Henry Wadsworth Longfellow

"He was my first and greatest love," Michele told our seminar group. "But because I was young and he was older, my parents forbade me to see him. Tearfully we parted, and although I grew up and went through two marriages, I held him in my heart, and he always lived in the back of my mind. Eventually we lost track of each other, and I always wondered how he was. I moved from the Bronx and started a new life in Florida. One day I walked into a 7-Eleven in Clearwater, and there he was—it had been 37 years. We talked and then we went out to dinner. I knew that our meeting was not about us getting back together. It was an answer to my prayer of completing with this man whom I loved so much."

What great mind could have known how to reunite these two people who cared about each other so deeply? Surely no human technology could draw two lovers together after 37 years and a thousand miles of distance. There is, however, a powerful organization that coordinates such events. It is called the C.C.C.C.—*the Cosmic Coincidence Control Center.* This invisible agency neatly arranges the meeting of any two people who need to connect for an important reason. The center works day and night to keep track of all hearts' desires and soul needs. All prayers for healing are referred to the C.C.C.C., and the agency makes sure that any incomplete soul issues magnetize the perfect people to work them out.

No one is ever more than a thought away. If it is right, you will draw them or someone similar to you so that your heart may rest.

Lift my vision beyond the limits of this world. Help me remember that I can and will be joined with everyone and everything I need. Thank you for bringing me the right and perfect people and events for the fulfillment of my purpose.

The spirit of love arranges all meetings in divine order for the highest good of all concerned.

79

The Holiest Orange

From you I receive, to you I give.
Together we share, from this we live.
— Rabbis Joseph and Nathan Siegel

On the Jewish holiday of Purim, it is the custom for neighbors to visit each others' houses with gifts of fruit. One Purim, three men on a business trip found themselves miles from civilization with but one orange between them. One man took the orange in his hands, held it close to his heart, turned to another man and told him, "My dear Chaim, with this orange I give you all my love, and I pray that God grants you a life of peace and plenty."

Chaim appreciatively accepted the orange and faced the third man, telling him, "My brother Yosef, this is a symbol of my deepest thanks for your friendship in my life. I wish you all the happiness your heart desires."

Yosef, nearly in tears, received the fruit and turned to the first man. "Beloved Jacob, you are a true man of God. May the angels of mercy walk by your side and return to you a thousandfold all the good you give."

Jacob received the orange and, brimming with ecstasy, gave it to Yosef again with an additional blessing. So the three men went on all night, adding more and more love to the orange until their souls were filled beyond measure.

The only gifts we truly have to offer one another are the gifts of spirit. Physical objects are but cups we fill with love. A gift, no matter how expensive, is not a gift unless it is given with sincerity and kindness. Even if our physical means are meager, if we imbue a gift with intention, it will bless the receiver in the deepest way.

Let my words and actions be filled only with love.
Let me use all the means of this world
to magnify the divine presence.

I give from my heart, and
I am filled in the giving.

Pray to Be Wrong

Would you rather be right, or happy?
— A Course in Miracles

When a friend and I were about to watch a video, the television screen showed only snow and distortion. My friend suggested, "Put in the video head cleaner," but I knew the problem was more serious, and I went on to spend a great deal of time fussing with wires and connections. Every now and then, she repeated, "Try the head cleaner," but I told her that was not the trouble. Finally, to appease her, I ran the head cleaner, and to my great surprise the picture completely cleared up. I was glad that I was wrong!

A problem is a call for us to open up our consciousness and view a situation from a different perspective. If we stubbornly cling to a position, we may miss the very awareness we need in order to master the situation at hand. No one knows it all. Be innocent enough to consider that the universe may be bigger than what you "know" to be true. You may gain more by being wrong than by tenaciously clinging to being right.

Make a list of all of your problems, troubles, and dilemmas. Then hold it in your hands and pray, "*Dear God, please let me be wrong about all of this.*" Your prayer will be answered because we are already whole, and as we allow Spirit to work on our behalf, our challenges are handled by grace.

I pray to be humble enough to see a grander picture than the one I have known.

I open my mind to live in a bigger universe.

Life Beginning

Fear not that thy life shall come to an end,
but rather fear that it shall never have a beginning.
— John Henry Cardinal Newman

"When I was diagnosed with cancer at the age of 17, I was sure that my life had come to an end," Edward told the seminar audience. "I hated the chemotherapy, all the medicalese, and the whole arena of sickness I seemed to enter. Sure, my body didn't feel good, but my Spirit was dying in all those morbid thoughts. Then, one day I was scheduled for chemotherapy when I discovered that there was a Grateful Dead concert the same night. The concert was much more attractive than the chemo, and I struggled with the decision over what to do. I realized that I had lived my whole life trying to please my parents and make everyone happy. I decided that this was my chance to make myself happy, and I went to the concert. Soon my condition was reversed, and I have been cancer free for years. I believe that it was my choice to be kind to myself that made all the difference."

It is not the years in our life that count, but the life in our years. We may live a long time in a small shell of fear, or a short time in a blaze of celebration. When we follow our spirit and live from joy rather than self-protection, the whole world opens up to us, and we have the power to make our dreams come true.

Cheri Huber declared, "I don't want to tiptoe through life just to arrive safely at death." What dreams have you been postponing? What steps could you take now to make them a reality? Do you live from fear or delight? What gift could you give yourself that would remind you that life is beautiful and worth living? Answer these questions honestly, and the road to freedom will be illumined for you.

I want to live today. I want to put my dreams into action.
I want to leave behind all that is not me and fully celebrate
my gifts. Thank you for showing me the way to freedom.

Today I begin my life anew.
I take my life in my hands and celebrate
every wonderful opportunity to soar.

82

Jesus and Judas

Life is a long lesson in humility.
— James Matthew Barrie

When Rembrandt set out to paint the likenesses of Jesus and the apostles, he walked the streets of Amsterdam to find men who embodied the character of his Biblical subjects. Rembrandt began with a tall, handsome man who bore the stature and purity of the Christ. Then, after setting the images of the disciples to canvas, Rembrandt was ready to paint Judas, and he searched for a man with a tortured soul. After combing Paris, he found a homeless man sitting outside a store. The man was dirty, unkempt, and his eyes spoke of deep sadness. After painting Judas, Rembrandt thanked the man for his assistance.

"Don't you remember me?" asked the man.

"I don't think so," answered the artist.

"I sat for your portrait of Jesus," the man answered.

Within every human being is the propensity to rise to the highest of the high and sink to the lowest of the low. That is why we can never judge others for their sins or errors. Given the same circumstances, we might be in exactly their position and take the same action they did. Mother Teresa became a nun when she recognized that "there is a bit of Hitler in every one of us."

While we strive to be the Christ, we must have compassion for the Judas, who simply played out his role in the Christ drama. In the end, we are not the roles we play. We are the light that animates every soul in the dance we call life.

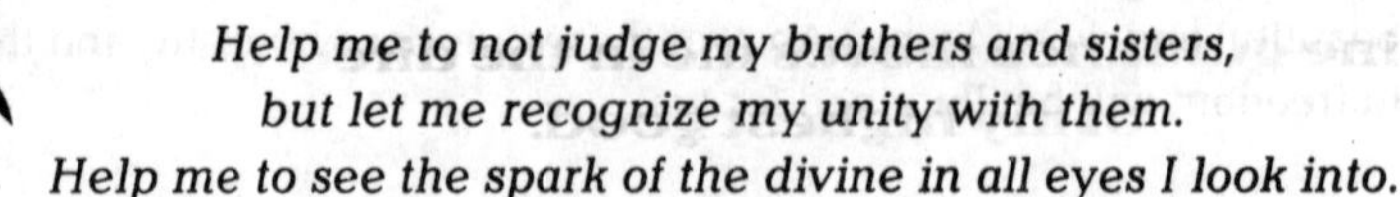

Help me to not judge my brothers and sisters,
but let me recognize my unity with them.
Help me to see the spark of the divine in all eyes I look into.

I am one with God and with everyone I meet.

Joy Is My Compass

Joy is the most ineffable sign of the presence of God.

— Leon Bloy

"Pick out a treat," I offered four-year-old Kate at the candy display. Quickly she grabbed a packet of M&M's with one hand and a Milky Way bar with the other.

"You can have only one," I told her.

"Eenie, meenie, miney, moe," she counted, finally landing on the M&M's.

"Okay, we get the M&M's," I confirmed.

Immediately, Kate threw the M&M's back in the bin and clutched the Milky Way bar. "I want this one."

Within our hearts, each of us knows what we really want. While our mind and emotions may go through all manner of drama and machinations, when we are confronted with the reality of choice, our heart will speak. Sometimes it is only when we receive what we do not want that we recognize what we do want.

When confronted with a difficult decision, flip a coin and imagine that you will be committed to the alternative the spin lands on. Then notice your *gut reaction* to the result. If you feel delighted, that is your path. If you are disappointed, go with the other alternative. Joy is the best compass.

Help me to be in touch with my heart's desires.
I trust you to know for me and through me.

Divine guidance moves me in the direction of my highest good.

Golden Moments

Do not wait for extraordinary circumstances to do good;
try to use ordinary situations.

— Jean Paul Richter

The phone blared at 6:45 A.M. I rolled over in the hotel bed, picked up the receiver, and heard the music for my wake-up call. Awkwardly, I pulled myself together and wandered toward the bathroom. Five minutes later, the phone rang again. Who could be calling at this hour?

"Good morning, Mr. Cohen," a pleasant voice resonated. "This is your wake-up call. Have a wonderful day." After she hung up, I stood for a moment and looked at the receiver. The key word was *wonderful;* she offered it quite sincerely, and I felt it. I tried to reason why a human being would call me after the automatic call, but I gave up and decided to just enjoy the gift. I went on to have a wonderful day.

It is not through world-shaking-triumphs that we build our life, but in the common daily interactions. The tone of our voice can win or lose a business deal, and a thoughtful hello can change a stranger's attitude. We never really know how far a little blessing will go. Go beyond the norm of expected kindness by even a little bit, and you will become a miracle worker.

Never underestimate the power of a kind word or act. Even if your gift does not seem to be received, your heart will soar. Love is always received in the heart of God, where we all live.

Today I will walk the path of kindness.
I will take the little moments of life
and weave them into gold.

My simplest words and acts change the world, beginning with my own.

At Faith Value

Faith is the substance of things hoped for,
the evidence of things not seen.
— Hebrews 11:1

"Hurry up, or we'll miss the bus!" shouted Paul. The streets of New York City became a blur as we jogged toward the bus terminal. Two blocks in five minutes—was it possible?

"You guys go up and catch the bus, and I'll get the tickets," offered Tom. We ran up the long escalator, brushing past less anxious passengers. At the top of the ramp, we saw the bus closing its doors. Running full speed, we reached the bus just as it was pulling out of its parking space. We pounded on the door, and the driver let us in. "Can you wait for our friend?" I implored. "He's getting our tickets."

"Sorry, fellas, I'm already late."

Paul stepped off the bus, looked toward the escalator, and exclaimed, "There he is!"

The driver rolled his eyes and indicated he would wait. Within moments, Tom showed up, short of breath, tickets in hand. As we made our way to the back of the bus, I told Paul, "It sure was great that you saw Tom coming; the bus would have left if you hadn't."

"That was good acting, don't you think?" Paul retorted.

"What do you mean?"

"I didn't see him coming; I only said that to stall the driver. We were lucky he showed up when he did!"

Real faith is acting as if your good is on its way even before you have evidence it is so. Jesus told us to give thanks for the answers to our prayers before we see the results. Faith is like a muscle. The more you use it, the stronger it becomes, and the more power you have to bring your good into visibility. Proclaim your good as if you already have it even before you see it, and you will see it.

Help me to celebrate my blessings before I can touch them.
Make the invisible visible to me.

I believe in my good, and I manifest it.

Stinkin' Thinkin'

You can't afford the luxury of a negative thought.
— John-Roger

When I was a child, my mother told me never to flush the toilet when I was sitting on it because "you might catch a cold in your tush." Trusting my mother's advice, I was careful not to flush imprudently, and I successfully avoided the dreaded tush cold. One day when I was 30 years old, I began to flush while sitting on the toilet, and I could hear my mother's voice warning me against it. But this time I decided to question her well-meaning advice. Would I truly catch a cold in my tush? Then it dawned on me: I didn't even know what a "cold in the tush" was! Could her fears be unjustified? So I flushed and did not catch the ominous tush cold, which helped me let go of a long-held program that had run me for years without ever thinking about it.

As little children, we regarded our parents as gods. They were bigger than we were, they gave us valuable advice that helped us navigate our world, and they purveyed rewards that made us happy, and meted out punishments that hurt us. Our tiny minds did not have the ability to discern illusions from truth, so we accepted all of what our parents told us—even if some of it was untrue.

Our psyche is like an iceberg, a tiny portion of which is apparent, and most of which lies below the surface of our awareness. The belief systems we adopted as children can control our entire lives unless we call them to consciousness. If you have the courage to question what you have always accepted, you may discover that you have been living out many false beliefs. From your heart and your own experience, what do you really know to be true? Meditate on this question, dare to live the answers you discover, and you will find unprecedented healing and freedom.

Help me to discard all illusions and live the truth of my own soul.

I release all past beliefs and march forward in the light of my own wisdom.

Where to Build a Sidewalk

Shift your sail with the wind.

— Italian proverb

When I attended a conference at a Pennsylvania college, I enjoyed walking through a huge grassy mall between the buildings. The area was landscaped beautifully, and the sidewalks were laid out in an interesting, irregular pattern. When I commented on this to a friend, she told me, "The sidewalks were designed by the people who walked on them. When the mall first opened, the architects did not designate sidewalks; instead they waited for a few weeks to see where students walked. After the engineers determined the footpath patterns, they laid down the sidewalks. They realized that no matter where they put the sidewalks, people would walk where they wanted and just trample the grass. So they decided to save themselves some work and make it easier for the pedestrians."

The sidewalk designers understood that there is a flow to life, and when we are one with it, we are empowered. When we tune into the energy flow, we can use it to our advantage, rather than struggling to make the world fit into our expectations. The ancient *Tao Te Ching*, recorded by Lao Tse, is a magnificent poetic instruction book on how to be strengthened by changes.

Jungle lore tells that monkeys learned how to evade capture by making use of ease rather than force. Hunters would put some nuts in a glass jar with a rim smaller than its base. A monkey of inferior intelligence would reach into the jar and grab the nuts, but because the hand with nuts in it was too large to fit through the rim, the animal would stand there struggling, and the hunter would grab him. The smarter monkeys, however, didn't reach into the jar; they simply opened one palm and tilted the jar so the nuts fell into it. If you are trying to clutch onto something that won't fit into your life naturally, that's when you get caught. Accept what shows up, and you are free. Take advantage of the tide of events, and life will support you in ways that you could not manipulate through anxious struggle.

Build on what is, rather than what isn't, and you will be one with life.

Show me how to live. Help me move with energy,
that I may be free and happy.

The door to my good is open now.

88

Let It Go

We must not conceive of prayer as an overcoming of God's unwillingness, but as laying hold of His highest willingness.
— Richard Chenevix Trench, Archbishop of Dublin

Day after day, I sat at the foot of my mother's hospital bed, worrying that she might die. She was not recovering after her surgery, and I was fogged with worry. Within a week, I contracted a staph infection and became ill myself. I had to go home and stay in bed, unable to do much of anything. After a few days of rest, I recovered, and so did my mom. My anxious doting in the hospital did no one any good. The best thing I could have done for both of us was to let her be.

Praying or holding an intention for a particular result is not intended to be a struggle or endurance contest. True prayer can bring us peace and illumination as easily and effortlessly as flicking on a light switch brings light to a room.

After you have prayed sincerely, release your prayer to God. When you mail a letter, you must let go so it can be delivered to where it is going. After dropping the letter in the mailbox, you do not stand there and make sure no one tampers with it, watch to see that the letter carrier tucks it away safely, follow him or her back to the post office and trail the letter through the sorting process, insist on sitting next to the mail sack while it is being flown across country, follow it through its next sorting, do a security check on the next postal deliverer, and make sure the addressee picks it up. At some point you must just let go and trust the postal service to do its job. To breathe down the neck of postal service workers would only annoy them and waste your energy.

Pray and act decisively, and then release your intentions so God can take care of you in ways that you could not take care of yourself.

I release my sense of struggle, and trust You to answer my prayers and fulfill my dreams.

God is my trustworthy source of Good.
I let go and let God.

89

The Answer Is You

I have good news and I have bad news:
The bad news is that we have lost the key to the door
behind which the secret of life is hidden.
The good news is that it was never locked.
— Swami Beyondananda

When human beings appeared on the planet, a group of gods got together and decided to play a game. "Let's hide the secret of life!" one suggested.

"Great idea!" another agreed. "Where shall we hide it?"

"Let's plant it at the top of the highest mountain," one proposed.

"No," responded another, "people will even climb to Mount Everest."

"How about at the bottom of the ocean?" asked another.

"No, they will invent submarines."

On and on the gods pondered, trying to find a suitable hiding place. Finally, one god had a bright idea: "I know!" he exclaimed. "Let's hide the secret of life inside each person—they'll *never* think to look *there*!"

We remain in darkness when we seek external solutions for internal needs. We believe our problems exist because of causes outside ourselves, and then seek to rearrange the outer world. Even when we succeed, we feel empty because the external situation was not the cause of our pain. To truly be healed we must deal with our experience at its source—our own beliefs, attitudes, and actions.

In their important book, *Conscious Loving*[6], Gay and Kathlyn Hendricks put forth the core principle that *each partner must take 100 percent responsibility for everything that happens in their relationship and their world.* Empower yourself by identifying yourself not as a victim of circumstances, but as the source of your experience. The whole game changes when you realize the answer is within you.

Give me the strength to release anyone else as the source of my experience and to own my responsibility for creating the life I choose.

I am the answer.

Results and Excuses

When you are just interested in something, you do it only when it is convenient; when you are committed, you accept only results, not excuses.

— Dr. Kenneth Blanchard

I had an employee, Tony, who should have been in the *Guinness Book of World Records* for "The Greatest Number of Different Reasons the Same Job Didn't Get Done." When I asked Tony about the progress of a project he was supposed to handle, he answered, "Sorry, I haven't been feeling well; I'll get right on it next week."

The next week he told me, "I had some car trouble; your job is first on my list for next week." The following week his explanation was, "I had some hassles with my girlfriend; I wasn't emotionally available." The week after that, "I had a little miscommunication with the phone company about my bill; they turned off my service, so I couldn't get the calls made." On and on the saga went, and a job that should have taken a few weeks remained undone after months. Finally, I hired someone else who did the job in a short time.

There are two kinds of people in the world: those who make excuses and those who get results. An excuse person will find any excuse for why a job was *not* done, and a results person will find any reason why it *can* be done.

I was an excuse person about being on time; I was 15 minutes late to everything. When I showed up, I would always have a different reason: *"Traffic"; "Got a phone call just as I was leaving"; "Had to feed the dog";* and on and on. Many of these situations had actually occurred, but none of them accounted for the reason I was late. My tardiness was a result of my choice, not external conditions.

We can tell our intentions by the results we create. Words mean little in the face of what we manifest. If you are going to do something, own it. If you are going to not do something, own it. You become most powerful, effective, and trustworthy as you acknowledge that you are the source of your experience. Be a creator, not a reactor.

Help me to live in integrity. I want to empower myself and others by being true to my word.

I can because I choose.

Get Your Bearings

Shake your souls. Awake!...The promised hour has come. Over the dark firmament of suffering, humanity is rising. The morning star is heralding the day when you will understand that man's most sacred duty is to...break the fetters with which ignorance and fear have bound unconscious humanity. You will stand up free and know yourselves to be the eternal manifestation of...that great All whom you call God.

— found in a Russian church after World War I

"I used to travel on business so much that some days I would wake up and not know where I was or what I was supposed to be doing," my friend Linda told me. "I became so disoriented that every night before I went to sleep, I would paste Post-its on the hotel TV screen, telling me what city I was in, and who I was supposed to see, when, and why."

We are all like voyagers in a distant city. We came from the world of Spirit to a world that has lost sight of its origin and purpose. It is easy to become distracted by fears and illusions and to forget who we are and why we came.

We must take care to remind ourselves often about our identity and purpose. Prayer, meditation, spiritual study, and uplifting fellowship are like Post-its we can paste on the screen of our consciousness to help us stay on our spiritual track. If you do not surround yourself with reminders of your spiritual nature, the world will teach you that you belong to it, and you will feel lost and alone.

Keep the high watch. Put up inspiring pictures and quotes in your home and office. Listen to music that nourishes your soul. Go to restaurants, movies, and social gatherings that honor the presence of God. Choose friends who uphold you on your spiritual path. Get regular massage, counseling, or training by persons attuned to higher laws.

It is within your power to build your life on the values you choose, but you must take an active role in staying awake. Step back often, take deep breaths, and check in with your spirit. Any investment you make in your spiritual growth will bless you many times over.

Help me keep You in my mind and heart,
that I may remember that I belong to the light.

Established in truth,
I fulfill my destiny today.

92

The Divine Fool

'Tis is a gift to be simple, 'tis a gift to be free.
— Shaker Song

In the Tarot deck, *The Fool Card* depicts a young man walking along gaily as he smells a flower. Unbeknownst to him, he is about to step over a cliff. The card has a dual interpretation: on one level, it is a lesson to pay attention; on the other hand, it is a celebration of holy foolishness—the innocent vision of a child who knows no bounds, obstacles, or dangers. Sometimes what appears to be foolishness is divine wisdom.

In the film *Being There*, Peter Sellers portrays Chance, a simple-minded man who grew up in such a sheltered environment that his mind never developed beyond that of a five-year-old. When he is suddenly cast into a cold and wily world, Chance retains his delightful innocence. No one who meets him knows quite what to make of him, but they really like him. Through a strange series of events, Chance meets the President of the United States, who is attracted to his earthy, unpretentious wisdom and makes him an advisor. Although Chance knows nothing about politics, he discusses the natural cycles of life in his garden, and the application of these principles makes Chance a national hero.

The final scene of *Being There* shows a group of politicians speculating about Chance being the next President. As they are debating the merits of his nomination, Chance wanders off to a nearby park and walks over a lake—no one ever told him that he couldn't!

Sometimes we are wisest to play the fool. Go with your sense of child-like innocence and wonder, and doors will open that intellectual manipulation could never force. Not only that, but you'll have a lot more fun as you play.

I pray to return to my innocence and
see the beauty of life as You created it.

I give myself permission to live
in childlike wonder.

The Man Who Planted Trees

In a gentle way you can shake the world.
— Gandhi

I saw an extraordinary film[7] about the life of Elzéard Bouffier, a humble shepherd who turned a wilderness into a lush forest. In a lifetime spanning two World Wars, while madmen killed each other for worldly power, this individual quietly and anonymously brought his world back to life, planting one acorn at a time. He not only created natural beauty, but contributed to healing an entire town that had fallen into despair—one man, working gently, living day to day, seeding love wherever he went.

Each of us has a forest we can plant to bring our world back to life. Our trees may not be spruces; they may be children, songs, art, ideas, massage, repairs, writing, or any other gift that comes to us and through us.

What impressed me most about Elzéard Bouffier was the humility with which he conducted his forestry ministry. He was silent most of the time, he did not seek acknowledgment and never asked anyone to follow him. He simply knew what he had to do and went about the business of doing it.

I met Scott and Helen Nearing, the famous couple who initiated the back-to-the-land movement in the 1930s. Although the Nearings had well-paying jobs and comfortable city lives, they moved to the mountains of Vermont, grew organic food, heated with wood, and nurtured their land. At the time, they were laughed at and criticized. Now they are considered pioneers and virtual saints. I asked Helen, "How do you feel now that so many are doing what you began?"

"It's wonderful," Helen answered, "but that's not why we did it. We did what we had to because it was right for us. If no one else ever followed, it would have been just as right."

What is your forest? How can you bring your world back to life? Begin today, one acorn at a time.

I pray to restore my world with color and beauty.

I bring my world to life.

Worth It

If you had but the faith of a mustard seed, you could say to this mountain, "Be thou moved," and so it would be.

— Jesus Christ

While I was writing my first book on a borrowed electric typewriter, I saw a similar one at a yard sale for $50. I questioned if the project was really worth it, and I passed. But the thought of the typewriter nagged at me until I decided to return to the (regular) yard sale a month later. The typewriter was still there (a sign!), and I purchased it.

The book became a bestseller, and along with my subsequent writing has created millions of dollars in sales. As I look back now on my hesitancy to purchase the typewriter, I laugh at how small I was thinking—a $50 investment eventually returned itself a hundred thousand times over!

Now I realize that it was not the worth of the typewriter I questioned, but my own worth. If I had known that such seeds of service and success lay within me and my writing, I would have gone out and bought the best typewriter on the market!

Every decision you make reflects what you believe about yourself. If you know your worth, you will act in ways that reflect your gifts.

Help me honor who I am and what I am here to do.

God inspires me to do great things.
I joyfully act on the guidance I receive.

95

Scars into Stars

Every minus is half of a plus,
waiting for a stroke of vertical awareness.
— Alan Cohen

On a shoestring budget of $150, Jim opened a clothing store with some sundry garments. Soon after the store opened, a wealthy woman came in to browse and soon walked out, complaining, "This place is nothing but a bunch of odds and ends." Her phrase rang like a bell in Jim's head, and he decided that that description would make a good name and theme for his store. He had a sign painted, proclaiming *"Odds and Ends,"* and set out on an advertising campaign with that motif. After a number of years, Jim owned five successful *Odds and Ends* stores, and eventually sold them for $475,000.

What seems to be a setback or an insult may be a gift from the universe, pointing you in a direction of greater good. When a phrase or idea resonates within you, it is probably the voice of Spirit trying to get your attention to act upon it.

Think and act as if everything that shows up in your field of consciousness is for your good. Imagine that there is only one power—love—and it is the force behind every experience. Even if something seems painful or insulting in the moment, use it as raw material with which to grow. Even repulsive manure is good fertilizer, when put in its proper place and recycled for the farmer's purpose.

Today let me recognize Your voice behind every voice.
Help me to take Your signs and signals and
build a life of beauty and abundance.

I receive the word of God and
use it to grow my life.

Divine Discontent

Lord, let me always desire more than I think I can do.
—Michelangelo

There is a part of us that will not let us be content until we become all that we are capable of being. Life is not about resting on our laurels and hanging out in our comfort zone; it is an adventure from good to better to best.

Rev. Jack Boland urged, "Do not let good be the enemy of better." Your current situation may be good, but if a greater opportunity presents itself, you must be open to expand. This does not mean you are to run away or violate your integrity. If, however, you can step ahead with honesty, honor, and peace, you will enjoy the benefits of living in a larger universe.

Muscles stay strong and flexible only by use and stretching, and so does our mind. Challenge is the universe's way of showing us that we are bigger than we thought we were.

Bless your dreams, your desires, and your sense that there must be more. There *is* more because you *are* more.

Give me the courage to ask for it all.

I leave behind my limits and step forward to live as large as God.

97

Reading Skills

The quality of mercy is not strained;
it droppeth as the gentle rain from heaven.
— William Shakespeare

I approached the desk anxiously and handed the tickets to the reservations agent. We needed to change our airline tickets at the last minute, and they were clearly marked "non-changeable/ non-refundable." While waiting in line, I had considered various excuses, but decided to just go with the truth.

"We would like to delay our return several days," I explained. "My friend needs to stop in Los Angeles, and I need to stay here in San Francisco." The agent studied the tickets and went into the computer record. After a few moments, he told us, "This record says that these tickets cannot be changed." My heart tightened. "It says here that if you want to make these changes, it will cost you an extra $900." Whoa. Then he looked at me and smiled. "But I'm not a very good reader. I don't see why you should have to pay all of that." He issued me a new ticket with my desired date and gave my partner a free ticket to Los Angeles. "Have a nice flight," he added.

Sitting on the airplane, tears welled up in my eyes. That man didn't have to be so kind. He could have quoted chapter and verse and enforced the extra payment penalty. But he didn't. I began to consider the situations in which I might give someone a similar gift by reducing my reading skills, or overlooking what the rules said in favor of mercy and forgiveness. I remembered Jesus telling the Pharisees that they were caught up in every jot and tittle of the law while completely overlooking the spirit.

Take a few moments to consider your reading skills. Whose day or life could you brighten by letting go of punishing laws and extending a little extra kindness? As you release, so will you be released.

Help me to grow beyond smallness.
Inspire me to show mercy.
Help me to overlook and forgive, that I may be forgiven.

My acts of mercy build a forgiving world.

Get Real

In a dream I saw myself as a great and colorful butterfly; now I am not sure if I am Chuang-Tsu dreaming I was a butterfly, or a butterfly dreaming I am Chuang-Tsu.

— Chuang-Tsu, Chinese Patriarch

Over the past decade, the word *real* has come into vogue. Coca-Cola insists that it is "the real thing." Our friends tell us to "get real." Before entering into business ventures, we do a "reality check." We can't help avoiding the questions, "What is real?" and "Who is the real me?"

At the completion of nearly every one of my retreat programs, someone wistfully notes, "Too bad we have to go back to the real world now." I always respond by saying, "This *is* the real world. The world of loving, honest communication and genuine caring reflects our true identity much more than the world we usually call 'real.'"

What world is real to you? The world that most people consider real is fraught with illusions. Money, fame, power, sex, and material security do not offer true reward and substance; they dissolve as soon as the tiniest light is shed on them. While the "real world" tells us that these commodities are worth living and dying for, those who have them are often desperate for love, relationships, communication, community, and peace of mind.

The real world is the world of kindness, caring, vision, and service. All of these qualities are attributes of our divine nature. As children of God, we can be only what God is, and that is everything that is good. We are born of light, and we return to the light. To live in light is to live in the real world.

Show me the real world.
Let me not forget my nature and my origin.

I live in the real world of love.

99

How Much Do You Want It?

Thy strength shall be according
to the measure of thy desire.

— Arab proverb

A young man came to a guru and asked him what he would need to do to become enlightened. The master took the student to a lake and pushed his head under water for a long time. Finally, the man became desperate for air and forced his way to the surface, shouting, "Are you trying to kill me?"

The guru calmly replied, "When you want God as much as you wanted air, you will find enlightenment."

While this world seems to be a place of haphazard results, each of us is getting exactly what we are asking for at any given moment. If we truly want freedom, we shall find it, and if we're not ready, so shall we remain bound.

If you seem stuck in any situation that is less than fulfilling, ask yourself if you are receiving any perceived benefits from staying where you are. While no one would reasonably choose illness, the subconscious perceives many hidden benefits: it gets us out of work, we get sympathy, we do not have to face the issues in our life that trouble us, we may be receiving some kind of monetary reward for our disability, and on and on. While no one would consciously admit to choosing illness, on some level we do.

Many people complain about their dysfunctional relationships, yet staying in them often seems to outweigh the benefits of leaving. One thing is for sure: The moment leaving becomes more attractive, staying will not have its way. We are free to choose, and we always are.

Place within my breast the burning desire for You alone;
You are all I want, and You are all I shall have.

I am determined to have
my dreams come true.

100

I Love You

Love always answers, being unable to deny a call for help, or not to hear the cries of pain that rise to it.
— A Course in Miracles

Half an hour into healer Patricia Sun's lecture, a man stood and announced, "I came in late—would you please tell me what happened?" This interruption seemed rather rude, considering that Patricia had spent time developing her theme for a thousand eager listeners. But Patricia did not play the judgment game. She smiled at the man and told him, "I love you—that's what happened." Patricia paused for a moment for him to receive the gift; then he replied, "Thank you," and sat down.

The man was not really seeking information, but love and acknowledgment. He felt left out and wanted to be included. Giving him the love he sought cut past the game he was playing to get it, and everyone was served to observe the gift Patricia gave him.

One of the most powerful ways to deal with irritating behavior is to reinterpret is as a call for love. I am fascinated by teenagers who drive up and down city streets blasting car stereos so loud that one can hardly carry on a conversation within a hundred feet. With each passing year, the speakers grow larger, now to a point where many of these aficionados have removed their back seats to fit in two giant speakers. When I hear one of these cars passing, I translate the gross noise into, "Please pay attention to me! Please listen to me! Please know that I am here!" I am certain that a sociological study would reveal these car owners to be children who have felt unseen and unheard by their parents or society. If we gave our kids more love and attention at home, they would not need to buy huge speakers to demand attention from the world.

The next time someone asks you for attention in an inappropriate way, stop, take a breath, and sincerely tell them, "I love you."

I pray to give only love today.
I know I can meet all needs by giving love.

Love is my answer,
no matter what the question.

Integrity

Have a purpose in life, and having it, throw into your work such strength of mind and muscle as God gives you.
— Thomas Carlyle

The telephone repairman showed me the cause of the terrible static on my line. "Do you see where all these wires come together?" he asked, pointing to the junction of wires from my four house telephones. "This one wire is faulty, and it is polluting the rest of the circuits." He removed the one wire and let me listen to the other lines, which became perfectly clear.

When one area of our life is out of integrity, it affects all the others. When you compromise or live a lie in an important relationship, it will create static in your career. When you clean up one area that is out of harmony, the other areas will advance at rocket speed.

Purify any parts of my life out of alignment with Your purpose, so I may live as a whole and powerful being.

One with God,
I am united with my purpose.
My life must succeed in every way.

102

My Invisible Partner

You and God are a majority.

— Anonymous

After Mr. Taylor experienced several business failures, in exasperation he turned to God and declared, "Okay, I give up trying to do it all by myself. I invite You to be my partner in all future endeavors. If You want something to be, I trust You to manifest it; if it is not Your will, I will not struggle."

Mr. Taylor's next venture was a small department store. True to his promise, this time he proceeded with ease and peace, knowing that with God as his partner, he would not have to fight for his good. As a result, the store flourished, and Mr. Taylor went on to create a hugely successful chain—*Lord and Taylor.*

Trying to do it all yourself leads to frustration, exhaustion, and failure. While it is important to be responsible and self-reliant, it is equally important to be open to receive support. Everything in nature gives to other living beings; we cannot do it all alone. All good things are overseen and supported by a higher power. Do all you can do without anxiety or struggle, and trust Spirit to do the rest.

I invite You to be my partner.
I allow You to do for me what I cannot do for myself.
I let go of fear and struggle, and step onto the path of joy.

I am empowered by Spirit.
Together we must succeed.

A Touch Can Change a Life

Never underestimate the power of a kind act.
— Anonymous

In the midst of a long meditation retreat, Rick was feeling tired, bored, and discouraged. Waking up to a cold, dark morning, he decided he would leave today. As Rick joined the line of students for the morning walking meditation practice, the man behind him placed his hand comfortingly on Rick's shoulder. "With that touch I felt renewed," Rick explained. "Although the man did not speak a word, I felt him tell me, 'It's okay. I know you are having a hard time; hang in there.' From that moment on, my attitude was transformed, and I went on to complete the retreat."

Kindness is powerful, contagious, and transformative. Never underestimate the potential of a friendly smile, gentle touch, or supportive word. So many people walk the world in pain and self-doubt. Your simple gift could make all the difference in a friend's or stranger's day, and even save their life. You are the light of the world—let it shine!

Let me be a positive influence on everyone I meet.
I offer myself to make a difference in the lives I touch.

God blesses the world through my words and hands. I am a messenger of love.

The Active Ingredient

Though I speak with the tongues of men and angels and have not love, I am a noisy gong and a clanging cymbal.

— Corinthians 13:1

Have you ever read the list of ingredients on a tube of toothpaste or patent medicine? There is usually a long roll of chemicals, colorings, and additives, followed by bold letters: **"Active Ingredient"**—the one that really gets the job done and makes the item worth buying. Everything else is a filler or enhancer. Without the active ingredient, the stuff would be useless.

Love is the active ingredient of life, the chemical that makes everything else worthwhile. You can have all the other amenities, but if love is absent, you are lost. You can feel victimized or abandoned, but if you add love, suddenly life has meaning again.

I met a woman who owned a booming ski resort. "I have done very well financially for many years," she told me. "But lately I have felt bored and irritable; my life and job seem to have no meaning. I meditated on my situation, and the answer that came was 'more caring.' I realized that my work had become distasteful because I had gotten caught up in the mechanics rather than the essence, which is taking care of people. So I rededicated myself to making my clients happy, regardless of the financial outcome. I even found ways I could reduce rates. Now my work is a delight, and I am even more successful."

Have you retained the active ingredient, or has it slipped away? If so, ask yourself how your work, relationships, or spiritual path could be enhanced by bringing more heart to them. Rearrange your priorities to give care first, and all else will follow.

Show me how to truly care, that I may bring Your peace to my daily activities.

Love is my function.
I am a servant of the heart.

Perfect

Heaven is not a place, and it is not a time.
Heaven is being perfect.
— from *Jonathan Livingston Seagull*, by Richard Bach

I used to think I was a perfectionist," Larry confessed. "I was constantly finding flaws and errors that other people overlooked. If there were many aspects of a job that were well done and one that wasn't, I would point out that one. But now I realize I was an *imperfectionist*. If I was a perfectionist, I would have found perfection everywhere I looked; instead, I saw only imperfection."

Whatever we focus on, we will find more of. The world we live in is the one we choose by virtue of the vision we use. Are you a perfectionist or an imperfectionist?

Jack and his wife Elaine were waiting in a lineup of cars on the Cross Bronx Expressway, sandwiched in an alternate merge at a construction zone. "This is hell!" Jack complained inwardly. "We're creeping along at a snail's pace."

Then Elaine pointed out, "Isn't this wonderful!"

"What's so wonderful about this?" asked Jack.

"It's really inspiring to see how people are cooperating here. One car goes ahead from this lane, and then one from the other lane. It shows me that people know how to work together when there is a challenge."

We can discover good in any situation if we choose it.

Help me find You in the events of daily life.

I am committed to beauty, and I find it everywhere I look.

How to Bless the IRS

Love is the only power. Love is the only way.
— Rabbi David Zeller

As Alice was writing checks to pay her bills last April, she penned a note of blessing on the memo line of each check, as is her custom. When Alice came to the check due to the Internal Revenue Service (IRS) for her tax payment, she asked herself, "Do I really want to bless the IRS? Would anyone there receive the gift?"

After some reflection, Alice decided that there are no exceptions to the law of love. "Perhaps," she reasoned, "the IRS is in greater need of blessing than most of the other people and companies I am paying." On the memo line of her check, Alice inscribed, *"Peace and joy be with you."*

Several months later as Alice was going through her canceled checks, she noticed the check she had sent to the IRS. On the back of the check, below the institutional stamp, she read these words, written by hand: *"And with you, too!"*

Somehow Alice's blessing found its way to someone's heart. Consider what a gift this was to the person who received it! The IRS is probably not the most delightful place to work. Hardly anyone enjoys paying taxes, and I expect that IRS employees are not the recipients of many blessings from their constituents. Can you imagine the pleasant surprise of the person who processed the check? Perhaps it changed her entire day. Perhaps that person went on to offer some extra kindness, caring, or forgiveness to the next person she dealt with. I am certain that Alice's blessing went a long way.

Any activity in life can be elevated to the level of blessing. The situations we encounter are templates upon which we imprint our heart's intentions. Every moment we make the choice between love and fear. Nothing in this world is outside the power of transformation by way of a loving heart. When we choose love, we bring the world closer to heaven. Fear makes the world hell. The choice is ours.

Help me to remember that everyone I encounter
is a child of God who will respond to pure love.

I use all situations as opportunities to prove and celebrate the power of love.

In Their Best Light

Treat your friends as you do your pictures,
and place them in their best light.
— Jennie Jerome Churchill

It was probably a grace that Brenda passed away, I thought. My elderly neighbor was a severely addicted alcoholic, and, from what I saw, her life had little meaning. The few times I attempted to converse with Brenda I looked into her eyes, and it appeared that no one was home. She had to be in a better place now, I imagined. Then I talked to Marvin, a man whom Brenda and her husband had taken in as a caretaker. Marvin felt a great sense of loss in Brenda's death.

"She was so good to me," Marvin tearfully confided. "Like a mother. I will miss her a lot." Through Marvin's words, I gained a profound realization: I saw only one limited aspect of Brenda's life. Even while I judged her life as empty, she had riches. She loved someone, and someone loved her. Her life, broken as it appeared to me, was a blessing to at least one other person. In spite of the ravages I beheld, God lived through her.

The Bible tells us not to judge—not because we *should not* judge, but because we *cannot* judge. When we hold a judgment about someone, we are focusing on one moment from one angle. At another moment or from another angle, we would see an entirely different person or story.

While visiting a children's zoo, I watched a man become very abusive at the snack bar, ranting and raving at the clerk over a minor mishap. I thought, This guy is one ornery hombre. A few minutes later, I saw a man feeding a fawn through a fence. As he tenderly stroked the deer's nose and gave it love, he reminded me of St. Francis. When he turned his head, I saw that it was the same man who created the scene at the snack bar.

When we release judgment, we find God in every person. Moreover, we free ourselves to be lovable and forgivable. Judgment is illusion, and love is real.

I pray to see Your children as You do,
through the eyes of love and appreciation.

I focus on the good and let all else go.

Don't Think

A man needs a little madness, or else he never dares cut the rope and be free.

— Zorba the Greek

"Are you really going to jump from there?" I asked Frank as he stood poised on a rock at the top of the waterfall.

"Sure, it's fun—you're going to join me, aren't you?"

I looked over the edge of the precipice. "I don't know."

"You'll love it!" Frank exclaimed, and took a flying swan dive into the pool below.

I stood atop the ridge looking down, adrenaline shooting through my system. "Can I do this?" I asked myself. An inner voice replied, "Don't think about it—just do it." I gazed for a few more seconds and felt as if a big hand was nudging me from behind. So without further delay, I leaped—and loved it.

Somewhere inside me I knew that if I jumped, I would enjoy it, and I also knew that if I thought about it, I would not do it. Sometimes we have to override our reasoning mind and just go with the energy at hand. As I climbed back up to the top of the ridge, I wondered how many times I have used my mind to talk me out of doing things that would make me happy.

I am not suggesting that you do anything foolish or do something that would be injurious to you. The place of knowingness inside you is always giving you good advice. When your head is in a quandary and your heart says yes, follow your heart. Use your mind to empower you, not limit you. The heart without the head is chaotic, and the head without the heart is a tyrant. Break free of the tyranny of overthinking, and become as a little child. That is how you get back into heaven.

Raise the volume of my inner voice of truth, that I may walk the way appointed by wisdom.

I have a passionate delight for doing what is right.

Consciousness, Not Conditions

Consciously selected miracles can be misguided.
— A Course in Miracles

One of the questions I am most frequently asked is, "How do I know if something I am praying for is in my best interests? What if I am imposing my will over God's will? How can I tell if my request is being inspired by love or driven by my ego?"

A rule of thumb that I suggest is to assume that your inspirations are coming from right intuition, and act with authority. Once in a while you will find that you have made a mistake, but in the long run you will be way ahead of where you would be if you assume that your intuitions are guided by ego and do nothing.

The real answer to the question is to understand that what you are seeking is not really conditions, but consciousness. You may be praying for a new BMW, but what you really want is to know that you are an abundant being living in a wealthy universe. You may be seeking a soulmate, but behind your search is the quest to know that you are lovable and cherishable. You may want to have a number-one hit on the pop charts, but behind that desire is the wish to feel acknowledged and important. You can get the conditions, but if you do not have the consciousness, you will be ever seeking and striving for more conditions. If you have the consciousness, however, the conditions will usually manifest automatically, and even if they do not, you will be secure in your wholeness.

If you aren't sure if what you are praying for is correct, complete your prayer with "this or better." Tell God (remind yourself) that you are doing the best you can with what you know, and if there is something more wonderful available, you are willing to give up your current idea for the bigger picture.

Help me to know that my prayers are worthy.
Show me that I am Your child, deserving of Your kingdom.

God's will for me is perfect happiness.

Guilt and Responsibility

Love and guilt cannot co-exist, and
to accept one is to deny the other.
— A Course in Miracles

While addressing a support group for cancer patients, I explained that we shape our lives by the thoughts and attitudes we hold. Illness is the universe's way of getting our attention so we can realign our life with the perfect pattern we deserve. Because our thoughts and energies have a role in manifesting disease, we can facilitate healing by shifting our vision toward wholeness.

After the lecture, the sponsor angrily told me, "I didn't like you making my people feel guilty for their cancers; they feel guilty enough as it is!" I was stunned. I had not said anything about guilt. To the contrary, my intention was to empower the patients to know that they were worthy of being healed and to open up to the possibility that they could take an active role in their healing.

The ego, which thrives on guilt, does not understand responsibility, for the separated mind cannot conceive of being at cause. Its very existence is built on the illusion of being an effect. The notion of creatorship threatens the ego's platform of victimhood. Someone who feels guilty will fight the notion of responsibility, as the ego cannot see beyond the blame game. In the game of creative living, however, each of us has the power to manifest the world we choose, regardless of the worlds that others are choosing for themselves or would choose for us.

Guilt is debilitating, while responsibility is liberating. Guilt focuses on what you did in the past, while responsibility looks at how the choices you make now will affect your future. Guilt is shrouded with blame; responsibility empowers us toward greater possibilities. Guilt is emotional and implies sin; responsibility is reasonable and points toward laws of success. Guilt calls for punishment; responsibility calls only for correction.

We are all responsible. Let us reclaim our power to be healthy and live the lives we choose.

Help me release guilt forever and walk in the power with which You created me.

The power of my life is in my hands.
I choose to love and be whole.

Don't Miss It

What is essential is invisible to the eye;
only with the heart can one see rightly.
— from *The Little Prince,* by Saint-Exupery

As he stood before a firing squad, French dissident le Bodoyère gently touched his hand to his heart and advised the soldiers, "This is what you must not miss."

We would do well to remember le Bodoyère's advice throughout our entire lives. We may have all manner of material success, but unless our heart is fulfilled, we have nothing.

When someone died in ancient Egypt, the priests removed the bodily organs they considered unimportant and saved the organs they believed sacred. The Egyptians discarded the brains but kept the heart. They believed that the seat of true wisdom was not the mind, but the heart.

The power of the heart goes far beyond feeling and emotions; in the heart lies great wisdom and peace. In our culture, we tend to try to think things through. Certainly the rational process is important, but it must be tempered with intuitive understanding. In my seminars, I tell audiences, "Please point to yourself." Nearly every person in the room points to their heart. Although they had a choice of many body parts, 99 percent of those asked sensed that they live in their heart. On some level, we remember that our heart contains the essence of who we are.

Practice consulting your heart before speaking or acting. If you are not sure what to say or do, take a moment, draw a few deep breaths, and feel what is happening in your chest. There you will find the most valuable guide to right action. If you find yourself upset or unhappy, ask your heart, "What would you have me know?" Employ all the worldly wisdom available, but when you want to know the most important truth, return to your heart. *"This is what you must not miss."*

I pray to know the wisdom of my heart and
act upon its sacred knowledge.

My heart guides me to right action.

Beyond Duty

There are three impediments to enlightenment:
Lust, fear, and duty.
— Buddha

Jesus told the parable of a wealthy man who went through a town inviting the important people to a great feast. "Sorry, I have to work," said one man.

"I'm on my way to bury a relative," answered another. Everyone he asked could not come because they had something to do first. Finally, the man invited all the poor people in town, and they accepted because they had nothing else more pressing. Jesus likened the banquet to the kingdom of heaven, which we miss if we are caught up in worldly activities. Time and again Jesus affirmed that the kingdom of heaven is at hand, and we may enter it if we are open to receiving it.

The kingdom of heaven is just as available today as it was when Jesus pointed toward it. Since that time, we have invented even more duties that we believe we must perform before we can have peace. Begin to examine your sense of duty, and ask yourself where it comes from. Do you respond to the needs and wishes of others because you will feel guilty if you do not? Do you believe that you must play out the roles others tell you that you should fulfill to be a good daughter, son, wife, husband, employer, student, or disciple? Do you postpone joy because you believe that you must first strive, suffer, or pay off karma?

Activities are valuable only if they bring us closer to peace. Relationships are healthy only as much as they reflect real love. Careers are important only for the aliveness they bring us and the service they render to others. To follow any creed that does not proceed from your heart is hypocrisy and psychic self-abuse. Begin to sincerely question your motives for social activities, and let go of anything that does not reflect a truth you believe from the inside out. Your life is too important to live for others. Come to the banquet now.

Bless me with the strength to live
my spiritual truth and ideals.

I walk the path I believe in
and let all else go.

A Better View of the Sky

Now that my house has burned down,
I have a better view of the sky.

— Zen saying

I was startled to receive this letter from a successful Los Angeles artist: *"During the recent fires, my house was leveled, along with my entire collection of paintings."* To my surprise, the next line read, ***"Now I am free!*** *I am packing to go to the island of Kauai, where I will fulfill my lifelong dream of leading wilderness adventures."*

When an apparent disaster strikes and our life as we knew it is undone, it may be a blessing in disguise. The event could be clearing out an old pattern to make way for a new and more fulfilling life. See the situation not as a curse, but as an opportunity. The Chinese language character for *crisis* is a combination of two other symbols: *danger* and *opportunity*.

A Hawaiian gardener told me that gardeners in colder climates have an advantage over those in the tropics. The winter frost kills all micro-organisms in the soil so that next spring's crops are not subject to contamination from the previous year's pests. Even when life seems frozen and desolate, growth and good are occurring behind the outer appearances.

In the Hindu religion, the god Shiva, ruler of destruction, is revered as much as Vishnu, the creator. The old must be cleared away to make way for the new.

Help me trust that changes beyond my control
are working on my behalf.

I surrender to change and call it all good.
I release the old to make way for
the new and better.

When the Time Is Right

To everything there is a season, a time to every purpose under heaven.

— Ecclesiastes 3:1

O.Y. O'Connor's dream was to build a water pipeline to irrigate parched terrain east of Perth, Australia. After years of planning and labor, the aqueduct was constructed, and throngs stood at the mouth of the huge conduit to see the first drops of liquid life. But when the valve was opened, nothing appeared. The next day, O'Connor was found dead in his home; the failure of his dream was too much for him to live with. Several days later, a trickle of water appeared at the mouth of the pipeline, and before long, water was gushing abundantly. The only thing that went wrong was his idea of when it would happen.

The early Bible, recorded in Greek, uses two different words for our word *time*. *Chronos* is the Biblical word for the time of day, which we translate into hours, minutes, and seconds. The other word, *kairos*, means, "in nature's time," or "in due time." There is a divine order to life, and timing is a part of it.

If you feel frustrated or disappointed over lack of results on a project, hang in there and have some patience. If your venture is a good one, you will see the results. Perhaps not in *chronos*, your idea of the right time, but in *kairos*, the right time—the one appointed by Spirit. If you have done all you can to make something happen, and nothing seems to be coming of it, turn it over to God. Nurture your Spirit, and trust the universe to support you.

Give me the trust to know that all things are working in my favor, even when it does not appear to be so.
Help me move beyond discouragement and see my dreams through to completion.

God's timing is perfect.
Divine order is operating now.

Nothing to Protect

Your days are short here; this is the last of your springs.
And now in the serenity and quiet of this lovely lace,
touch the depths of truth, feel the hem of heaven.

— Adlai Stevenson

When my mother was undergoing chemotherapy, she lost her hair. At first she joked about it, but then she became self-conscious and bought a wig, which she wore at all times. During the final weeks of her life, she was too ill to care about how she looked, and she renounced the wig. I felt jarred to see her without hair, and yet in my heart I applauded her for going beyond her concern for appearances. She was finally free.

Children and older people are the most honest because they have no investment in the games other people believe they have to maintain. The elderly and the very young do not have a vested interest in power, money, sex, prestige, status, and appearances. They are not trying to change the world or get a lot from it. They can tell the truth without fear of losing. Their delight in being what they are far outweighs any glitter the world may offer.

Some of the greatest wisdom is uttered by the young and the elderly. While we usually notice children's jewels, often we overlook the wisdom of the aged. One of the great tragedies of our culture is that we do not respect our ancestors. By not doing so, we dishonor the elderly who live among us, and we hurt ourselves by missing out on the wisdom and blessings they have to offer. My Japanese friend told me that every Oriental home has a place of honor for the family's ancestors. The family prays and makes offerings daily to the memory of their forebears.

Let us learn from the young and the old, that we may be as free as they are and rise above the distractions of the years in between. Is anything really worth compromising the truth? Let us bless our young and elders for the wisdom and legacy they impart.

I pray to keep the flame of truth burning
above all other desires.

In the truth I am free.

116

Best When It's Worst

Consider that people are like tea bags.
They don't know their own strength
until they get into hot water.

— Dan McKinnon

In the film *Starman,* an extraterrestrial comes to earth to study life on this planet. Like many such visitors, he does not receive a very kindly welcome and spends most of his time fleeing from authorities. In the process, he falls in love with a woman who befriends him. Finally he must leave, and he has a few short moments to say good-bye to his beloved. "Do you know what I learned about human beings?" he asks. "I learned that when things are at their worst, you are at your best."

Adversity is a gift if we make it work on our behalf. Challenge is not a curse or a punishment, but an opportunity to shine. If life were easy all the time, we would not deepen in love, compassion, and wisdom, or learn how to sink a pipeline into the well of true strength within us. Often we do not know how powerful we are until we are faced with a challenge that draws forth our greatness.

In high school I took a typing class. By the end of the course, I had built up my speed to about 40 words a minute. The time came for the final exam, on which a large part of my grade depended. I focused intently and scored a smashing 64 words a minute—over 50 percent faster than my regular speed! Why did I do so well? I knew it counted for a lot.

When an act in life counts, there is a source of strength within us that grows to meet the challenge. Some people demonstrate superhuman abilities, such as pushing a wrecked car off an injured person. Where do they find the strength? It was within them all the time; the worst brought out the best.

I pray to be big enough to handle
whatever comes before me.
With Your help, I can and will do anything.

The power of God is within me.
The Grace of God surrounds me.

117

When to Pray

You got to pray if you want to make it today.
— Hammer

My friend Tami, a guidance counselor in a Los Angeles elementary school, conducted a staff meeting to determine how to help a five-year-old girl. At the age of four, Janet had watched her father commit suicide and was then sent to live in her aunt's home, where she was abused by her uncle. The little girl, emotionally traumatized, became aphasic and registered an I.Q. bordering on retardation. After Janet left the meeting room, the staff sat in stunned silence; they all felt the deep pain this child had undergone at a tender age. As the teachers rose to leave, Tami called them back, inviting them, "Let's pray." The group held hands, and each person, in their own way, asked God to take care of this child. As human beings, they had hit a dead end, and they acknowledged that they needed help from a higher power.

Perhaps it is time we started to pray again in schools—and homes and offices and hospitals and government buildings and everywhere. I am not referring to rote prayer in which we parrot meaningless verse; I am talking about real prayer that emanates from the hearts of sincere human beings to the heart of a receptive God.

Prayer is our greatest power, for it connects us with the power of the entire universe, which is love. Often we leave prayer until the last resort, while it will help us just as readily if we use it as our first response to fear. Pray for your peace and that of others. God will answer.

Be with me today, and help me remember that
You are the source of true healing.

God is my best friend and
my fountain of strength.

118

Blessed Death

Death is delightful. Death is dawn, the waking from a weary night of fevers into truth and light.

— Joaquin Miller

As my friend Deborah was about to leave for a vacation, her 11-year-old son told her, "Mom, I'm afraid that when you leave, you'll die, and I'll never see you again." Deborah sat down and talked with him about her vacation, and explained to him that sometimes when we or the people close to us change, it feels like a death. In a way he was correct; his mother was changing her life, and she was going through a symbolic death. She communicated that she loved him and would always be there for him. Her vacation was deeply transformative, and she returned feeling more whole and able to reach her son on a new level.

While writing my first book, I had the strangest feeling I was going to die. After meditating on the feeling, I realized that what was dying was the old me. I knew that when the book came out, I would have to own the strength, vision, and intimacy for which I was making a stand in my writing. "Then let it die," I declared, trusting that the me who was being born was far more rewarding than the one that was passing away.

Death is not a bad thing; with every death comes a birth. The key to moving beyond the fear or pain of death is to ask, *"What is being born in place of what is dying?"* When you discover the blessing death brings, you can walk through the valley of the shadow of death and truly fear no evil.

Help me find life where I once saw death.
Lead me from the darkness to the light.

God is life.
I gracefully accept endings, knowing each completion brings a greater beginning.

119

You Won't Get Over It

As soon as you trust yourself, you will know how to live.
— Goethe

In the film *Doc Hollywood*, Michael J. Fox portrays a young doctor who becomes stranded in a tiny southern town, where he falls in love with a young woman named Lou who is engaged to a man named Hank. Although Lou is not in love with Hank, she feels she must go through with the marriage because it would be too embarrassing to cancel it. Fox confronts Hank, reminding him, "But she is not in love with you!"

"That's okay," Hank answers nonchalantly. "She'll get over that."

Many women in my seminars have told me they wish they had listened to their inner voice when it told them not to go ahead with a particular marriage at an early age. Sooner or later, after a certain amount of hardship, such women or men trace their steps back to the point where they sold out; they begin to tell the truth they were denying, and confront the issues of their relationship. Because they learned a great deal in the process, the experience is not a total loss, but they do gain the awareness that they must honor their instincts and not go along with something just because it is socially expedient.

I discovered a challenging Zen koan, a riddle to contemplate throughout the day: *Where does your self end and where does society begin?* What do you do because you honestly choose it, and what do you do because it is expected of you? If you were living to fulfill your heart's intentions rather than the wishes of others, what would you be doing differently?

When we violate ourselves out of fear, we don't get over it. The universe asks us only to be true to ourselves, and if we deny self-integrity, eventually we must return to the same point and choose again, this time in our favor.

I must live my truth.
Give me the strength to be what I am.

I honor my heart. I live my own dreams.

120

The Answer in the Question

Go to your bosom, knock there and
ask your heart what it doth know.
— from *Measure for Measure*, by William Shakespeare

"I am dating two men who have both proposed to me. Which one should I marry?" the woman asked Dr. Norman Vincent Peale, author of the classic book, *The Power of Positive Thinking.*

"Neither," he answered in his gravelly voice.

"Why do you say that?"

"Because you are not in love with either of them."

"How do you know?"

"If you were, you wouldn't be asking me whom to marry; your heart would speak to you directly."

As divine beings, we contain the knowledge of everything that is right for us. At any moment we can turn within for guidance and discover the next step on the path of our highest good. Others may illuminate the way or remind us of what we already know, but they cannot give us something we do not already have. A consultant is someone who borrows your watch to tell you what time it is. The only thing more valuable than a good consultant is the ability to read your own watch.

Experiment with agreeing to only those activities with which your whole heart resonates. To enter into a venture with half a heart will create half a result. If you have doubts, do not try to override them. Lay them out on the table, and look at them in the light. If you sincerely ask for guidance, the doubts will either reveal themselves to be important factors to be dealt with, or they will dissolve and give way to full participation.

Do it with a full spirit, or do not do it at all.

Thank You for placing the seeds of all wisdom within me.
I will look for You in the temple of my own soul.

I turn within for my answers.
I know my highest good.

Blaze Now

On the planes of hesitation lie the sun-bleached bones of untold millions, who while on the verge of victory stopped to wait, and while waiting, died.

— Anonymous

In the film *Spies Like Us,* Chevy Chase and Dan Aykroyd portray a couple of bumbling secret agents who come upon a Russian nuclear installation and inadvertently launch a missile that will lead to atomic devastation. Once the Americans and Russians at the site realize what has happened, Chase asks, "How much time do we have before the end?"

"About 45 minutes," answers Aykroyd.

Chase looks at the woman he loves and suggests, "Then let's go out in a blaze of glory!" His beloved smiles, and the two go off to light up the finale in high style. Then the others in the group look at each other and pair off to leave the world with a smile. At that moment, the notions of Russians and Americans, separate languages and nations, disappear. Ultimately, the missiles are recalled, and the end is averted, but not before the couples make love like there is no tomorrow.

Watching this scene, I wondered why we would wait until the end is near to make love. I am not suggesting that we indulge in licentious sex; I consider the scene a metaphor. Sometimes it is only when our life or livelihood is threatened that we give ourselves permission to express the love we deeply desire. Why put off your good? Follow your spirit now, and avoid the rush later.

Make a list of the things that you would love to do, but are waiting until the time is right. Now imagine that you have a month to live, and prioritize what you would do with your time. Then go out and do the things your heart desires. Your sense of joy and vitality will be so great that you will wonder why you ever waited, and you will add years of health and enthusiasm to your life. Don't wait for the end of your world to be a meteor. Blaze now.

Give me the courage to live my dreams now.

I celebrate my heart's deepest desires by expressing them enthusiastically.

Treasured Wounds

The only appropriate response to your brother is gratitude.
— A Course in Miracles

Charles Dickens' character Miss Havisham was jilted by her fiancé. As a lifelong reminder of the pain he caused her by leaving her at the altar, Miss Havisham keeps the wedding feast on her banquet table, just as it was. Although it has become stale and moldy, she regularly looks upon it with regret and resentment.

If we have an investment in not forgiving someone, we carry a "treasured wound" that reminds us of the injustice done to us. This wound might be an actual physical injury, pain, or illness; an article symbolic of our relationship; a photo; a piece of jewelry; a letter; or another person who connects us to the person. In all of these cases, we harbor one purpose: to keep the pain alive as we focus on the feeling that we have been victimized.

From the standpoint of the Spirit within us that loves to be free and happy, treasured wounds make no sense whatsoever. The voice of fear urges us to hold on to any memory or symbol that proves we were dishonored. The voice of love, on the other hand, holds on to any mementos of the love and blessings a relationship brought us.

Are you keeping any moldy wedding feasts on your banquet table? You may not be holding on to a literally stale meal, but perhaps you are still getting mileage out of an old hurt. Perhaps you have told the same story a hundred times, believing you gain justification by framing yourself as a victim. But with every shovelful of resentment we cast at another, we dig our own grave. We only lose when we cling to treasured wounds.

Instead, let us treasure the blessings we have gained. *A Course in Miracles* reminds us that "all that is left of your past is a blessing." Let us clear the dead banquet from the table and invite someone wonderful for a new feast.

Help me find blessings and release any pain I have held onto through unforgiveness.

I release the past to make way for a brighter future.

Lord of Your Kingdom

Make your life a mission, not an intermission.
— Arnold Glasgow

One of my favorite literary characters is the beloved Don Quixote, Man of La Mancha, brought to life by Miguel de Cervantes. Through worldly eyes, Don Quixote appears to be a foolish itinerant, but his spiritual vision reveals him to be a knight on a mission to bring truth, love, and purity to a dismal world. He vanquishes a windmill he fancies to be a fire-breathing dragon; he ceremoniously dons an old brass shaving bowl as "The Golden Helmet of Umbrino"; when he meets the town harlot, Aldonza, he gives her his handkerchief and humbly adores her as Dulcinea, "The Sweet One." Aldonza laughs in his face and jabs, "I am no Dulcinea, you fool—I am a slut!"

Don Quixote objects, "No, my lady, you mustn't speak that way about yourself; you are my lady Dulcinea, and I your knight, the Lord of La Mancha."

Like many visionaries, Don Quixote poses a threat to those who believe in worldly power, and his foes devise a plot to break him of his delusions. They capture him in a room of mirrors and convince him that he is not a knight, but a fool. They succeed in breaking his spirit, and he becomes ill and despondent.

In the final scene of the play, Don Quixote lies weakly in a dungeon after he has been convicted of heresy and sentenced to death. There, Aldonza and Don Quixote's sidekick, Sancho, visit him and try to remind him of his quest. "I know of no quest," he retorts sharply.

Aldonza takes his hand and kisses it. "Don't you remember?" she asks. "You are the Lord of La Mancha, and I your Lady Dulcinea!"

A light begins to gleam in Don Quixote's eyes, and soon he reclaims his quest. "Sancho, get my armor!" he commands, and sings the classic song, *The Impossible Dream.* As the guards call Don Quixote to his execution, it is clear that although they may annihilate his body, his spirit has triumphed.

Give me the strength to believe in my quest and live it.

My visions are given to me by God.
I will live my dreams.

124

First-Class Flying

Above all things, reverence yourself.

— Pythagoras

The movie *Defending Your Life* suggests that when we leave this world we review the experiences in which we succumbed to fear rather than choosing love. As Daniel reviews his life, he realizes that he consistently denied his own good, until the following event: After a devastating divorce, Daniel was left with a small amount of money and an airline ticket for a vacation in the Orient. When Daniel arrived at the ticket counter for his pleasure outing, the agent told him, "You have seat 38B."

"Does that mean I'll be sitting in the back of the plane between two other people for ten hours?" he asked.

"I'm sorry, sir, there are no other seats available."

"How about in first class?"

"There is one first-class seat left; to upgrade will cost an additional $3,000."

Daniel deliberated for a moment, then exclaimed, "I'll take it!"

Do you love yourself enough to give yourself what would make you happy? Can you trust that your happiness will not take away from another's good, but will only add to the sum total of joy in the universe?

Asking for what you want is not selfish; it is your responsibility. The more you honor yourself with beauty, play, and joy, the greater will be your capacity to love and serve others.

I open myself to receive all the gifts You would offer me.

I accept the best that life has to offer.

Swimming Naked

Few is the number of those who think with their own minds and feel with their own hearts.
— Albert Einstein

One day a friend and I set out to swim *au naturel* in the mountain pools near my home. Soon after we arrived, a few people showed up. I should probably put my bathing suit on, I thought. These people may find my nudity offensive. Then I thought, But I was here first. Besides, most people swim naked here. I'll just carry on as I am and trust that everyone will be fine.

A short time later, a family showed up. Now I should really put my suit on, I thought. But we were here first, I remembered. Kids usually go naked anyway. I'll just trust that everyone will be okay with it. Half an hour later, a tour group arrived. Off the mini-van the Japanese poured, camcorders rolling. Now I really better get dressed, I figured. By this time, however, I was enjoying myself immensely. If they don't like it, that's their problem, I reasoned. Besides, I was here first. So went the day. Everyone else wore swimsuits, but they seemed fine with us being naked, and we all enjoyed ourselves. When we finally left, I felt a deep sense of peace.

Do you have the courage to swim naked even when others are wearing their suits? I am not referring to being physically naked; it is infinitely more important to be spiritually naked—to be who you are, whatever you are, where you are, and to act from a sense of inner vitality rather than social accommodation.

Give me the courage to be what I am.
In the presence of Your love, I have
nothing to hide and everything to celebrate.

Who and what I am is enough.

Gambling for God

Do as the heavens have done, forget your evil.
— from *A Winter's Tale,* by William Shakespeare

A man knocked feverishly on the rabbi's door one morning. "Rabbi, I came to tell you that Shlomo, Samuel, and Ben were up all night gambling!"

"Wonderful!" exclaimed the rabbi.

Shocked, the man complained, "How can you say that? It is against the laws of our religion to gamble!"

"I know," answered the sage, "but these men are finding the energy to stay awake to do something they love. When their hearts turn to love the Lord, they will have the ability to stay up all night to serve God."

We cannot judge or condemn another person's act because we do not know how it fits into the bigger picture of their life or the lives of those they touch. At any given moment, we see only a tiny sliver of a huge jigsaw puzzle that only makes sense on a level that is broader than any human being can understand.

Ultimately, every experience contributes to spiritual awakening. The Holy Spirit sees only love, and when we lift our vision, we behold a miraculous universe.

Help me to see all persons and events
in the loving light of spiritual perception.

My eyes are God's eyes.
I exchange judgment for compassion
and look upon a forgiven world.

What Could Be So Important?

Make not treasures on earth, where moth and rust corrupt and thieves break in and steal. Find your treasures in heaven. Wherever a man's treasures are, there will be his heart.

— Jesus Christ

When I travel, I carry a black briefcase that contains all of my important materials, including a computer, airline tickets, checks I have received, and an address book. Because these items are so vital, I keep the briefcase with me almost all the time. Before delivering a lecture one evening, I set the briefcase down next to the stage, and when I looked for it after the talk, it was not there. Suddenly my heart seemed to skip a beat, and I felt a sinking feeling in my chest. My fear that the satchel had been stolen was almost debilitating. When I asked the lecture sponsor if she had seen the briefcase, she answered, "Oh, yes, I put it in my office for safekeeping."

While I was relieved that the briefcase was safe, I could not help but notice how I had tied my peace to it. I asked myself, "What in that briefcase could be so important that I would lose the peace of God with it?" I wondered how much the anxiety over protecting the property had cost me in the long run. It was a poor trade. What you possess, possesses you. Whenever we value a thing more than happiness, we pay a dear price. Things can be replaced, but peace cannot.

Is there anything you value so much that you would lose your happiness if you lost it? Have your succumbed to worshiping at the altar of fear rather than the citadel of trust? What is *your* black briefcase?

The Sufis suggest, "Do not value anything that could be washed overboard from a ship." When we remember we are here to love, all else becomes secondary.

Help me keep You first today.
Let me not make any false gods before You.

I live to love. I am safe. My heart is at peace.

Make Today Count

To enhance the quality of your relationships,
imagine this is your last day with whomever you are with.
— Og Mandino

The morning started out like any other. Mrs. Magliano drove her husband John and son Ted to the train station, kissed them good-bye, and wished them a nice day. But the day was not like any other. En route to New York City, a crazed gunman opened up fire on the train car, killing a large number of people including John Magliano, and seriously wounding his son.

I saw a television show documenting Ted's recovery. With the help of loving friends and a positive attitude, he was making a remarkable come-back. I was struck by his mother's reflections: "My last memory of my hus-band is kissing him good-bye and telling him, 'I love you.' I did that every day for 30 years, and I meant it. It brings my heart peace to know that we parted with a blessing."

We never really know if we will see any particular person again. That is why it is important to resolve conflict and bring our relationships into peace and healing without delay. In college I broke up with a girlfriend on bad terms. We avoided each other for a while and then saw each other at a party. "We need to talk," she told me. We sat down and gently resolved our upset. A year later, I learned that she was killed in an auto accident. I was very glad that we had spoken words of kindness when we did.

Make a list of any situations or relationships with which you are out of peace. Pray and ask for guidance about what you can do to heal them. Go about your business of bringing them back into harmony. Then you can enjoy them, yourself, and your life.

Spirit of Love, open my heart.
Help me to be at peace with all of my relationships.
Let me not settle for upset or separation. I want my life
to reflect Your love and blessings.

I create peace with my loved ones and myself.

The Case for Forgiveness

Forgiveness is the only sane response.
— A Course in Miracles

Successful attorney Michael Rembolt was dealing with an especially grisly divorce case. Both parties were making huge demands, and neither seemed willing to yield. When Michael sat down to pray on the morning of the court date, he remembered a lesson from *A Course in Miracles: "Forgiveness offers me everything I want."* He began to send prayers of forgiveness to his client and her husband. These thoughts felt so good that he extended his blessings to the opposing attorney, and then to the judge and everyone else scheduled for court that day. Michael arose from his prayer feeling a deep peace.

When he arrived at court that morning, Michael found no one there. He went to the judge's office to find out what had happened, and the magistrate asked him, "Didn't your secretary tell you that your client settled out of court?"

"That's amazing!" Michael responded.

"What's even more amazing," the judge went on, "is that we had 32 cases on the docket today, and every one of them settled out of court!"

Forgiveness is not just a wimpy act of withholding an attack for a wrongdoing; it is a dynamic, creative, and practical force that has the power to manifest miracles. When we let go of judgment, we free ourselves to enjoy a peace that surpasses anything the world has to offer. The power of forgiveness is misunderstood and underused. It is a sacred gift employed by those who recognize that their true safety comes not from worldly manipulation, but from faith in a higher power. There is nothing in this world that cannot be healed by forgiveness.

Give me the strength to extend pure love
and release to everyone I meet.
I trust You to take care of me as I let go of my fears
that would prompt attack.
I take refuge in blessing,
that I may live in a forgiven world.

I forgive and I am forgiven.
My world reflects the beauty of heaven
because I love as God loves.

Truth and Greatness

If any man seeks for greatness, let him forget greatness and ask for truth, and he will find both.

— Horace Mann

Years ago, I taught yoga in a local adult school. I enjoyed it so much that I decided I wanted to make it my profession. I launched a massive promotion campaign, calling and writing every health spa and adult school in the phone book. After great efforts, I manifested two contracts, one which was eventually canceled due to low enrollment, and the other in a health spa. Our class was located on the floor next to exercisers who walked over the relaxing yogis and joked about us en route. I began to wonder if a publicity blitz was really the way to go. In the wake of my fruitless efforts, I decided to simply focus on the classes I was already teaching and give them 100 percent of what I had to give. As a result, word-of-mouth spread, and before long I had more invitations than I could accept.

Many of us have the cart before the horse when it come to establishing a career. We believe that if our presentation is slick enough, we can wedge our foot in the doors we desire. But do you really want to be where you are valued for presentation alone? We earn our right place by giving quality service. Treat your customers like God, and God will provide for you like the heir to the kingdom that you are. Put aside your desire for fame, power, riches, and worldly success, and make it your first priority to give true caring to your clients. Deep in every customer's heart is the knowledge and appreciation of integrity. Quality is the best promotion.

Help me serve through being what I truly am.
I put aside my illusions of grandeur and trust
that if I am grand in love,
I shall live in abundance and joy.

I give my best to life, and life gives its best to me.

131

God's Payroll

Seek ye first the Kingdom of Heaven,
and all else shall be added unto you.
— Jesus Christ

"I feel so guilty," my friend Don told me. "I have a word-of-mouth auto sales business in which I sell a few cars a week and make pretty good money. I spend most of my time as a sponsor for people in 12-step recovery programs. Yet I work just a few hours a week, and all my needs are met."

"No need to feel guilty, Don," I told him. "You are on God's payroll."

The universe will pay you to do what serves it best. To be in your right place and enjoy the benefits of right livelihood, release the idea that work is something you must slave at. The notion that work is a necessary evil and that we must violate ourselves to receive money is not a principle of God, but a tenet of fear. If God is love, then God would not make you do something you hated in order to receive support. To the contrary, the universe will rush to take care of you when you follow your bliss and do what you most enjoy.

You came to earth with talents, intuitions, and visions. As you follow them, you draw to yourself all the material and spiritual support you need. If abundance does not seem to be flowing your way, ask yourself if there is something that you would love to be doing more than what you are doing. Have you had urges or intuitions that you have not acted on? Your secret dreams or delights may be exactly the keys to shifting your energy and results. When you do what you love, you will be serving others in the highest capacity, feel fulfilled, and enjoy the support of the universe.

Give me the courage to follow my heart. Help me do what You would have me do, that I might enjoy the fullness of Your blessings.

I do what I love, and the universe loves to support me for it.

A Bit of Myself

Know then that the world exists for you...
Adam called his house heaven and earth; Caesar called
his house Rome; you perhaps call yours a cobbler's trade,
a hundred acres of ploughed land, or a scholar's garret.
Yet line for line and point for point your dominion is
as great as theirs.... Build therefore your own world.
— Ralph Waldo Emerson

"I prefer doing oil paintings," John told me, "but occasionally I take a commercial art job. Even in my commercial work, I imbue my essence. My brother-in-law, a contractor, commissioned me to do a painting of his backhoe. I depicted the backhoe realistically, and where the backhoe was digging into the ground, I painted a scene of the starry cosmos. He loved it!"

Everything we do has our flavor in it. To do anything without your essence would be as impossible as the sun shining without heat. Your essence is the unique dimension you add to any act you express, from walking your dog to building a skyscraper. It is the special energy that you came to deliver to the world. Just as no two snowflakes or fingerprints are alike, every individual has a uniquely beautiful contribution to offer.

When I walked into a bookstore after I published *The Dragon Doesn't Live Here Anymore,* I was shocked to find hundreds of books with similar themes, some written by famous and gifted authors. Suddenly I felt glad that I hadn't studied the market before I wrote the book; I would have felt intimidated and doubted there was anything I could add to the field. I might have even quit before I started. But I was blissfully naive, and I went ahead, motivated by the sheer joy of expressing myself. Now my books are on the very shelves I would have shied away from.

Never shrink from expressing yourself. *Your* perspective is the one that will carry you. Follow your unique instincts, and you will be uniquely successful.

Help me know that what I am is good enough.
I honor the uniqueness in which You created me.

Confident in my gifts,
I shine my own light and bring quality to
life through my individuality.

Soulmate Knocking

When you are no longer compelled by desire or fear... When you have seen the radiance of eternity in all the forms of time...When you follow your bliss...doors will open where you would not have thought there were doors... and the world will step in and help.

— Joseph Campbell

In one of my seminars, a young girl anxiously posed this question: "I live in California; what if my soulmate is in South Carolina? How am I supposed to find him?" Many of my friends have tried all kinds of techniques to hasten the crucial connection: some of them place and answer personal ads; others join video dating services; some pray and recite affirmations; others make lists of desirable mate traits and read them aloud; some hire matchmakers; and others wear crystals and use flower essence formulas.

My friends John and Susan met in a way that defies methodology. John was a hermit living in the Halawa Valley, a remote jungle reachable only by a long and winding road at the far end of the sleepy Hawaiian island of Molokai. One day, John's friend William showed up to visit him, accompanied by his traveling companion, Susan. Instantly, John and Susan hit it off, fell in love, and before long, wedding bells rang. Eventually, they moved to another island and John re-entered society.

The season of the heart was ripe for the couple to meet, and destiny had its way. John could not have been situated more off the beaten path, and Susan was simply on vacation. Geography means nothing to destiny. If two people are meant to find each other for any reason, they will. We don't have to worry or scheme. Simply be what you are, where you are, and your good will find you.

I pray to release anxious struggle.
You know my best interests. I believe in love.

I place my destiny in the hands of God, trusting that my good is manifested through a hand greater than my own.

All in the Attitude

Always give them the old fire, even when you feel like a squashed cake of ice.

— Ethel Merman

"You are a fantastic rider!" trail guide Frank called to eight-year-old Shanera, who felt awkward and looked self-conscious on her first horseback ride. "You look so beautiful on that horse," he continued. "I can't wait to get your picture!" The child lit up. Frank works magic with his riders, constantly bolstering their confidence, affirming their strengths, and lightening awkward moments. Fifteen years ago, he came to Maui with a dream of taking visitors on unique horseback treks through secret jungles and unspoiled mountains. With hard work and a dynamic attitude, his *Adventures on Horseback*[8] has attracted a steady stream of appreciative clients who ride to majestic cliffs and then picnic and swim at secluded waterfalls. He is living his dream and helping others to live theirs.

Much of Frank's success is a result of the caring he brings to all his riders. A trail ride with Frank is not just a jaunt on a horse; it is a journey into self-esteem. While some customers are nervous riding through obscure jungle trails, Frank's unwavering attention, full presence, and unconditional support have filled his guest log with superlative comments and increasing word-of-mouth business.

You can live your dreams, too—the more unique and outrageous, the better! Your best investment in making them a reality is an attitude of confidence, joy, and true caring. Make your career an exercise in giving love, and you will succeed beyond your secret hopes.

Help me remember that everything I do is an opportunity to share love.

My dreams are God's dreams for me.

Gas or Brake?

Hast thou attempted greatnesses?
Then go on; back-turning slackens resolution.
— Thomas Herriot

A student in Suzanne's self-hypnosis class complained that after she practiced the method to lose weight, she gained five pounds. "Tell me about your technique," Suzanne said.

"I sat down, closed my eyes, and went through the induction," answered the student.

"What suggestions did you use?"

"I said just what we did in class last week: *'My shoulders are getting heavier...my arms are getting heavier...my legs are getting heavier...*"

When we attempt to apply positive thinking and do not get the results we desire, we must look not to the principles, which always work, but to our *application* of the principles. The laws of manifestation are impersonal; the universe will put them to work for or against us, depending on whether we apply them intelligently or erroneously.

We may be praying, treating, or visioning for one result consciously, while affirming the contrary subconsciously. We pray for more abundance and then let our mind go into a tailspin of worry when we see an ominous newspaper headline. We envision a more rewarding relationship and then absorb our mind in trashy talk shows that splash abusive relationships before us like mud. We affirm good health and then get significant mileage out of telling the story of our illness. We insist we want a better future, but then protect ourselves from things that happened in the past. It is no wonder that we lurch in fits and starts when we drive with our foot on the gas and the brake at the same time!

To move ahead, we cannot afford to cancel out our good work by feeding our holy mind thoughts and words to the contrary. Become aware of your subtlest indulgence in thoughts, feelings, and energies that negate the good you are trying to create. Keep coming back to what you want. Your vehicle will really begin to travel when you take your foot off the brake.

I pray to keep my mind and heart on track.
Help me to be faithful to my vision.

I affirm the best of my visions and
I let all else go.

136

A Better Deal

When one door shuts, another opens.
He that would struggle with the world, and bear up
in adversity, ought still to resolve not to be discouraged,
for resolution is the mother of fortitude, and...
very much conducive to our deliverance.
— Samuel Palmer

While searching for an office to rent, I found an attractive space for a reasonable fee. I had a few reservations about the place—it was at a noisy intersection and the rooms were small—but I needed to move in a short time, and the quarters seemed adequate. I told the Realtor I would take it, but when I did not hear from him after a few days, I called to remind him that we had a deadline and we needed to get the lease signed. He assured me that everything was in order, and not to worry. Another week passed and I called again, with the same response. Finally, a few days before the first of the month, I told him we could wait no longer for a confirmation. He sheepishly informed me that the owner did not want to rent to me; he had looked at some of my writings and did not like my philosophy. I felt insulted and outraged. "That sounds like discrimination to me!" I righteously claimed.

The Realtor tried to defend the position, but it was clear there was nothing he could do. My mind raced with anger as I felt I had been deceived and mistreated. Meanwhile, an inner voice said, "No use getting upset; this is all working on your behalf." While driving home, I decided to take a scenic route, where I saw a storefront with a large *"For Rent"* sign in the window. The landlady was a lovely woman who had sold tea and held tai chi classes in the space, which was large, beautiful, inexpensive, surrounded by green life, and minutes from my home—in every way superior to the place I had lost. I rented the space, and we have been happy there ever since.

Nothing is withheld or taken away from us unless something better is in store. Remember this, and bitterness will fly away forever.

Help me trust that Your wisdom is operating behind the scenes at all times.

I have no use for sorrow.
God is in charge of my well-being.

Crazy Works

You have to be a little cracked to let the light in.
— Anonymous

My friend Darryl is a crazy genius. He spent time in and out of mental institutions, and I could never quite decide if he was a saint or a madman. Once I went to visit him in the day room of a locked ward where the patients milled around and had contests to see who could do the strangest things. "Do you see that man over there?" Darryl asked me. "He murdered his family." Oh. "And that guy over there is a chronic rapist." I got the picture. "Jerry over there ate 12 cats before they brought him in." I checked my jacket for the odor of my cat, hoping Jerry wouldn't confuse me with a feline.

Just then, two of the patients got into a loud, violent argument and started to push each other around. Not seeing any attendants, I began to feel frightened that I might be pulled into a maniacal fray. Suddenly, Darryl, a frail vegetarian, jumped up, forced himself between the two bulky brawlers, and shouted, *"Now you guys cut that out right now—do you understand?"* To my utter amazement, instead of squashing Darryl summarily as they could easily have, the two lugs sheepishly parted and retreated to different corners of the day room.

I was stunned. "Darryl, man," I asked as he returned, "how did you manage to get those wild men to listen to you?"

"The most amazing thing happened the first day I was here," Darryl explained. "I had no space in my room to do yoga, so I did it right here on the floor of the day room. When the other guys saw me, they thought I was a martial arts expert, and now they're all afraid of me. They do whatever I tell them."

The Lord works in mysterious ways, and takes care of His own.

Place within me the intuition to succeed in all situations;
speak to me from inside my heart.

I am always safe because
God is always with me.

The Temple

While God waits for His temple to be built of love,
men bring stones.

— Rabindranath Tagore

"When the church board interviewed me, they asked if I would spearhead a building campaign for a new sanctuary," the minister recounted. "I told them that I could not promise a new sanctuary, but I could guarantee that I would build a new consciousness."

The movie *Field of Dreams* taught, *"If you build it, they will come."* But what is it that you must build? Because we are spiritual beings, we must nurture our thoughts and attitude above all else. If we think in harmony with truth, the outer forms will take care of themselves: *"Seek ye first the kingdom of heaven, and all else shall be added unto you."*

What is the use of building a sanctuary, home, or business if it is not filled with love, light, laughter, and service? There are huge edifices built to God that are conspicuously devoid of caring, compassion, and acceptance. And there are small and humble churches, businesses, and families that are holy temples because they are founded on love. Remember that essence is always more important than form, and all else shall be provided.

Make my life a temple to Your love.
May everyone I meet feel safe, cared for, served,
and uplifted in my presence.

My life is my gift to God. My religion is love.

Screams or Music?

Be aware that a halo has to fall only a few inches to become a noose.

— Dan McKinnon

When the Beatles' 1995 reunion was accompanied by an in-depth television documentary on their incomparable talent and success, the band members spoke candidly about their experience. Being the best-known and most sought-after people on the planet wasn't all fun and games. "After two years of intense touring and fending off all kinds of people who wanted something from us, we were bored, frustrated, and going buggy," one of the Beatles noted. "Our music was stagnating because we couldn't hear a note we were playing, and neither could the screamers. You can't grow, improve, or be creative in that kind of atmosphere." Subsequently, the group quit touring and put their energy into innovative recording, which proved to be the most productive and rewarding segment of their career. During that period, the Beatles released *Sergeant Pepper's Lonely Hearts Club Band,* which became a landmark in music history and one of the most celebrated albums of all time.

We cannot breathe or wax creative in an atmosphere of inappropriate adoration or limelight. Nor can we truly enjoy the object of our affection if we are hysterical over it. The world would tell us that fame, fortune, and worldly approval equal success. Yet these men who were the most famous in the world eventually wanted no part of the mania.

The only true measure of success is peace, happiness, and spiritual reward. Worldly accolades mean nothing in the Kingdom of Love.

I pray that my intentions remain pure and that I put Spirit before any worldly illusions or distractions.

**I move forward with my vision on peace.
I succeed because my heart is pure.**

Sleeping Beauty

My soul, sit thou a patient looker on;
judge not the play before the play is done;
her plot has many changes, every day speaks
a new scene, the last act crowns the play.
— William Shakespeare

Rob and Angela had a very difficult time with their teenage daughter Mindy, who went through many turbulent adolescent trials that caused her parents to wonder if they had somehow failed. On the eve of Mindy's departure for college, the family went out to dinner. As soon as everyone was seated, Mindy handed each of her parents and her younger brother an envelope. As the family read the enclosed cards, tears began to flow. Mindy had written long, sincere, heartfelt letters of appreciation to all of her family members, carefully thanking them for all the gifts of love they had given her, honoring them for preparing her so well to go out into the world as a whole person. "In that moment," Angela told me, "it was all worth it."

When you serve or support someone, do not be fooled by appearances. Temporary circumstances may not be a true reflection of long-term benefits. Just keep offering the highest gifts you can, while trusting that one day you will be able to say, "It was all worth it."

Help me to serve today without being attached to results.
I will do my part, trusting You to do yours.

The love I invest in my relationships returns to me multiplied many times over.

Stand by Your Plan

Believe that with your feeling and your work you are taking part in the greatest; the more strongly you cultivate in yourself this belief, the more will reality and the world go forth from it.

— Rainer Maria Rilke

The story behind the making of the blockbuster film *Forrest Gump* is as fascinating as the movie itself. After the script was pitched for nine years, Paramount finally took it on. When the movie went ten million dollars over budget (due largely to the special-effects scenes in which Forrest Gump visits well-known historical figures), the studio decided to finish the film without those scenes. Actor Tom Hanks and two producers urged the studio to invest more money in completing the special effects, but the studio refused and countered with the offer that if the principals wanted to invest two million dollars of their own funds, they could have a larger share of the box-office gross. The principals felt the movie was worth it, and took the risk. To everyone's surprise, *Forrest Gump* became the third highest-grossing film of all time, earning over $300 million. The principals laughed all the way to the bank, and Tom Hanks received $30 million as his share.

If you believe in what you are doing, you will be asked to stand behind it fully. If you are true to yourself, you will act as if your goal is worth enormous support. Why would you be involved in any project that you could not put your whole heart and soul into? The *Forrest Gump* investors gave it 100 percent; they could not bear to stop with less.

Throw yourself wholeheartedly into the task at hand. Anything worth doing is worth doing well. Live what you believe in, and the world will reward you many times over.

Inspire me to give all I have to what I believe in.

I support my visions with my whole heart.

Hang in There

If well thou has begun, go on foreright;
it is the end that crowns us, not the fight.
— Robert Herrik

I was inspired to establish a weekly community dinner at which spiritually oriented friends could get together for fellowship. I set the date to begin, invited my friends, cleaned the house, and baked an eggplant Parmigiana dinner as my offering to the potluck. When the appointed time arrived, no one had shown up. "Maybe they are fashionably late," I reasoned, and waited. Half an hour later, there were still no guests, so I sat down to begin the dinner myself. Another half-hour went by, and there I sat with my eggplant and no guests. I felt very disappointed and wondered if I had made a mistake with the project.

I persevered and went on with the plan the next week, and two people joined me. The following week, we had half a dozen. Within a few months, the community dinner was booming, and the house was bursting at the seams with guests. We went on to share creative meals, music, and presentations for over five wonderful years. After I moved from the area, the program was carried on at various homes, and it became a source of support and friendship for many people. Looking back on my first night romancing the eggplant, I realized how foolish I was to judge the value or success of my project based upon the initial response. The idea was an excellent one; it just took a little time to get rolling.

If you have a good idea, don't give up on it because your initial returns are not what you expected. Hang in there, hold the vision, keep the faith, and before long you may find your house bursting at the seams with success.

Help me be true to my visions,
even when the outer world does not seem to support them.
I know that the inspirations You give me are good
and must succeed.

Steadfast I march on, secure.
With God I am never alone.

Now I'm Sure

Come, my friends, 'tis not too late to seek a newer world...
We are one equal temper of heroic hearts.
— Alfred, Lord Tennyson

In the film *Lost Horizon*, a group of air-crash survivors find their way to Shangri-La, a Utopian community high in the Himalayas where everyone lives in harmony and enjoys tremendous longevity. One of the survivors, Robert Conway, senses that he has finally come home and plans to live out his life in Shangri-La. But when some of his fellow passengers convince him that he has been deluded, he rejects the community and ventures back into his old world. It is not long before he realizes that the peace of Shangri-La was genuine and the life he attempted to regain was the illusion. Conway tries to find his way back to Shangri-La, but because the community is tucked away beyond bottomless chasms and unsurpassable blizzards, he must persevere fearlessly and tirelessly to regain the paradise he renounced. Eventually, he does locate the land of peace, and the wisdom he gained during his quest earns him a position as a leader in the community.

When we say no to love, the contrast between what the love offered us and what we tried to exchange it for is obvious. We recognize without a doubt that the good we renounced was indeed in our best interests. Then we can pursue it with a whole heart. When we regain it, we know it is ours, and we deserve it by right of our consciousness. In the big picture, perhaps we had to say no first so we could become sure of the yes we eventually declare.

Let me hearken wholeheartedly
to the call of love and renounce any delusions
that fear could offer me more.

Love is my refuge and my salvation.
I choose it with all my heart.

Time Out

If you ever feel that you ***should*** *do something,*
lie down until the feeling passes.
— Arnold Patent

Every activity of life is enhanced by rest. From golf to boxing, players are given time between their performances to step back, renew themselves, and get a perspective. The greatest creators and inventors make use of frequent periods to tap into their creative unconscious: Thomas Edison and Albert Einstein were known for taking cat naps in the midst of their experiments and returning with powerful insights. The Bible tells us that God created the heavens and the earth in six days, and on the seventh day He rested.

If the Creator of the Universe took a day off to rest, certainly you and I can! Yet how many of us stop to recharge our batteries and remember that there is more to life than incessant activity? We live in a society obsessed with terminal doingness. We believe that our worth is determined by how much we produce, and we fear that if we step back for even a moment we will get behind and someone else will get ahead. Insanity!

The cycle of activity and rest is as natural as day and night, as colorful as the seasons, and as vital as breathing. If you are always on the go, stopping to catch your breath will only empower you. Effective resting is an art that truly successful people have mastered.

The next time you feel overwhelmed, have the presence of mind to stop and catch your breath—it will make all the difference.

I pray to be renewed by the breath of life You give me.
Help me to step back and allow You to be reborn in me
that I may be reborn in the world.

I breathe deeply. I am empowered by the cycles of creation.

Be Good to Yourself

When I tune into my beautiful self, I get happiness.
Everything in the universe belongs to me.
— Dick Gregory

One of my favorite places to speak is at a chapel overseen by Rev. Chris Chenoweth, one of the most gracious and generous people I have ever met. Chris just loves to say "Yes!" Whenever I speak at his church, he does everything he can to support my work, materially and spiritually.

Rev. Chenoweth inspired me when he gave me some insights into his own life. "I just love my new hot tub!" he exclaimed during one visit. When I saw him the next year, he suggested, "You'll have to come to my house and enjoy my new big-screen TV." A year later, Chris was eagerly awaiting the arrival of his new Honda motorcycle. Chris's delight with his toys showed me that he had a complete prosperity consciousness—he was just as generous with himself as he was with others. He proved that when Spirit showers love, It does not leave anyone out.

Real humility is not denying the gifts of God; it is accepting them. Material gifts are just a symbol of God's abundance. The real gifts are the gifts of spirit—joy, aliveness, laughter, love, appreciation, compassion, and many more. If you give to others, materially or spiritually, and you leave yourself out, you cannot say that you are a true giver. Accept for yourself what you are giving to others, and your life will be a more valuable teaching than your words.

Help me love completely.
Let me enjoy the blessings of giving.
I am willing to receive as much as I give.

All that I give is given to myself.

Then I Saw the Picture

If we could read the secret histories of our enemies,
we should find in each man's life, sorrow and suffering
enough to disarm all hostility.

— Henry Wadsworth Longfellow

"After I killed him, I went through his pockets to search for valuables," Jack soberly told our seminar group. "It was standard practice in Vietnam." Jack's eyes began to tear, and his voice started to shake. "What I found changed my life: In this soldier's pocket was a photo of his wife and young child. I stopped in my tracks. Although I had killed many Vietnamese in the war, they always seemed just a faceless enemy. Suddenly I realized I had killed a real person with a family like my own. I could not do it again. As soon as I could, I made arrangements to be transferred."

We keep enemies by not looking at them. The moment we look into the eyes or the heart of one we call enemy, we recognize ourselves.

If there is someone from whom you feel estranged, look into their eyes. If you can do this in person, you will see their innocence behind the drama and feel your oneness with them. If it is not possible to do this with them physically, call them to you in spirit, and mentally look into their eyes. When you touch someone's soul, you cannot long hold resentment. The eyes are the windows of the soul, but they are also the mirror of yourself.

When I visited the Soviet Union with citizen diplomacy groups, we shared family photos with the Russians. We placed their pictures on mantels or altars at home, and they did the same. It is quite difficult to imagine dropping bombs on people who are just like us.

War will end when we realize that people are not our enemies. Fear is the root of separateness, and the consciousness of our unity is the healer.

I pray to release all thoughts of separateness and enmity.
From this day on, may I call everyone I meet
and know my friend.

I am one with all of my sisters, brothers,
and the earth.

When the Student Is Ready...

When you pray, you pray amiss.
Give thanks for the answers to your prayers before you see them manifested.

— Jesus Christ

The men were huddled round the cassette player, listening intently. As I entered Victor's room, I heard a strong voice from the tape: "*You are a divine being, created in the image and likeness of perfection. Live the life you were born to live, and never compromise with fear.*" I was magnetized to the power and authority with which the speaker delivered a stirring address. After the lecture, I asked, "Who was that? Where can I get that tape?"

The three fellows looked at each other sheepishly, and Victor answered, "I don't know."

"How can you not know? Isn't there a label on it?"

"The label is blank," Victor answered. "I got the tape at Radio Shack. I bought a new package of three blank cassettes, and this was one of them."

When Spirit wants to get through to you, It will find a way. We never need to struggle to connect with the right people or teachings. When the student is ready, the teacher appears.

Everyone and everything that shows up in our life comes to us by vibrational attraction. When you are vibrating at a particular frequency, you draw to yourself all that is in harmony with that frequency. That is why it is useless to try to force the universe to do anything. The level at which human force operates is puny, trivial, and impotent in light of the mighty strength of Spirit to manifest your highest good without struggle on your part.

If you want to attract the right job, mate, or living situation, give up fighting to make it happen. Instead, bring yourself into vibrational harmony with the object of your desire. In meditation, prayer, and affirmation, visualize and feel your oneness with the thing you want. When you are energetically unified with your vision, the universe will lay it at your doorstep in miraculous ways.

 *I pray to attract my highest good easily, gently, and joyfully.*

I let go of struggle and allow Spirit to manifest my good. 

148

Find the Miracle

While there is a chance of the world getting through its troubles, I hold that a reasonable man has to behave as if he were sure of it.

— H.G. Wells

On a journey through a jungle, a king accidentally cut off his toe while chopping a coconut. "That's wonderful," exclaimed his advisor. "There is a blessing here." The king, angered at the advisor's flippancy, threw him in a pit and left him there.

The next day, the king was apprehended by a band of headhunters who decided he would make a good sacrifice. When the tribal priest noticed that his toe was missing, the headhunters released him as an imperfect specimen. Suddenly the king realized that the advisor was correct, and he returned to the pit and apologized profusely.

"No apology necessary," said the advisor. "It was also a blessing that you threw me in this hole."

"How is that?" asked the king, incredulous.

"Because if I was with you, the headhunters would have taken *me* for the sacrifice!"

Imagine that everything that happens to you is assigned by divine order. If you look for miracles, you will find them.

Help me see the good in everything.

I am in the presence of love, taken care of at all times in all ways.

149

Leap of Faith

Only those who dare to go too far can possibly find out how far one can go.

— T.S. Eliot

In one of the popular Indiana Jones movies, Indy (played by Harrison Ford) surmounts a long series of harrowing challenges to arrive at the temple where the chalice of Christ is kept. Our hero stands before a vast bottomless chasm, wondering how he will get across. Then he remembers the instruction he was given to help him at this point: *Faith*. Indy grits his teeth and steps off the ledge onto nothingness. Then a miracle occurs: a bridge appears beneath his foot, enabling him to reach the grail and save his father's life.

The only way we grow is by taking leaps of faith. Such a leap means that we are willing to step into the abyss without any obvious security or guarantee of success. ("If you want a guarantee, buy a toaster.") Even the simple act of walking requires us to be out of balance. When you shift your weight from one foot to another, there is a tiny in-between moment when you are not secure on the old footing or the new.

Bless insecurity as an opportunity to be supported by a higher power. It is only when we have exhausted our resources that God can prove His mighty presence.

I step ahead knowing that You are here for me.
I trust Your arms to comfort me when
nothing in the world can.

God is my strength in every need.

Blessed Interruptions

Life is what happens while you are making other plans.
— John Lennon

The film *The Accidental Tourist* tells of an emotionally wounded man who shuts down his heart after losing a child. Although he is a renowned author, Macon Leary (played by William Hurt) is lonely and aching for love. He meets a kooky young woman (Geena Davis) who, with her son, invites him to come back to life. At first he resists, but then he recognizes that she is not a threat, but his salvation.

"I used to get annoyed when someone pulled me off my track," a friend told me, "but then I discovered that the best parts of my day are the interruptions."

Thank God when you are interrupted from your plan. If something comes up that is unavoidable, ask to find the gift in it. Consider the possibility that this person or event has been sent to serve and bless you in some way. Perhaps you are being asked to open your heart more, make a stand for something you believe in, or take a new direction that will ultimately be more meaningful than the one you were headed in. There are no accidents—only opportunities to dance in a bigger universe.

Help me be open to opportunities to know myself better.
Let me recognize that everyone who comes to me
is a teacher, and empower me to do
the things that love would have me do.

I allow God's plan to substitute for mine.
I find the jewel in every encounter,
relationship, and experience.

151

Tell Me Before I Forget

You will remember everything the instant
you desire it wholly.
— *A Course in Miracles*

The parents of a four-year-old boy arrived home with his new baby brother. Soon the elder child began to pester his parents to leave him alone with the infant. Fearing that the four-year-old might hurt the baby, they refused. Finally, after the boy persisted, the parents consented. As a safeguard, they turned on the intercom to monitor the boy's visit. Listening from the kitchen, they heard the older brother approach the crib, lean over, and ask the baby, "Tell me about God—I'm starting to forget."

We have all forgotten about God, and we are starting to remember. We love children because they still bear the innocent light of heaven, and they have not yet been sullied by the pain and small thinking of the world. They are our connection to the divine.

The light that children shine still lives within us. It has not been lost, just covered over. The spiritual path is not one of attainment, but return. We are returning to our innate wisdom that the beauty we seek shines in us, through us, as us.

Help me remember my divine origin.
Let me rediscover the innocence within me and all of life.

I am innocent. I am free.
The God I seek lives within me.

Crossing the Line

The obligation of the comedian is to find where the line is drawn, deliberately cross it, and make the audience glad you took them with you.

— George Carlin

In the film *Meetings with Remarkable Men,* young George Gurdjieff comes upon a Russian country village where some children are playing a cruel trick on one of their peers. Gurdjieff finds a young schoolboy trapped inside a chalk circle drawn by the other children. Under the superstitious belief that anyone caught inside such a circle is trapped by the devil's power, the boy cannot escape, and he is terrified. With compassion, Gurdjieff rubs out a portion of the circle, and the boy flees.

Many of the beliefs that hold us hostage are no more real than the chalk circle. When we examine our perceived limits or someone else demonstrates that they are not valid, a portion of our chalk line is rubbed out, and we grow beyond our imprisoning perceptions to gain the freedom we deserve.

What do you believe you cannot do? Are you wiling to call to question your sense of limits? Would you rather be right, or free?

Make a list of all the things you would like to do, but believe you cannot. Then examine each of your reasons and consider whether they are real, or simply represent a belief you are holding. You may be pleasantly surprised to find that you are not as constrained as you believed. Look fearlessly and honestly upon your limits, and you will find that you are more powerful than any of your fears.

Show me the way to freedom.
Dissolve my limits, that I may live the life You intended.

I am unlimited. I am free. My life is an ever-expanding adventure.

Happily Even After

Use no relationship to hold you to the past,
but with each one each day be born again.
— A Course in Miracles

On Father's Day, my friend Danielle took her two former husbands out to dinner. "I wanted to honor the two most important men in my life," she told me. "They are the fathers of my children, and we are all related." I respected and honored Danielle for keeping her former mates in her heart and acknowledging the good they had brought into her life.

Most of us are taught that when a relationship is over, both parties go their ways upset; one is a villain and the other a victim. But what if suffering is optional? What if we can create our partings in any way we choose? What if we don't have to separate in anger or guilt, but go on to enjoy a friendship that lasts a lifetime and beyond?

We can let go of our old models of isolation and separation and replace them with kindness, caring, intimacy, and support. Because we are spiritual beings, it is not what our bodies do that determines the quality of our lives, but the state of our spirit. Although our bodies may go in different directions, we can remain whole and joined in the heart. The end of a marriage or relationship does not mean the end of love. True love spans far beyond the boundaries we have laid over it, and it does not die; it simply goes on gathering force until everyone and everything we look upon is blessed by our appreciation of each other as gifts from God.

I pray to honor the people in my life no matter what the voice of fear tells me. I will give love no matter what.

My relationships reflect the love of God.

Buddha on Board

Take care of you.
— advice given to Julia Roberts' character in *Pretty Woman*

Years ago, little yellow *"Baby on Board"* signs began showing up on rear windows of cars. The message meant that other drivers should be especially careful to avoid an accident with an auto containing an infant. A good idea, to be sure. But does this mean that we can be less careful to avoid colliding with a car containing an adult?

We all have a baby on board wherever we go. No matter what our age or status in life, we carry a fragile inner child in our bosom. That child requires tender care and protection, and we must do everything we can to keep it from being injured.

Before a seminar I conducted, I asked each participant to send me a baby picture. I had these photos enlarged and transferred to T-shirts. The first night of the program, I gave out the shirts and told everyone, "In case you become angry at someone, look at that person's T-shirt. Imagine that you are dealing with a sensitive child rather than an armored adult. Speak to that child with patience and kindness." The group loved the exercise, the program was a huge success, and everyone took their T-shirts home. I still wear mine when I want to remember my inner child.

You not only carry an inner child within you, but an inner Christ, Buddha, and any saint or angel you can imagine. These inner divine beings are much closer to your true identity than the person you usually identify with. Honor the Buddha on Board, and your outer life will reflect the respect you deserve.

I pray to treat myself and others with the gentle respect we truly merit.

God lives within me as me.
I honor the light I am.

The Unaffordable Budget

In my defenselessness my safety lies.
— A Course in Miracles

On the *Star Trek* television series, the crew of the Starship Enterprise regularly faced a tough dilemma. While holding up their force-field shields to ward off an attack, the ship would lose power to do anything else. Engineer Scotty would report to Captain Kirk, "Our shields are draining our energy. If we are going to make a move of any kind, we are going to have to drop them." The crew would then have to come up with some ingenious plan to triumph, and they always did.

Any energy we invest in defense robs us of creativity and diminishes our ability to move forward. Our country spends a billion dollars a day on our war machine; imagine the service that money could generate if it were invested in education, social medicine, the arts, housing, and human services. How much is defense worth?

On a personal level, the more energy we spend in hiding, the less alive and creative we are. Any game that requires defense does not befit the son or daughter of God that you are. Consider bringing your hidden self into the light, and you will liberate the riches of your soul. You might think that if people knew who you really are, you would be crucified; but if *you* knew who you really are, you would be exalted.

Show me how to live in the light. I do not want to hide anymore. Help me trust that my true strength lies in authenticity.

I am as God created me.
I renounce fear and regain my soul.

Get a Job

Thank God every morning when you get up that you have something to do that day which must be done. Being forced to work, and forced to do your best, will breed in you temperance and self-control, diligence and strength of will, cheerfulness and content, and a hundred virtues which the idle never know.

— Charles Kingsley

My friend Stanley seemed to live an enviable life. At a young age, he inherited a fortune from his father, and subsequently never held a real job. Stanley spent most of his time traveling, visiting friends, and dabbling in various projects for fun. As I got to know Stanley, I noticed that he made poor choices in managing his life and his money. He was easily influenced, and he was a bad judge of character. When I discussed Stanley with my counselor, she noted dryly, "He needs a job."

A life that is too comfortable and cushy may weaken us. While there is nothing wrong with having a lot of money, and we are certainly not required to slave at an occupation we hate, there is a value in engaging in work that teaches us to manage our resources wisely and learn the importance of right service, activity, and integrity. Dealing in the marketplace moves us to stretch and enter into situations that challenge us to see and tell more truth, communicate, and grow.

After years of intensive traveling, lecturing, and dealing in the business world, my spirit needed a rest, and I took a sabbatical from work for a year. I spent the first month of my retreat doing nothing, thinking to myself, "This is the life! I am never going back to work again!" As the months went by, I felt more and more healed, and by the time the year was over, I was ready and enthusiastic to return to activity. I needed the rest, but I also needed the stimulation.

Work is not a bad thing; it builds muscles and opens doors that we would not access on our own. Right livelihood brings forth the greatness inherent in our soul and assists us to fulfill our purpose as creative beings.

I pray to put my strengths and talents to their best use, that I may serve and grow.

My work is a joyful and productive expression of my inner spirit.

Where Is the Jungle?

Calm soul of all things!
Make it mine to feel amid the city's jar
That there abides a peace of things man did not make,
and cannot mar.

— Matthew Arnold

My parrot was swept on a gust of wind and deposited in a jungle valley across a gulch from his aviary. Yogi landed in a tree near the hut of a hermit, a bearded mountain man named Tom who had holed up in seclusion for many years. As I approached Tom's makeshift dwelling, I saw he was living on a wooden palette under a thin plastic tarpaulin. A few meager possessions were scattered around the palette, but what caught my eye was his television. Tom was engrossed in watching the news on an old TV hooked up to a car battery.

"Armageddon is on its way!" he announced. "It's all over the news; just watch what's going on—the Bible tells us these are the end times!" Well, I thought, anytime you watch the news it looks like the end times. It turns out that Tom spends most of his time in the jungle watching disaster news on television. While it might appear that he has renounced the world, he has actually taken it with him.

In an old *Honeymooners* episode, Ed Norton longed to return to work after he was fired from his job in the sewer department. Ed's classic comment to Ralph Kramden was, "You can take the man out of the sewer, but you can't take the sewer out of the man!"

By contrast, my teacher Hilda lived in one of the toughest sections of New York City, and she carried heaven with her wherever she went. She regularly encountered drug addicts, thieves, prostitutes, and murder victims, but the light within her was so strong that she transformed everyone she met. You can take the person out of heaven, but you can't take heaven out of the person.

We may live in a jungle, but whether it is heaven or hell depends on the thoughts we carry within us.

I pray to carry the light with me wherever I go.

I live in the world I choose with my thoughts.

A Silver Platter

At every moment the universe is making you an irresistible offer.

— Anonymous

The movie *Dumb and Dumber* depicts the trials of a pair of goofy guys traveling cross-country in search of the girls of their dreams. After many disappointments, the duo is stranded on a desert road when a busload of gorgeous bikini-clad babes pulls up. Three mega-attractive women step off the bus, and one greets them, "Hi! We're on the Hawaiian Tropic Tanning Oil tour, and we're looking for a couple of guys to travel with us and rub suntan oil on us before our demonstrations." Then she coyly asks, "Do you know where we could find these guys?"

One fellow smiles and answers, "Sure! There's a town about three miles down the road!"

Disappointed, the girls climb on the bus and leave the two in the dust. "Look at that, Harry," one of the pair complains. "Some guys have all the luck."

While it may seem that life is passing us by, quite often it is laying golden opportunities at our doorstep. Before doubting or missing an invitation, consider if there might be a divine gift in this meeting. Imagine that everyone you meet is sent to you by God for a reason. Although you are not required to accept every invitation, there is a gift in every encounter.

Today I will regard everyone I meet as Your messenger, come to teach, heal, or bless me in some way.

My good is seeking me. I accept it now.

The Key

Boldness has genius, power, magic in it.

— Goethe

"I am at a crossroads in my life," John confessed. "Last year I quit a successful job in the oil industry so I could explore my spiritual path. Recently I received a lucrative offer to work for another company, and I'm tempted. If I take it, my soul will shrivel, for I would be going backward, not forward."

"Would you be willing to trust the universe to support you to live your dream, even if you cannot see how that would happen?" I asked.

John thought for a while and smiled. "Yes, I am willing for that to happen."

A few weeks later, I received a letter from John, who reported, "The most amazing thing happened. I went to visit my father, who has never really understood or been very supportive of my spiritual path. He took me into his study and told me, 'Son, I am proud of you for what you're doing with your life.' He took out his checkbook and wrote me a large check that will keep me going for at least a year." Within four months, John had gotten his massage teacher's license at Esalen, a yoga teacher's certification from Kripalu Institute, and attended a Mastery Training in Hawaii. The last I heard of him, he was trekking in Nepal.

The key to John's transformation and his unexpected gift was his willingness to allow the universe to support him. It was an internal shift from, "I don't see how this could happen" to "I am willing to have this happen somehow." When you start an automobile, the key is just a tiny piece of metal, minuscule in comparison to the might of the engine that will drive the vehicle. Yet, all of 300 horsepower depends on the flick of a small key.

You don't need to know the *how* of it; just know the *what*, and be willing for an unfathomable force to work wonders on your behalf.

I surrender to Your wisdom and strength.
Do for me what I cannot do for myself.

I am willing to have the universe support me to live my dream.

Just Testing

All things are lessons God would have me learn.
— A Course in Miracles

"My engagement is off, and I'm really bummed," Wendy told me. "He turned out to be a real turkey. When we first got together, he promised me everything. Then I found out that he was carrying a lot of baggage from his past; his ex-wife is a cocaine addict who owes a hundred thousand dollars on her credit cards. I can't believe I wasted six months with that jerk!"

While I understood Wendy's disappointment, I saw that she was hurting herself by assuming a victim position. A little while later, I asked her, "What kind of work do you do?"

"I work for the army, training soldiers to protect themselves against biochemical warfare. I take them into a room where noxious chemicals have been released, and I take away their gas masks. My job is to see how they react under pressure. Some of them follow the emergency procedures they have been taught, and others freak out. Some become angry at me, call me horrible names, and try to grab their mask back. They don't realize I'm trying to help them by training them."

Then a thought occurred to me: "What if your fiancé has offered you the same service you provide your soldiers?" I asked Wendy.

"What do you mean?"

"Your fiancé showed you where you feel small and unprotected. When you got angry and blasted him for your discomfort, you are like the soldiers blaming you. You might consider this experience a training for you to find strength and wholeness within you, in the presence of a noxious environment."

Everyone we meet serves us. Some help us by bringing us peace and joy; others help us by challenging us to find clarity within ourselves. Let us honor both our friends and foes as teachers who lead us to greater power and truth.

Help me to appreciate all my relationships, and find the gift in every encounter.

Everyone is my teacher of peace.
I learn and grow from all my relations.

Good News

Your defenses will not work, but you are not in danger.
— A Course in Miracles

At a cavalry outpost in the Old West, two soldiers vigilantly fended off an Indian attack, determined to fight to the death if necessary. One of the soldiers tapped the other on the shoulder and informed him, "I have good news, and I have bad news. The bad news is that we are out of ammunition, and there are no reinforcements."

"Then what's the good news?" asked the other soldier.

"There are no Indians."

We may spend much of our life trying to protect ourselves against the calamities that threaten to destroy us. We may invest vast amounts of time, energy, and effort to armor ourselves against people, institutions, and ideas that we believe have the power to take away our good. Yet if we would step back for even a moment and call to question the power we have ascribed to evil, we would find that our entire defense strategy was based on a faulty premise. "Logic" has been defined as "a system of reasoning by which you arrive at the wrong conclusion with confidence." If we build our world on fear, every action that follows on its heels will result in self-diminution because we erected our world on a misunderstanding.

What actions do you undertake in the name of self-defense? Do they truly bring you more peace, or do they edify your sense of powerlessness and abandonment? I chuckle as I read magazine ads for radar detectors. Every year the companies come out with a new method to outwit the current state-of-the-art police technology, and the next year the police invent new methods for overriding the latest radar detectors. Like the *Mad* magazine cartoon, "Spy Versus Spy," everyone is trying to trick everyone else, and no one ever wins.

We are most powerful when we give up trying to defend ourselves and allow Spirit to take care of us.

Help me to let go of my human defenses and rely on You for my safety and support.

The Lord is my shepherd; I shall not want.

The Pig of God

Trust would settle every problem now.
— A Course in Miracles

As a man was driving around a dangerous hairpin mountain curve, a woman in a little red sports car tore around the bend from the opposite direction, cutting him off and forcing him to veer off the road. To add insult to injury, as the woman sped by, she yelled "Pig!"

Furious, the man shook his fist at her and shouted, "Sow!" He kept going around the curve, where he ran into a pig sitting on his side of the road.

Sometimes when it appears that life is attacking us, it is trying to help us. Those who challenge us bring us valuable life lessons that we might miss if we are caught up in feeling insulted or unappreciated. Imagine that everyone you meet is here to assist you to go deeper in your wisdom, healing, and joy. Do not be fooled by appearances; use your higher vision until you find the gold.

When I attended a lecture by Ram Dass, he announced that several people in the audience needed rides to a nearby city. When no one in the auditorium raised their hand to offer assistance, he added, "And the person you take in your car may be the Christ or Buddha in disguise." Immediately, half a dozen hands went up! Cultivate the ability to say, "Thank you for everything," and you will find that everything is a gift.

Open my vision to see the gifts I have been missing.
Open my heart to love in situations I judged as unlovable.

I name all things "good," and I welcome life as a brilliant teacher.

Fearless

I am at home. Fear is the stranger here.
— A Course in Miracles

In the film *Fearless,* Jeff Bridges portrays a man named Max who narrowly escapes death in a plane crash. In surrendering to imminent death, he loses all fear, and when he goes on with his life, he finds himself unafraid in a world motivated by mistrust and deception. His lawyer wants him to lie to exact a larger settlement from the airline company; his wife cannot handle the truth he is now unafraid to tell about their numb relationship; and his psychologist thinks he has gone mad (while he has actually gone sane).

In a poignant scene, Max momentarily gives in to pressure to lie, which leaves him painfully contracted. To vent the horror he feels, he climbs onto the roof of a tall building and screams at the top of his lungs. Watching this symbolic scene, I wondered how loud would be the cries of humanity if we all went up on a roof and screamed at the top of our lungs in proportion to the pain and constriction we have experienced by living in ways that are inconsistent with our true nature.

Fear is not our ordained condition. Psychologists tell us that infants are born with only two fears—that of falling, and loud noises; every other fear is learned. Fear is not a reality, because if it were, everyone would be afraid of the same things.

To live in fear is not natural, and neither is it our destiny. Our destiny is to live in peace and express joy. Dump fear by trusting life to provide for you as you live your truth.

Help me to see beyond the illusion of fear
and walk in strength and freedom.

Love is my nature.
My trust manifests miracles.

Tigers or Strawberries

The past is a canceled check, the future is a promissory note, and the present is cash in hand.

— Anonymous

A man being chased by wild tigers scurried down a vine hanging over the edge of a cliff. Looking down, he saw two more hungry tigers waiting for him at the bottom of the vine. Unable to move backward or forward, he noticed a succulent, ripe red strawberry growing out of the side of the cliff near him. He smiled, plucked the fruit, and enjoyed the sweetest strawberry he had ever tasted.

While our past and future seem to threaten us, we can take refuge in the current moment. Anxiety springs from regret or resentment over past events or fear of anticipated pain. When we relax into the now moment, we are not vulnerable to the past or future, and we discover that eternity is a golden necklace strung of an infinite number of present moments. We can live quite well on fresh strawberries.

Help me to relax into the beauty of now.

I open my eyes and heart to the miracle of now, and leave time behind.

Beyond the Rap

Turn your melodrama into a mellow drama.
— Ram Dass

T*he Heartbreak Kid* is a hilarious film that chronicles the misadventures of a young man named Lenny (played by Charles Grodin) who attempts to bamboozle his way through social situations. When Lenny meets the girl of his dreams (Cybill Shepherd), he tells her, "I think it's time we stopped taking from the earth, and started putting back into it." A good philosophy, to be sure—except that Lenny is full of hot air; he uses the same spiel with everyone he meets.

Eventually, the couple gets married, and the final scene of the film depicts our hero at his wedding reception sitting on a couch between two 10-year-old children. "I think it's time we stopped taking from the earth..." he drones. The kids, bored to tears, look at each other, roll their eyes, and promptly get up and walk away. His rap fails to impress anyone.

Many of us, too, have our "rap"—a story we've told a thousand times. We tell it because it gets us attention, upholds our chosen image (often as a victim), and relieves us of social malaise. But falling back on our rap is always self-defeating because we're hiding behind our story line. We use our rap to escape from being fully present.

If I find myself telling a particular story based on my drama more than three times, a little "rap alarm" goes off in my head. I recognize that I'm trying to milk the story for more than it's worth, and I'm hurting myself by hiding behind it. I see if I can tell a deeper truth, or just let it go. My rap has become shorter and shorter, and has mostly disappeared, allowing me to be fully present rather than fall back on a story.

Today I walk naked as myself.
I discard any armor and allow myself to shine.

The truth about me is greater than any story I could fabricate.

Leave the Lady at the River

Keep your eye on the road and use your rear mirror
only to avoid trouble.

— Daniel Meacham

Two monks were walking through a forest when they encountered a woman stranded at the bank of a stream. One of the monks graciously carried the woman across the stream, and the men continued on their way. The other monk fumed for a long time, and then blurted out, "You know it is against the rules of our order to touch a woman!"

"Yes," answered the first monk, "but I put her down an hour ago."

Carrying the past with us is always more burdensome than any mistake we have made. Guilt, resentment, and criticism of self or others for past deeds is far more debilitating than a momentary error. Any energy we invest in reliving or resenting the past detracts from the life at hand.

The movie *The Mission* tells of Mendoza, a slave trader who, after murdering his brother, is filled with remorse. In seeking to do penance, Mendoza carries over his shoulder a massive sack of heavy steel weaponry. He climbs a huge waterfall with this weighty burden, only to be met by the tribe from which he extracted slaves. The chief approaches him with a long knife, and Mendoza bares his breast to be slain. Instead, the chief severs the rope to the sack, which tumbles far down to the river below. While Mendoza inflicted a lifelong sentence of pain and misery upon himself, the Indian taught him how to forgive.

Are there any sacks of self-inflicted penance you've been carrying? Cut them now and be free.

Take from me the pain I have inflicted on myself.
Show me the grace I have missed,
that I may know Your love completely.

I take refuge in the peace of this moment,
and I am free.

Could Be Your Ring

To get thine ends, lay bashfulness aside; who fears to ask, doth teach to be deny'd.

— Thomas Herrick

At summer camp, I developed an industrial-strength crush on a girl named Roberta Horn. Roberta was pretty, sweet, and friendly, and when I stepped within ten feet of her, my heart quickened and my stomach did flip-flops. I talked to Roberta a few times and once, when we went roller skating, I got to hold her hand. (I didn't wash it for a week.) At the age of 15, I was too nervous to approach her since I knew that someone as beautiful and wonderful as she would never be interested in someone as weird as I was. Several years later, I saw Roberta and she showed me her hand again, this time with an engagement ring on it. By that time, I had developed some courage, and I told her about the crush I had felt.

"I had a crush on you, too," she told me, "but I didn't think you liked me very much." Whoa. "Funny, huh?" she waxed philosophical. "Who knows? If either of us had been more honest, this might have been your ring on my hand." While the pain of missing out on a potentially wonderful relationship shot through me like an arrow, the lesson was a gift. It was a primer in telling the truth even when it's scary. I learned that asking for what you want is a prerequisite for getting it.

If you feel a deep resonance with a person, whether in romance, friendship, creativity, business, or the spiritual path, it is likely that person feels the same way. Be honest about your enthusiasm, and take a step in that direction. Even if you get a "no," you will have the satisfaction of being true to yourself and knowing that you honored your feelings. In the long run, you will do better by voicing your intuitions rather than hiding them.

Give me the courage to act on my inspirations.
Help me put Your visions into action.

The good I seek is seeking me.

The Margin of Greatness

Ride on! Rough-shod if need be,
smooth-shod if that will do, but ride on!
Ride on over all obstacles, and win the race!
— Charles Dickens

In major league baseball, a batting average of .250 is respectable. If a player with this average is also a decent fielder, he can expect a secure and lengthy career. If a player hits .300, he is a star. He will receive multimillion-dollar contracts, you will see his face on shaving cream commercials, and his baseball card will be pricey. Consider the difference between an average player and a star: a .250 average means 5 hits out of 20; a .300 average is 6 hits out of 20. The margin of greatness is but one hit out of 20!

Sometimes just a little extra effort is all we need to put us over the edge to huge success. In your career, family, or spiritual path, try to stretch beyond your perceived limits. A little extra patience with a customer could make her a lifetime client and bring you her friends' business. A seminar participant told me that she signed up for an intensive workshop simply because I had responded to a letter she had written me. An extra kind touch, one more deep breath, or a willingness to listen could make the difference between a modest salary and a million-dollar contract, or a life of mere survival and a glorious adventure.

Move me to be all I can be. I don't want to simply glow;
I want to shine.
Help me fulfill my highest potential today.

Today I go beyond anything
I have done before.
I am willing to be great.

There You Are

Wherever you go, there you are.
— Anonymous

My friend Gil left his lucrative practice as an electrician in southern California to move to a remote jungle section of Maui where he rents a tiny ramshackle cabin for a hundred dollars a month and collects unemployment. Gil did some electrical work for me because he needed the income to pay his phone bill. "But I thought you lived out in the jungle?" I questioned him.

"I do, but I have this massive addiction to talking to people on my computer."

"You have a computer in your shack?"

"I ran a line through the bush and got a state-of-the-art computer. But then I got into trouble. I was totally compulsive about communicating with people all around the world, and I ran my phone bill up to $900. I told the phone company to cut me off—it was unmanageable. This was no mild addiction; I was mainlining—they might as well have just wired the phone line into me intravenously. I could escape L.A., but I couldn't escape myself."

Geographical cures rarely work. You can extricate yourself from a place, but you cannot escape your own thoughts. Move somewhere to get away from an uncomfortable situation, and you will likely recreate the drama with a new set of actors playing the same roles. Heal your mind, and you are free anywhere.

Dr. Michael Ryce teaches a seminar called *Why Is This Happening to Me Again?* "You leave New York to get away from a painful relationship," Dr. Ryce illustrates, "and the person who picks you up at the airport in Los Angeles completes the sentence the person in New York began."

Our first and foremost responsibility is to face ourselves and heal our minds and hearts. Then we may go anywhere and live in peace.

I pray to be unafraid to look within
and find the light I am.

I create my world with my consciousness.
I choose to live in peace.

170

I Feel Your Peace

He that is in me is greater than he that is in the world.
— Jesus Christ

When my mother passed away, I received many thoughtful expressions of sympathy. The message that touched me most deeply was one I received on my telephone answering machine from my friend Cisley. "I feel your peace," she lovingly affirmed. As soon as I heard her words, I felt peaceful and comforted.

When a friend or loved one is going through an emotionally stressful time, the greatest gift we can offer is an affirmation of their strength. True spiritual support consists of using a higher vision than fear would show us. We must pierce beyond appearances and recognize wholeness and strength. When we reflect our friend's power, we remind them (and ourselves) who we really are.

Let me be a messenger of strength.
Remind me to use my thoughts and words to affirm
the presence of God.

I behold perfection, and I bring healing.
My vision illuminates God.

In-Body Experiences

When Mahatma Gandhi was asked,
"What do you think of Western civilization?,"
he answered, "I think it would be a very good idea."

While discussing the phenomenon of mysterious crop circles, my friend asked, "How do you think it would change life on our planet if extraterrestrials showed up?"

His question evoked another one from me: "How do you think it would change life on the planet if human beings showed up?"

Many people on the spiritual path have spent a great deal of time trying to leave the planet. We are fascinated with near-death experiences, astral travel, transmigration of souls, and many other aspects of nonphysical reality. I am quite interested in all of these phenomena and have gained much from studying them. Yet many of us have become enamored with other worlds at the expense of this one. Yes, God is in the heavens and on the other side of life, but God is also here on earth. When someone asked me what percentage of my friends have had out-of-body experiences, I answered, "I know quite a few people who have yet to have an in-body experience."

The earth plane is a wonderful classroom to learn and master spiritual principles. Every truth of spirit is observable on earth. My favorite church is nature. As I observe the trees, animals, water, sky, sun, and moon, I find profound evidence of the Creator's majesty. I see God shining through the eyes of my loved ones, and I feel God's love in their embrace. Surely a loving God is not absent on earth, but very present.

Begin to look more closely at the way your body and earth life teach and bless you. The food you eat, the health and energy of your body, and the way your physical world plays out all contain valuable messages for spiritual growth. "On earth as it is in heaven."

Help me to find You everywhere. I open to Your gifts and teachings in my experience.

The spirit of truth speaks to me through all my senses.

172

Perfect as Usual

Miracles are natural.

— *A Course in Miracles*

As my 11-year-old friend Tasha sat down to eat some noodles she had cooked for lunch, I asked her, "How did your noodles turn out?"

Tasha smiled and answered, "Perfect—as usual!"

Tasha's answer reminded me that perfection is our natural state. Life was intended to work perfectly; it does and it will. Those who attune their vision to behold perfection will find it, create more good, and enjoy it. Those whose sight is set on loss, victimization, and death will continually manifest those experiences.

Some psychologists did an experiment on children's attitudes. They took a child who was considered negative and unappreciative and placed him in a room with a collection of new toys. He played with each toy for a few minutes and then complained that he was bored. Then the scientists took a child described as positive and optimistic and put him in a room with a huge pile of horse manure. Soon he smiled and exclaimed, "This is great!"

"Why is that?" one of the researchers asked him.

Quickly he answered, "There must be a pony somewhere!"

Miracles, perfection, healing, and happiness are not elusive and remote conditions. They represent our natural state, given as our birthright from God. We were not born to suffer; we were born to be happy. To find and live the truth, we must reverse the "laws" taught by the world. If something can go right, it will. Death and taxes are not sure things. The purpose of relationships is love. To find the good is not Pollyanna; *it is the only way that works.*

Experiment for a day, week, month, year, or lifetime by claiming, *"Perfect as usual,"* and refuse to settle for less. The life available to you is far greater than the one we have accepted.

Help me remember that I deserve love.
Show me the world You intended for me to enjoy.

I live in a world of good.
I claim perfection now.

Go to the Beach

For fast-acting relief, try slowing down.
— Lily Tomlin

"After five frustrating attempts to get in touch with people who were renting houses, I got the message that I wasn't supposed to be trying." John recounted. "I told my wife, 'Let's just go to the beach.' While we were there, we saw a friend who asked us, 'Do you know anyone who would like to rent my house?' We made a great deal for his beach house and thoroughly love it!"

If something you're doing is not working, doing more of it will probably not work any better. If you're butting your head against a wall again and again, stop. Rest. Breathe. Let go for the moment, then try a different approach. Whatever you do, don't keep trying to swim against the flow of life.

If a door is not opening organically, there's a good chance you are to go through another door. The moment you perceive struggle, step back and reassess your strategy. Commit yourself to success by way of ease, and you will open doors you never could have opened by trying to kick them down. True power is gentle, not forceful.

Imagine that the universe is set up for you to have what you want without struggle. Imagine that for every need you have, there is someone out there who has a need to offer the thing you want. Watch for signs and hints that you're on the right path or that you're looking for your good in the wrong place. Dare God to bless you without pain, and Spirit will answer with peace.

Help me to take the light path. I open myself to receive my good gently and joyfully.

I do not have to fight for my good. Love will provide me with all that I want and need.

Beyond Velveeta

Living out your dreams can be more therapeutic than analyzing them.

— Advertisement for a Hawaiian hotel

Two psychologists were walking down a corridor when they passed one of their colleagues. The fellow smiled, greeted them with a "Good morning!" and continued on his way. As soon as the man passed out of earshot, one psychologist turned to the other and said, "I wonder what he meant by that."

Many of us have been involved in self-analysis, introspection, therapy, and processing our relationships for a long time. There is no end to emotional processing; some of us have been more processed than Velveeta. There comes a time when we must quit trying to figure it all out and just go out and do something. While delving into our subconscious motivations is valuable, eventually we must extricate ourselves from the caverns of analysis and start to live. We will learn more from doing than trying to figure it all out.

Woody Allen quipped, "When I went into psychoanalysis, my biggest fear was that I would emerge with the personality of a 19th-century Jewish Viennese neurotic cocaine addict. Now after eight years of therapy, I would have gladly settled for that!" In his movie, *Sleeper*, Allen is accidentally frozen in a hospital and wakes up 500 years in the future. When the technicians who revive him tell him what year it is, he exclaims, "My God! I'd almost be done with therapy by now!"

The goal of therapy is to get us up and functioning. Therapists or patients who make a religion of keeping the patient in analysis forever have substituted the form for the goal. The best therapists are those who encourage patients to live their own lives, make their own decisions, and move on to the next level. It's time to get on with life, which will teach us in joyful ways as we live from celebration.

Give me the simple heart of a child
that I may enter the kingdom.

I trust life to reveal my riches to me.

Original Innocence

Open your eyes! The world is still intact;
it is as pristine as it was on the first day, as fresh as milk!
— Paul Claudel

I saw a 20-year-old prostitute being interviewed on a talk show. When Candy was 14, her mother took her to a street corner in Los Angeles, gave her $20, and left her there. She hadn't had a home since that day. I was struck by the hardness of this young woman's face. Although tender in age, she seemed haggard, tired, heavily defended, and old beyond her years. The show's host announced that his staff had found Candy's father, whom she loved and had not seen for many years. Moments later, he walked onstage and embraced his little girl, whose makeup was now streaming down her cheeks with her tears. I wish I had a picture of Candy's face when she saw her dad. In an instant, those horribly painful years fell away, revealing the tender child who had been cast unprotected into a cold world. Candy's innocence was not lost; it was just hidden.

Like Candy, we have all covered our light with many layers of armoring in the wake of pain. But the pure child within us has not been destroyed by the challenges through which we have passed. We have gone through dark times, and we are still here. There is something inside us that is bigger than our circumstances. We must remember who we are in the midst of appearances that would tell us that we are something else. We can reclaim our innocence.

Today I return to You. Show me my original innocence.

I do not belong to the world.
I belong to love.

It's Not About You

What you think of me is none of my business.
—Terry Cole-Whittaker

A black man tried unsuccessfully to gain admission to a white church. Year after year, the church gave the man and his family a different excuse for rejection. Finally, the man got down on his knees and prayed, "Dear Jesus, every year I try to become a member of this church, and every time they deny me. Can you help me?"

Suddenly a deep voice boomed, "Don't feel bad, George—I've been trying to get into that church for a lot longer than you, and they won't let me in either!"

Other people see us through their own eyes, perceptual screens, and belief systems. Anger, prejudice, and rejection are statements—not about the recipient, but the giver. If you're treated unfairly, your most powerful response is not attack, but truth and prayer. Be honest about your experience, and pray that fear is lifted from the other person's heart and that forgiveness flows into your own. While we're not asked to put up with abuse, we must maintain the knowledge that we are whole and lovable no matter what anyone else says or does.

Let me remember that love is the only reality.

I align myself with love,
and I am invulnerable in forgiveness.

Will You Bless Me?

No man is so poor as to have nothing worth giving....Give what you have. To someone it may be better than you dare think.

— Henry Wadsworth Longfellow

Hugo and Sylvia asked me to be the best man at their wedding, which was to take place on the last day of a conference we were attending. By the end of the program, I was feeling frazzled and tired. Although my energy level was low, I went to Hugo's room to see him before the ceremony. Hugo invited me onto the balcony, took my hands, and sincerely asked, "Will you bless me?"

My initial internal response was, "I am too weary and scattered," but I could not resist his sincere request on this important occasion. I closed my eyes, took a breath, and prayed for assistance. Immediately, I felt a deep peace and a miraculous renewal of energy. I opened my eyes and spoke a powerful blessing, which Hugo appreciated.

We always have the energy we need when love calls. When life asks you to serve in a way that will bring healing, the little ego must step aside. The windfall of Spirit will enable you to do whatever is necessary to serve God's plan. We always have infinite energy and resources to magnify the voice of love.

Breathe through me today.
Give me the energy to do what will truly serve.

I can do all things through God who strengthens me.

Free to Live Anew

Never look for the birds of this year in the nests of the last.
— Miguel de Cervantes

One of the most profound acts of healing I have witnessed was that of a couple whose teenage son had sustained a brain injury. Before his auto accident, Tim had been a vital, popular, and athletic young man. Now he was slow of speech and motion, and although he was making progress with therapy, he still struggled to do simple acts that before he had taken for granted. At a seminar, his parents asked to create a release ceremony. "We need to say good-bye to the son we once knew so we can embrace the person he is now." Amid profuse tears and with tremendous courage, this couple each read a statement of love, appreciation, and release for the son who was no more, and made a declaration of acceptance and commitment to the person he had become. The healing and empowerment that accrued to them was tremendous, in sharp contrast to the pain they experienced in attempting to hold on to someone who no longer was.

Are you freezing yourself or a loved one in a cast from the past? Are you trying to force someone to be who they were rather than honoring who they are now? No one wants to be treated like the person they once were; we want to be appreciated for who we are. Come fully into the present with yourself and others, and you will liberate tremendous energy to love and bless what is, rather than bemoan what was, or what you wish would be.

Help me to see clearly and to honor
the beauty before me now.

I accept the gifts before me,
and I accept the highest in everyone,
including myself.

Lottery Winners

You cannot serve both God and money.
— Jesus Christ

I was stunned to learn that New York now has support groups for lottery winners. Apparently, for some people, winning the lottery causes more problems than it solves! Those who hit the jackpot have to deal with all sorts of situations they're not prepared for. Suddenly they have friends they never knew they had; they have to be responsible for managing the money, create productive free time after they quit their job, deal with ex-spouses who want a cut, hire bodyguards to protect their kids from kidnaping at day care, and on and on. Some lottery winners spend it all on shoes, others fight with their relatives, others turn to addictions and, sadly, some commit suicide. In many cases, the windfall does not end the recipients' problems; it just substitutes new ones for the old.

What these lottery winners really need is not the money, but the consciousness to handle it. The ego tells us, "If I just had this brass ring from the outside world, I would be happy." But because we are spiritual beings, it is the *inside* world that determines our happiness.

I worked in a store that was losing money because the owner had a negative and irresponsible attitude. He asked for a large capital loan from a local entrepreneur, who came to me for a reference. I had to tell him the truth. While the owner blamed his failure on every external circumstance, the source of his problems was his own way of thinking. He could have received millions of dollars of capital, but it would have all gone out of the same consciousness hole that his original money had slipped out of. What the owner needed was not more money, but more wisdom.

Do not pray for a particular external event; pray for the consciousness to sustain the quality of experience you desire. Then you will not only attract your good—you will be able to enjoy it.

Show me how to use Your gifts wisely. Let me know who I am, that I may manifest real success.

My good flows to me effortlessly by right of my divine thoughts.

A Place for God

Welcome me not into a manger, but into the altar to holiness, where holiness abides in perfect peace.
—A Course in Miracles

For many years, I have kept an altar in my home. An altar is a place where the presence of God is remembered and honored. To establish an altar is far more than a ritualistic observance; it is a high and holy gift to yourself.

We decorate our homes with photos, works of art, statues, plants, and memorabilia that lift our minds and hearts and remind us of the people, places, and experiences that make us happy. Since God is the source of the deepest happiness, we magnify our joy when we adorn our home with symbols of Spirit's presence.

While all religions have altars, an altar need not belong to a particular religion. You can build an altar that represents you. Set aside a table, corner, or room as your sacred space. On your altar, place photos of great beings who inspire you, books or quotations of wisdom, candles, crystals, feathers, or any symbols of love and beauty, such as special rocks or seashells. Do your prayer, meditation, or spiritual practice at your altar space, and keep the energy field clear of jangling influences, such as chit-chat, arguments, or television. Keep the area clean and beautiful, and before long it will generate a magnificent peace and healing energy. The moment you enter your altar area, you will feel the presence of God and your sacred self. Any space you dedicate to Spirit will bless you many times over.

I pray to keep You in my life. Help me to remember Your presence throughout each day.

God gives my life meaning.

More Than Four

How can love survive in such a faceless age?
— from "Forgiveness," by singer/songwriter Don Henley

The Center for Lifestyle Management reported that the average American couple spends approximately four minutes a day in meaningful conversation. This is a sobering statement about the meager level of intimacy for which most people have settled. At the same time, many people report a sense of emptiness in their lives. How can we expect to feel fulfilled if we do not tell each other the truth about who we are and what we feel?

The quality of communication may be mapped out on a diagram similar to an archery target. The most shallow level, indicated by the outermost ring, is *news and gossip,* which requires no personal disclosure or investment and moves attention away from the speakers. The next level is *my opinions and judgments,* in which we reveal a little bit of ourselves, but restrict our communication to intellectual chatter. A deeper and more rewarding level embraces *my feelings;* at this level we begin to bring into the light what is going on unseen within us. The next ring is *my most vulnerable feelings and experiences,* which are the most difficult (and most rewarding) to share, as we make ourselves naked in our pain and ecstasy. At the bull's-eye, we enter into *unspeakable unity.* At this level, we feel so joined with our partner that words would only detract from the golden beauty of the moment.

To create more fulfilling lives, we must speak to each other with more intimacy. The word *intimacy* is built on *"into me see."* If you want more intimacy in your life, let others see into you more, and let them know that you can see into them. Then, meaningful communication will not be resigned to a few scraps, but will nourish you like a rich banquet.

Help me penetrate to the heart in my communications with others.

I am intimately joined with my beloveds and with God.

The Supervisor

Be not afraid, neither be thou dismayed:
for the Lord God is with thee whithersoever thou goest.
— Joshua 1:9

"I'm sorry, sir," the telephone company representative told my assistant Mick, "we have no private lines available in your area; you can have a party line if you like."

Well, that wouldn't quite do. We had just built a new office after the phone company had told us they would install two private lines.

Mick began to contact every phone-company supervisor who might be able to help us. He spent 20 hours working his way up the telephone company chain of command, until he was on a first-name-basis with the Director of Consumer Affairs. To our chagrin, everyone he spoke to told him that all of the private lines in our rural area were spoken for, and no new equipment would be installed for over a year.

"Do we have a contingency plan?" he asked me, frustrated.

"Let's talk to the Supervisor," I suggested. "Let's ask God for help. We are wasting our time talking to people." Mick and I clasped hands and affirmed that God was in charge of this situation. We agreed that we live in an unlimited universe, and God can do anything. We knew our need was justified, and we asked Spirit to create a solution that would work for us.

When the telephone installer arrived, we told him our predicament, and he told us he would do what he could. You can imagine our delight when he packed up his equipment and told us he had just installed two private lines.

We always have recourse to a higher Supervisor than the world indicates. Be willing to turn to the Real Source when you have a challenge. If your need is real, it will be met.

Help me remember that I always have recourse in the love and grace of God.

God is my source.
I can do all things by the power of Spirit.

Supersoul

To be all that we were meant to be and
to do all that we were meant to do,
is the only end in life.

— Spinoza

The first *Superman* movie offered a striking metaphor for the way we learn our purpose on earth. In the film, baby Superman's parents place him in a space capsule and send him off to Earth to escape the destruction of their planet. As the infant is hurtling past the stars, he listens to a series of audio tapes teaching him about himself and his purpose. The tapes, preprogrammed by his parents, remind him of his origin, his strengths, and his mission on Earth. By the time he arrives at his destination, he is clear about his identity, and he goes about the business of being Superman.

Our story is remarkably like that of Superman: We arrived on Earth with great innate wisdom, seeded with the knowledge of our purpose. Before we were born, we consciously chose, in co-creatorship with Spirit, who we would be and what we would accomplish while we are here.

But here our story departs from Superman's in that when we arrived on Earth, we forgot. Quickly we were distracted by the limits that our body imposed on us and the negative messages laid upon us by a world that had forgotten to look within for truth. Before long, we wandered with the masses, puzzling, "How did I get here, and what am I supposed to be doing?"

The moment we ask these questions, we begin our spiritual adventure of returning to the wisdom we forgot. We set out to reclaim true vision, which rewards us infinitely more deeply than seeing through the body's eyes and playing out the world's beliefs. Gradually, the veils of illusion and ignorance are lifted, and we regain the sense of purpose we came to live.

Help me remember my purpose and
live the highest life possible.

I honor my purpose of divine expression.
I am here to love, learn, and serve.

No Psychic Required Here

Call on God, but row away from the rocks.

— Indian proverb

As I was leaving a restaurant with my professional psychic friend, Denise, a fellow approached and asked if I wanted to buy a stereo. Since I was in the market for a car stereo at the time, I told him, "Maybe," and he invited Denise and me to his showroom in the trunk of his car. There he displayed an extensive collection of unusually shoddy stereos at remarkably high prices. When I asked him if he offered any warranty, he told me that his boss did not like people coming to the warehouse (for insurance purposes, you understand). When he asked me if I wanted one of the stereos, Denise leaned over and whispered in my ear, "I don't think you should buy anything from this man."

I whispered back, "I don't need a psychic to tell me that." I thanked the fellow, bid him a good day, and off we went.

Many on the spiritual path have a difficult time differentiating between judgment and discernment. Some feel that to say no or acknowledge that someone is hurting himself or another would be an act of judgment. While we must not judge, we must discern. Judgment is distinguished by turbulent emotion and fear, while discernment is based on clarity and peace. You serve another if you refuse to participate in an activity that would hurt him or yourself.

It is loving to tell the truth and hurtful to put up with a lie. If someone is not coming from a place of integrity or is endangered by an addictive behavior, it is your duty to call the situation as you see it. Perhaps God is giving you the insight that this situation needs correction. You don't need a psychic to see the truth, which is always trying to make itself obvious, if you are open to seeing it.

Give me the wisdom and the courage to call the truth as I see it.

My divine mind guides me on my right path.

Heaven and Hell

Heaven is the decision I must make.
— A Course in Miracles

A samurai warrior came to a Zen master and commanded him, "Teach me about heaven and hell."

The master looked at the warrior and laughed, ridiculing him, "Why would you think I would waste my time teaching an ignoramus like you? You are an uneducated buffoon!"

The samurai, severely insulted, began to breathe heavily and grew red in the face. Furious, he drew his sword and lifted it to chop off the master's head.

"That, sir," the master interrupted, "is hell."

Immediately, the warrior was overcome with humility. In deference to the profundity of this lesson, he fell at the master's feet and began to thank him profusely.

"And that, sir," continued the master, "is heaven."

Heaven and hell are not eternal dispensations that await us after we die; they are states of mind we experience even while on earth. Whether we live in ecstasy or torture depends not on an outside agent, but on the thoughts we think and the attitudes we hold. Love is the door to heaven, and fear is the path to hell. At any given moment, we hold the key that will unlock either door; the choice is ours.

I want to experience heaven even as I walk the earth.
Assist me to love so deeply
that I live in paradise continually.

I open the door to heaven
with the key of appreciation.

Declaration of Inner Independence

If I have freedom in my love, and in my soul I am free,
Angels alone that soar above, enjoy such liberty.
— Richard Lovelace

Today we celebrate the birth of our free nation. Yet even more important than national freedom is internal freedom. We may live in a democratic society, but unless we are free of the inner bondage of fear and separation, we are not truly free.

Today, break free of the power you have given others to make or break your life. While others may invite, suggest, guide, or influence you, ultimately you alone must live with the choices you make, and so you must choose in accordance with your heart's guidance. If you have given any person power over your life, take back your power now. No one can hurt you, and no one can save you unless you ordain it.

Today, declare a revolution of consciousness. Oust the old dictators of self-doubt, attack thoughts, jealousy, and the replaying of old negative patterns of thought and feeling, and replace them with a belief in yourself, trust in the wisdom of life, positive visualization and speech, and the willingness to be grand.

Today, move beyond human politics, and find unity at the core of your being. At the center of yourself, all states of consciousness within you merge into wholeness. Your economy is based on love: the more love you give, the more you have.

Today, let the world know that you are a sovereign and powerful nation, comprised of all the experiences and wisdom you have gleaned over a lifetime. Raise the lamp of liberty high, that all may know that you stand for truth.

I pray to walk in peace and freedom,
shining as a model of integrity to all.

I am free, and I give freedom.

Whose Dream?

To thine own self be true.
— William Shakespeare

In the motion picture *Out of Africa*, Karen Blixen uttered a haunting confession: "My biggest fear was that I would come to the end of my life and discover that I lived someone else's dream."

Many people live, grow old, and die without recognizing the power to manifest their personal destiny. Others seize every opportunity to celebrate their gifts and potential.

What is your dream? If you had unlimited time, money, and support, what would you love to be doing? Take a moment to explore your soul, and unearth your secret fantasy. Would you write a book? Travel to exotic places? Have a family? Learn photography? Open up a specialty restaurant? Establish a healing center? Your dream may be more available than you realize. Perhaps even now you could take a step in the direction of your vision. You could send away for a brochure, talk to an expert, take a class, or make a "treasure map"—a collage of magazine photos and words clustering around your goal.

Live as if your life depends on it.

I am here for a purpose.
Show me what I am to do in the name of joy.

Confident and whole,
I step forward to claim my destiny.

Do You Agree?

Where two or more are gathered in my name, there am I.
— Jesus Christ

"You need to replace a small metal roller about the size of a pencil," my laser printer technician told me. "Although it's a little part, you have to buy the cartridge to which it is attached, which costs about $700, plus a hundred dollars labor."

I could not believe that I needed to pay $800 for a roller the size of a pencil. I turned to my assistant Noel and asked her, "Do you agree that I can get this job done for less money?" Noel agreed enthusiastically.

I called another technician who offered to sell me the cartridge at wholesale cost which, with labor, would total $550. The estimate still sounded too outrageous to be true. Again, I turned to Noel and asked her, "Do you agree that I can get this machine fixed for a fraction of the original estimate?"

"I know you can!" she answered.

I made a few more calls and found a technician who told me, "Sure, I can replace the roller." The next day he showed up at my office, sat down, took out a screwdriver, disassembled the machine, replaced the roller—without a new cartridge—and put the machine back together, all in about half an hour. As he walked out, he presented me with a bill for $88—one-tenth of the original estimate!

We create our reality by agreement. When two or more agree that something is so, we attract results consonant with our belief. We can agree that we are small and powerless, or we can agree that we are co-creators with God. Never agree to your limits, but always agree to your infinite power. The universe will grow whatever you plant with your intentions.

I pray that my thoughts and beliefs deliver me to an ever more loving and expansive universe.

I agree with my good and reject all else.

Heir Pollution

A man is made impure not by what goes into his mouth, but by what comes out of it.

— Jesus Christ

A man at a Hindu ashram came to Swami Muktananda and complained, "You must get rid of my roommate! He is a smoker, and his foul smoke is polluting the atmosphere in my room. Someone as vile as he should not be allowed here!"

Muktananda thought for a moment and responded, "I will change your room—for his sake, not yours. Polluting the physical atmosphere with smoke is an offense, but polluting the psychic atmosphere with judgment is worse. You are hurting yourself and the universe more with your anger and judgment than he is with his smoke."

What we do with our bodies is important, but what we do with our minds and hearts is even more important. Because we are spiritual beings, the condition of our spirit is more real and meaningful than the physical atmosphere. Of course we must take care to keep a clean physical environment, but before that, we must be sure our thoughts are in harmony with a loving and forgiving universe.

We are heirs to the Kingdom of Heaven, which we magnify by thinking and acting in accordance with our identity as godly beings. Fear and judgment muddy our vision of love. Let us claim our inheritance by aligning our minds and hearts with the pure spirits we are.

Let my thoughts reflect divinity;
help me walk in the golden atmosphere of truth.

My mind is the mind of God.
My heart is a vehicle of pure love.

Beyond Appearances

The light of the spirit is invisible, concealed in all beings.
It is seen by the seers of the subtle,
when their vision is keen and clear.
— The Upanishads

A man in search of enlightenment found his way to a remote village in India, where a saint was known to live and teach. After a long and grueling quest, he was told by a local merchant that he could find the guru on the steps of a certain house near a particular intersection. The man rushed to the site, where he found a tipsy man drinking. Disappointed, he returned to the shop and complained that he had found only a drunkard. The shopkeeper laughed and told him, "That was the saint!"

Astonished, the man argued, "But no saint would be sitting there drinking!"

"This one does," answered the merchant. "You see, he is a very advanced soul who has mastered nearly all the lessons of life. The only experience he needs to complete is compassion for those with addictions. Once he has mastered that, he will have finished his incarnations on earth. If you would have talked to him, you would have discovered that behind his worldly guise, he is a great and illumined master."

We must not let our judgments and expectations stand in the way of receiving blessings when they are offered. We may have preconceived notions about what a holy person would look like or how one would act. But wise and holy people come in many different packages, sometimes very unlike the ones we expect. The truth is knowable not by its form, but by its essence.

I pray to keep my mind open to find You in all places.
Let me be bigger than my judgments and expectations.

My mind and heart are open
to receive the gifts of Spirit.

Hands to Earth

The labor of the body relieves us from the fatigues of the mind; and it is this which forms the happiness of the poor.

— La Rouchefoucald

On my way to speak at a conference, I shared the back seat of a car with a Middle-Eastern man who was also scheduled to lecture there. When he asked me about myself, I proudly told him I had written several books. Then I asked him, "What do you do for a living?" expecting him to tell me he owned a falafel stand in Manhattan.

"I'm a brain surgeon," he answered dryly.

Feeling somewhat intimidated, I tried to keep the ball rolling: "So, how did you get into brain surgery?" I asked, not unlike the way I would have asked someone else, "How did you develop an interest in needlepoint?"

"It's part of my religion," he answered. (I know there is a joke that doctors think they are God, but this was taking it too far.) "In the Sufi religion, there is a rule that everyone must take a profession in which they work with their hands. This is the vocation I chose."

It seems like a wise rule. I know many people who work with their heads and many people who work with their hands, and by far, I find that the people who use their hands are a happier lot. The elements of nature ground and heal us. All of the principles of Spirit are reflected in nature. To work with the elements is to be constantly reminded of our source. When we live in our intellect, we lose touch with the power of nature. When the European culture moved west and overcame the indigenous peoples, a great treasure was ravaged. We must re-establish harmony with the earth that nourishes us.

Welcome opportunities to work with your hands. Gardening, pottery and crafts, massage, carpentry, and any earth-oriented endeavor will restore balance and harmony in a way that thinking alone cannot.

I pray to live in harmony with the elements.
Great Spirit, restore my connection with nature.

As I touch the earth,
I am healed and I give healing.

192

Immediate Results

Only infinite patience begets immediate results.
— A Course in Miracles

In my rush to leave my house one morning, I walked through a screen door. As I hastily reached to take a patio chair out of the rain, I did not see that the sliding screen door was closed, and I rammed right into it, tearing the bottom. This got my attention. I stepped back, took a few deep breaths, and asked, "What is the lesson here?" Quickly the inner voice answered, "Slow down."

The thought that your life is moving too slowly is a sign that you are moving too fast. Rushing never improves the quality of our life or the results we seek; to the contrary, it muddies our vision and causes us to make errors that cost us twice as much time and energy to repair.

The universe is proceeding with perfect timing; if you believe it is not, it is not an error in the universe, but your perception. My friend was late driving to her therapy session and got stuck behind a slowpoke on the highway. After honking and cursing at the driver in front of her, she finally had a clearing to pass. When she did, she discovered that the driver was her therapist.

Trust that you have enough time to do everything that needs to be done. Love does not worry or force; it flows. Relax into what is happening, and the peace you enjoy will be accompanied by the clarity and efficiency you gain.

Help me to know that all things are unfolding naturally.

God's timing is perfect.

I Read the News Today, Oh Boy

Truth in journalism is usually found on the comic pages.
— Frank DeGennaro

A radio commentator noted that the news we generally receive through the media is "a proctological view of life." What is presented as the news is a carefully distilled entrée of mayhem, culled for commercial saleability, playing on base fears and sensationalism. Much of the news we receive is not honest, for it is not an accurate reflection of the truth. While the media lets us know that a rape occurs every five minutes, it does not tell us how many acts of kindness occurred in that time. We rarely receive statistics on how many children were brought into the world with delight and appreciation; how many teachers told their students, "You are destined for greatness"; how many athletes dug into themselves for the stamina to complete their jogging; how many creditors extended extra grace to their overdue accounts; how many drivers slowed down to allow cars from a side street into the lineup on a main thoroughfare; or how many times anyone said, "I love you." When the news reflects the whole of life, not just its sordid aspects, it will be honest, serviceful, and worthy of our attention.

If we wish to get more accurate news, we must withdraw our fascination from evil and reinvest it in peace. A San Francisco newspaper published two different versions of a day's news, one with a sensational headline about a murder, and the other with a more modest banner about progress in peace talks. The sensational headline outsold the more mellow edition by four to one.

Invest in a better world by placing your attention on what works, rather than what doesn't. Do not start or end your day by listening to newscasts. Celebrate all the good you hear about, and pray that we learn from our pain and suffering, rather than dwell on it. Make the news of the day better by shining the light of your consciousness on the good, the beautiful, and the true.

I pray to be a beacon. Give me the strength to bless the good and heal the sorrow.

I change the world by focusing on the light.

Unseen Help

If you knew Who walks beside you,
fear would be impossible.
— *A Course in Miracles*

While visiting a prison, I was required to walk through a series of five thick electronically secured steel doors and gates, connected by a maze of sidewalks and corridors. As I reached each door, I wondered if anyone would be there to guide me and open the door. As if by magic, the moment I approached a door, it was buzzed open electronically. After going through a few doors, I realized I was being watched via remote television cameras. At one point, I made a wrong turn at the intersection of two sidewalks, and I heard a voice call out of nowhere, "You are going the wrong way." I returned to the intersection and stood at the crossroads, puzzled. The voice returned. "Now, just continue in the direction you are facing."

On the path of life, we come up against locked doors and wonder how we will get through and whether anyone is available to help us. As I discovered at the prison, if we are in our right place, the door will be buzzed open; it would have been useless for me to try to open the doors manually. But there was someone watching me who had the power to release the door without struggle on my part.

The same guide will assist us if we take a wrong turn. A voice will call out, "You are going the wrong way." It may not be an external voice we hear, but an internal knowingness. When we return to the intersection and reposition ourselves, the same inner guide will let us know, "Just keep going in the direction you are facing."

Although we do not see our watcher, we are seen and known. On my way out of the jail, I noticed a guard booth adjacent to one of the corridors. The glass windows were heavily tinted so I could not see in, but the guards could see out. While we may be unable to peer into the guidance booth of the universe, those in charge of helping us can see us. We are never alone. Every door will open when we are ready to enter.

I trust You to open locked doors for me.
I do not have to fight to do the will of God.

God is watching over me,
making my path easy.

Table with a View

Make love now, by night and by day, in winter and in summer...You are in the world for that and the rest of life is nothing but vanity, illusion, waste. There is only one science, love, one riches, love, only one policy, love. To make love is all the law and the prophets.

— Anatole France

"Excuse me, sir, we are going to need this spot," a deep voice awakened me from my sunset reverie. I looked up and saw a young man wearing black tuxedo trousers and a short white waiter's jacket, setting up a dinner table on the grassy hill. He and an assistant laid out elegant white linen and cutlery befitting a fine restaurant.

"Is there some party happening?" I asked.

"It's a wedding anniversary."

"How many people are you preparing for?"

"Two. It's the couple's 25th anniversary. The husband is surprising his wife with a private catered dinner overlooking the beach."

In just a few hours on a verdant knoll overlooking a Maui beach, a happy woman would have the surprise of her life. As she and her husband would be strolling along casually, he would suggest, "Why don't we rest here, honey?" She would sit, perplexed, as a gourmet restaurant crew would emerge from behind the bushes and serve them a meal fit for a king and his queen, before one of the most spectacular backdrops on the planet.

Let's hear it for romance. Passion is a very holy thing. It is the very juice of life—the electricity that sparks all growth, achievement, and expression. Passion is the hand of God reaching into humanity to animate it to divinity.

Today, put some romance into your life. If you're in a relationship, surprise your beloved with a gift that you know will make him or her happy. And if you're in relationship with yourself, give yourself flowers, get a massage, or do something for yourself that a lover would give you. Don't miss a moment of the adventure of life. Make love now.

I will celebrate all the gifts You have created for my happiness.

The universe is my palette. I paint a glorious picture and step into it.

Easy Way Out

Teach only love, for that is what you are.
— A Course in Miracles

I saw a news story about a woman named Elsa who had been held hostage by an escaped criminal. Robert, a man fleeing from the police, broke into Elsa's country home and held her captive at gunpoint while a large SWAT team surrounded her home with an arsenal of firearms. Fortunately, Elsa was a psychologist, and she applied her listening skills to her interactions with this man. Over the two days that Robert occupied her home, Elsa did her best not to panic, and invited him to speak of the pain in his life. Quickly, she recognized that he was like a frightened beast trying to escape from his own wounds. She showed him kindness and cooked for him. As a result of their conversations, Robert calmed down and turned himself in, leaving her unharmed. When he was being tried, Elsa testified on his behalf, stating that he was acting out of fear and desperation. When Robert went to prison, Elsa visited him, and when he got out, she became his friend, a compassionate listener. Both Elsa and Robert reported that although their initial encounter was extremely dangerous for both of them, they felt grateful that they had dealt with it as they had.

The choice for peace is always empowering. When we refuse to give in to fear, we are able to see solutions that we would miss in hysteria. Any situation can lead to great pain or great freedom, depending on how we handle it. Even a hardened criminal can be healed and corrected with the touch of love. Practice being kind in situations where you are tempted to panic; that is how to become a true miracle worker.

Help me to remember that love works better than fear.

I can find the heart of anyone I seek to reach.

Listen

Do you know why we have two ears and one mouth?
We are supposed to listen twice as much as we talk.

— Anonymous

A successful psychiatrist saw eight patients a day and obtained excellent results. Each patient would walk out of his office with a smile and give the doctor a warm handshake. Many observers speculated on the secret of his success, but only his secretary knew it. At the end of each day, he would call her on the intercom and tell her, "Okay, Cindy, you can bring me my hearing aid now."

The only talent more effective than being a good speaker is to be a good listener. Most people are ready to offer advice, but few are willing or able to listen. Real listening is an art and a skill. Cultivate your ability to be fully present with someone who sincerely shares about their life, and you will be the best friend this person has.

In my seminars, I lead an exercise in which one partner speaks for five minutes, and the other simply listens. The speakers are instructed to express what they feel in their heart, and the listeners are instructed to listen without interrupting, giving advice, or telling their own story. Often the listeners receive more from the exercise than the speakers. They report that they felt relieved and refreshed not to have to respond with advice or feedback, and as a result, they were able to pay more attention to the speaker and feel with them as they shared. One speaker, elated, reported, "This is the first time in 20 years of marriage my wife heard me out!"

To truly bless your friends is much simpler than you may have thought. More than anything else, they would probably appreciate your undivided attention. Give them an open ear, and you will bless yourself as well.

Help me to be there for my friends
in the highest and most helpful way.

I listen with my heart and hear myself.

Feed Each Other

One thing I know: The only ones among you who will be really happy are those who will have sought and found how to serve.

— Albert Schweitzer

A man was being given a tour of the kingdoms beyond this world. His guide opened a door where he saw a group of unhappy people standing around a sumptuous banquet. Although the tables were spread with inviting, delicious food, the people were starving. When the man looked closer, he saw that the spoons the people were holding were longer than their arms, and they could not get food into their mouths. "This," the guide explained, "is hell."

"Then show me heaven," the man requested.

The guide opened another door where the man saw another group of people standing before a similar banquet with spoons longer than their arms. In this room, however, the people were happy and their tummies were full. The people in heaven had learned to feed one another.

When Jesus was saying goodbye to the apostle Peter, he asked him three times, "Peter, do you love me?"

Three times Peter answered, "Yes, Lord, I do love you."

And three times Jesus told Peter, "Then feed my sheep."

All philosophy and rhetoric pale in the face of true kindness and caring. When we take care of one another, we fulfill our highest function as divine beings. We can feed each other on many levels: physically, emotionally, mentally, and spiritually. There is no greater joy and service than to fill one another with whatever we have to share.

Let me know the joy of giving love. I pray to be a channel for love and blessing at every level.

I am an instrument of God's healing love.
I delight in feeding my brothers and sisters.

No Small Plans

Make no little plans:
They have no magic to stir men's blood.
— Daniel H. Burnham

"Quit your job; you are to work with Robert Redford," a firm voice spoke from a place deep within Judy. The intuition was so compelling that she had to follow it. Soon Robert Redford's production company came to Salt Lake City, and Judy signed up to be an extra in a movie. After a few days, she learned of a need for volunteers in the office, and the work she did there won her an invitation to join the paid accounting staff. At that time, Robert Redford was searching for a personal assistant, and Judy was offered the job. She went on to work closely with Mr. Redford for years.

As divine beings, we are here to do magnificent things, and smallness does not befit us. Anyone who has ever improved her life or changed the world has had to think big, think radically, and be willing to venture into unknown worlds. The voice of transformation begins with a tiny hint whispered to our inner self. If we follow it, we will be on our way to the life we wish for.

What visions or dreams have you denied because you believe they are too big for you? What would you love to do that you have shied away from pursuing because it feels like too much of a stretch? What possibilities send a current of enthusiasm through your body and spirit? These are precisely the avenues that you must pursue to live on the cutting edge of your own destiny.

Help me to think big and act on my dreams. I trust that if You give me an idea, You will give me the means to manifest it. Help me to move beyond fear into magnificence.

I can do great things because a great Source guides and supports me.

Velcro Relationships

All minds are joined.
— A Course In Miracles

While Carla was teaching a seminar, a woman told her, "I feel that my marriage is over. My husband and I have been together for a long time, and we have grown in different directions. I want to leave, but I cannot because I know it would crush him."

A month later at another workshop, a man confessed, "My marriage is empty, but I'm staying with my wife because I know she would never survive a divorce." Then Carla discovered that he was the husband of the woman who spoke at the first seminar.

Relationships are based on matching energy. Like strips of Velcro fasteners, partners contain hooking energies that conform by agreement. Often couples have similar or polarized underlying feelings that go unspoken. When you speak your truth, you invite your partner to do the same, and together you bring the relationship into more light and integrity. Invite your partner in a relationship, business, or friendship to greater intimacy by being honest about what you're experiencing. You may be surprised to find that you are more joined than you realized.

Show me my oneness with my brothers and sisters.
Let me meet them in the deepest and richest truth
of the heart.

I attract the perfect co-creators for my adventure into greater light.

Let It Be Easy

Life was never meant to be a struggle.
— Stuart Wilde

A friend of mine invited author Arnold Patent to participate in a project she was sponsoring. After considering the invitation, Arnold told her, "I don't think I'll be a part of this venture. When I try the idea on for size, it feels like a struggle for me. My life is about ease."

My life is about ease. Now there is a powerful affirmation! Imagine how much more joyful and creative you would be if you refused to participate in anything that was a struggle, and relaxed into what you're doing so that it became a dance instead of drudgery. You just might end up living heaven on earth!

Whenever you feel a sense of strain, ask yourself this question:

How would I be doing this differently
if I were willing to let it be easy?

Letting it be easy does not mean sitting back, succumbing to laziness, and expecting everyone else to do everything for you. Letting it be easy means honoring your aliveness, acting from the place in you where life is meaningful, and releasing any notion that you must participate in activities that deaden you.

When you proceed from joy rather than rote obligation, you will have so much more creative energy and health that you will be infinitely more powerful to manifest the life you choose, and serve others in the process.

Lead me from struggle to ease that I may reflect the Light of the world.

I magnify peace as I do what I love.

Today's the Day

The only time you fail is the last time you try.

— Anonymous

My friend Judith worked as a scuba diver for Mel Fisher, the indefatigable explorer who searched for a sunken Spanish galleon off the Florida keys. For 16 years, Fisher and his crew probed relentlessly for the fabled *Atocha*, going through many investors' capital to find a treasure that was speculative at best. The crew adopted the motto, *"Today's the Day!"* and wore T-shirts proclaiming this affirmation in huge letters. Day after day, year after year, the crew went out, motivated only by the hope that one day today *would* be the day.

Then, at 1:05 P.M. on July 20, 1985, Fisher's marine radio in Key West, Florida, carried the voice of Fisher's son Kane calling from the vessel *Dauntless: "Put away the charts. We've got the Mother Lode!"* Thus, history was made as Fisher's crew unearthed over $400 million worth of gold, jewelry, and buried treasure.

If you have labored long and hard for a project you believe in, don't give up. At any moment, you could have a breakthrough that will make all the difference in your life and your world. Richard Attenborough struggled for 18 years to get his film *Gandhi* produced, and he went on to win numerous Academy Awards. Thomas Edison went through 50,000 experiments before he perfected the first alkaline battery. All of these productions made the world a better place for many, and perhaps your project will do the same.

I pray to hold firmly with my vision.
I am open to a major breakthrough.

I will do my part and trust God to take care of the details.

Dare to Be Grand

To belittle is to be little.

— Anonymous

My friend Ernst was a regular fellow. We played in a band together, went out for pizza, and I felt his pain as he went through a divorce. When I saw him after an absence, he told me, "I've been spending a lot of time in South America. I went to visit a friend, and one evening a neighbor came for dinner. She told me that she had a headache, and I asked her if she wanted me to pray for her. After I did, she felt better. That night she came back with her daughter, who was suffering from menstrual pain. I offered the girl prayer, and she experienced relief. The next night all of this woman's relatives showed up at the door! She had told them I was a healer. Hoping I could be of service, I prayed for them. The next day half the town was lined up for healing. After I came home, I received a call from a town representative who told me that the people would pay my airfare back if I returned. So I did, and now I go back regularly; they fly me from town to town in a helicopter, and the prayers have had wonderful results."

Upon hearing this amazing account, my first thought was, "Ernst? Last year a bass player, this year a saint?" I had a hard time reconciling the two pictures, but then I realized I had a choice: I could negate the good that he was doing, or I could rejoice in the blessings. It felt a lot better to be excited about his success than to try to keep him small.

I realized that the cup in which I held Ernst's good fortune would be the die I cast for my own. *"You will be as big as you allow him to be in your thoughts,"* an inner voice told me. *"Keep him small, and you will be small. Let him be great, and so will you."* I decided it would be a lot more fun if we were both—and all—great.

Help me accept and celebrate the divinity in every being I meet.

I open to my full potential by blessing the good fortune of others.

204

On the Threshold

Do not look to the god of sickness for healing,
but only to the god of love,
for healing is the acknowledgment of Him.
— *A Course in Miracles*

My friend Bobbi is a successful anesthesiologist. When she sustained a leg injury, she had to deal with her own pain, which was humbling for her since she spent her life helping others numb theirs. Ironically, no practitioner that Bobbi consulted could alleviate her distress until she discovered an acupuncturist. After just a few treatments, her pain dissipated. "As much as we know in medicine," Bobbi confessed, "we know very little; the frontier of healing is much grander than any of us ever imagined."

Modern medicine has relieved much pain and saved many lives and is to be richly applauded. I am very grateful that my mother's life was comforted and extended through surgery. Yet, reparative medicine is but one aspect of healing. Physical manipulation of organs is rudimentary in the face of what truly heals. In one of the *Star Trek* films, Dr. McCoy travels from the 23rd century to visit a 1980s hospital. His eyes bulge as he observes what he considers Neanderthal medical procedures. "Unbelievable!" he exclaims.

True healing is based on light, sound, prayer, right use of the mind, and living in harmony with nature. Even now, laser and sound therapies are coming into vogue. When I last had my teeth cleaned at the dentist's office, the hygienist used an ultrasound pick that shook plaque off my teeth through inaudible vibrations.

Let us usher in the next level of healing now. Begin to pray, chant, send light, hold positive mental images, and reconnect with nature. Healing can be easy, gentle, and illuminating. We appreciate medicine as we know it, and we take our next step toward healing from the inside out.

Help me know the true essence of healing.
Let me give and receive healing as You do.

God is the healer. God can heal anything.
I am whole now.

Is That So?

That that is, is. That that is not, is not. Is that it? It is.

— Anonymous

When a young Japanese woman became pregnant by a sailor, she did not want the responsibility of raising the child, and named a local monk as the father. The woman's father angrily took the child to the gate of the monastery where the monk lived and informed him, "My daughter has told me you are the father of this child; now you must raise him."

The monk thought for a moment and answered, "Is that so?" He took the child and cared for him as if he were his own son.

Seven years later on her deathbed, the boy's mother confessed that the child was not the monk's. Her father returned to the monastery and humbly apologized to the monk. "My daughter has admitted her dishonesty. I will take the child back now."

Again the monk thought for a moment, and answered, "Is that so?" Then he let the child go.

True mastery lies in flowing with the events of life. We are empowered when we assume that everything comes from God and goes back to God. Nothing in form lasts forever, and when we can accept change, we are free. All pain is born of resistance. An attitude of nonresistance liberates tremendous energy. Pain arises when we fight against what is happening, and peace comes when we accept what is.

What in your life are you resisting? How much peace could you gain by letting what is, be? Practice the art of allowing, and you will come close to heaven as you discover the hand of God behind everything.

Help me trust in the flow of life. Show me how to accept what is, with love and appreciation.

Divine order is operating here and now.

More or Better?

We pray to be changed at depth.
— Alcoholics Anonymous tenet

In the movie *The Jerk,* Steve Martin plays Navin, a poor Southern boy who grows up in a ramshackle old house that looks like it's made of toothpicks and would blow over if a strong breeze came along. Navin grows up and heads for the big city, where, through a quirk, he makes a fortune and sends large monthly contributions to his parents for many years. Finally, Navin goes home, looking forward to seeing the big, beautiful house his parents have built with the money he sent. When he arrives, Navin discovers a sprawling version of the same shack he left. Although the "mansion" is 20 times the size of the original, the quality of construction is the same, and it too looks like it would blow over in a moment. It is not really better, just bigger.

If we truly wish to change our life, we must change its quality, not just its quantity. *More* does not necessarily mean *better.* Cosmetic improvements are meaningless; it is internal advancement we seek. A country singer ruefully likens her lover's insincere attempts to change himself to "rearranging chairs on the deck of a sinking ship."

In 1960, FCC chairman Newton Minow described the world of television as a "vast wasteland." At that time there were but five or six television channels in each city. Now with the advent of cable and satellite, many areas have over 100 channels, and we hear talk of expansion to 500. For the most part, however, the wasteland has simply expanded. We have *more*, but not necessarily *better*. By contrast, a few solid enterprises such as public television are making huge contributions to quality entertainment and education.

Before you ask for more, be sure you are not inviting more of the same. Ask for better.

I want to grow in peace and awareness.
Help me deepen my love.

My life expands as my consciousness grows.

Right Mind, Right Time

Miracles wait not on time.
— A Course in Miracles

Harbin Hot Springs[9] is a lovely spa in the northern California mountains where the pace of life is slowed to a gentle flow. In that place, anxious rushing seems other-worldly by contrast. One morning on my way to the mineral baths, I saw a clever sign: *If you are in a hurry, you are in the wrong place.*

We can extrapolate that principle to all of life: *If you are in a hurry, you are in the wrong consciousness.* Hurry is usually motived by fear and anxiety; we worry that we will be late or not have enough time to do what we need to do. Rushing is a symptom of lack thinking, indicating we believe in "not-enoughness." The principle of abundance applies not only to money or things; it applies equally to time. If you know you live in an abundant universe, you trust that you have enough time to do what you need to do.

When we are in the consciousness of peace, time becomes elastic; it will expand or contract to accommodate our purpose. One Saturday I arrived at the post office to mail a package ten minutes before the noon closing time. When I reached the window, the clerk informed me that I had not sealed the box properly and that I would have to buy some tape. I decided I would not rush, and if Spirit wanted the package mailed, It would have to create time for it. I drove to a shopping center two blocks away, found the tape in the back of a department store, grabbed a package of laundry detergent on sale, paid for the items, and drove back to the post office, all at a relaxed pace. I arrived at two minutes to noon. Physically, what I accomplished seemed impossible, yet it had all gotten done in that time. The choice for peace creates miracles.

Help me to relax and move through my day with a sense of ease and joy.

I always have enough time to do what Spirit asks.

Pygmy Thoughts

Be not content with littleness.
— A Course in Miracles

While visiting a farm, I noticed some tiny horses not much larger than big dogs. "Are those Shetland ponies?" I asked Sara, the owner.

"No," Sara answered, "they are pygmy horses, bred for their small size. The breeders try to make each generation smaller than the last."

Breeding for smallness is symbolic of the way we paint ourselves into a corner by thinking diminutive thoughts. When we believe in lack and act as if it were so, we manufacture a world smaller than the one we were born into, and generate a new wave of little thoughts that leads to even more limitation in our experience. Eventually, we live in a tiny world, miniature in comparison to the world we were intended to enjoy.

My teacher Hilda described the spectacular flowers she saw in her mystical visions. "I've seen some huge flowers," she reported. "They were gigantic in comparison to the ones in our physical world. I was told that the great flowers are actually the ones offered at creation, but stingy thinking has shrunken the world of beauty to a mere fraction of what is possible."

Jesus taught, "To him that hath, more shall be given, and to him that hath not, it shall be taken away." When we think magnanimously, we expand our universe, and when we think small, we shrink it. Let us open our minds to the highest possibilities, that we may enjoy all that is available.

I pray to think with You, that I may live in the largest universe possible.

My magnificent thoughts create a magnificent world.

Right in Front of You

Just open your eyes and realize the way it's always been.
— from the song, "The Balance," by The Moody Blues

While Frank Baum was writing his classic series of children's fantasy books, he had not yet chosen a name for the kingdom in which his characters would play out their adventures. As Baum was sitting with a friend in his office, the fellow asked, "What is the name of the land that will be the setting for your books?" The author shifted his eyes as he pondered, and his vision fell upon his file cabinet, in particular the drawer labeled "O–Z."

"Oz," Baum answered. "I shall build the story on Dorothy's adventures in the land of Oz." Thus was born the setting for the perennial and beloved *Wizard of Oz.*

While we may search high and low for an answer to our need, sometimes it is right in front of us. Hilda used to say, *"Take whatcha got and make whatcha want."* Life is not a mystery to be solved; it is a game to be played. Rather than spending a lot of energy hunting and pecking, we sometimes do better to just take what is before us and use it to our advantage.

Many of us have been taught that the best solution is the most complicated one. We believe that we must strive and strain and pay a high cost for what we want. But often the reverse is the case: The simplest answer is the one that will work best. God does not play hide-and-seek. The truth is simple; it is obvious, and it works.

Bless the simple things in your world. Appreciate your friends for the simple gifts they offer you. Rather than seeking to replace what you have, look for ways that you may more fully tap into the gifts that you have been given. You are already rich.

Show me the good I already possess.

Everything I need comes to me at the perfect time in the perfect way.

The Main Thing

The main thing is to keep the main thing the main thing.
— Anonymous

The rascal Nasrudin stood on the bow of a boat next to a pompous intellectual who began to quiz him on his education. "Have you ever studied astronomy?" asked the professor.

"I can't say that I have," answered the mystic.

"Then you have wasted much of your life. By knowing the constellations, a skilled captain can navigate a boat around the entire globe." Then he asked, "Have you studied meteorology?"

"No," answered Nasrudin.

"Then you have wasted most of your life," the academician chided. "Methodically capturing the wind can propel a sailing ship at astounding speeds." Then he inquired, "Have you studied oceanography?"

"Not at all."

"Ah! What a waste of your time! Awareness of the currents helps sailors find food and shelter."

A few minutes later, Nasrudin began to make his way toward the stern of the ship. As he ambled forward, he nonchalantly asked the fellow, "Have you ever studied swimming?"

"Haven't had the time," the professor haughtily responded.

"Then you've wasted *all* of your life—the boat is sinking."

Each of us reaches a point in life where we must decide what is really important and live from our highest values. We must put aside lesser pursuits in favor of what truly satisfies our soul. When all is said and done, we will remember our moments of love and kindness, and all else will fall away. Do not be distracted from your soul's true purpose. Do what is meaningful to you, and trust that all else will be taken care of.

Help me to stay on purpose today.
I pray to live from my heart.

My priority is peace.
I do what I am here to do.

Why Wait for Heaven?

Heaven is here. There is no other place.
Heaven is now. There is no other time.
— *A Course in Miracles*

When I landed after a long airplane flight, I was disappointed not to find my friend who was supposed to pick me up. When I called her house, she was still home, which meant that I would need to wait for nearly an hour in a hot and crowded airport. After grumbling to myself for a while, I decided to play a game I called "Heaven." I imagined that everyone and everything I saw was a part of a scene in heaven. People were stepping off airplanes, happy to finally arrive in paradise; families were greeting one another with open arms; and porters were assisting passengers with luggage to get them settled in heaven. Soon I enjoyed the game so much that I hardly noticed an hour go by.

When my friend arrived, I invited her to sit and play the game with me. Just then a man asked us if we would watch his bags while he made a phone call. In heaven, we had nowhere to go, and we gladly said yes, which he very much appreciated. Because we were at peace, we were in a perfect position to serve, and we brought his world closer to heaven.

Right where you are, there is just as much joy, peace, and happiness available as there is anywhere and anytime. The remedy for unhappiness is not geographical; it is attitudinal. If you choose to find peace where you are, you will bring it wherever you go and invite others to join you.

Help me remember that love is everywhere.
Wherever I go, there I will find You.

I carry the peace of God with me wherever I am.

212

Turtles All the Way Down

There is only one question that all of science and philosophy seek to answer: "Is the universe a friendly place?"

— Albert Einstein

A king woke up his advisor late one evening, anxiously reporting, "I couldn't sleep because I began to fear that the world would fall into the abyss."

"Not to worry," comforted the advisor. "The earth is held up by a giant bear."

"Thank you," answered the king, breathing a sigh of relief. Half an hour later, the king knocked again. "What is holding up the bear?" he inquired.

"A great turtle," the sage answered. "He will not let the bear fall."

"That's good," responded the king.

The seer was not surprised when half an hour later, the king knocked again. The advisor opened the door and, just as the king was about to speak, he raised his hand and told the monarch, "It's turtles all the way down!"

If we begin to question our support, we can enter into an abysmal tailspin of worry. Eventually we come to the point where we either trust implicitly or doubt compulsively. If we do not trust, we will find more and more reasons to fear, and if we trust, we shall confirm our vision of safety. We can short-circuit the experiment by practicing trust in the universe at every level, knowing that for every turtle we question, there is one below it.

I pray to have faith in things unseen,
knowing Your loving hand sustains me.

I am always safe because
God is always present.

Honest Courage

The art of life is to show your hand.
There is no diplomacy like candor.

— E.V. Lucas

Although Mike and Cindy were getting divorced, they continued to socialize and made plans to invest in a piece of real estate together. Meanwhile, the couple was at odds with each other emotionally and fought openly. As I sat on the beach with them and a woman named Sharon, I felt jarred by a constant flow of barbs and sarcasm the couple directed toward each other. If they disliked each other that much, I wondered why they even spent time together, let alone planned to buy real estate.

"Would you two like to come and look at the property we are considering?" Mike asked.

"Thanks for the invitation," I answered quickly, "but I have another appointment." ("Another appointment" meant "anything but this one.")

"How about you?" Mike asked Sharon.

"Generally, I would like to take the ride, but I am very uncomfortable with the hostility both of you are generating. I don't think I could be with it for several hours."

I gulped. I could hardly believe that Sharon had laid the truth out so plainly. She said what I wished I had the honesty to say if I had not feared insulting the couple. I watched Mike and Cindy for their reaction.

"We totally understand; thanks for being honest."

Sharon's directness showed me how often I have glossed over the truth (or outright lied) unconsciously because I feared the truth would be socially unacceptable. Sharon pierced through the veil of false politeness and cleared the air. Her intention was not to hurt Mike and Cindy, but to answer their question honestly. In this case, the couple was well aware of their energy; in other cases, other people may be well served to learn how they are affecting others. The truth is not always comfortable, but it has the power to remove the darkness.

Give me the courage to speak honestly
so I may bring the truth to light.

I speak my truth with the intention to heal.

The Most Powerful Prayer

When you pray, think. Think well what you're saying, and make your thoughts into things that are solid. In that way, your prayers will have strength, and that strength will become a part of you in body, mind, and spirit.

— Walter Pidgeon's character in the film *How Green Was My Valley*

An angel attempting to earn his wings was given the mission of finding the person on earth whose prayers had the most power to reach heaven. He journeyed for a long time and then returned with this report: "I circled the entire world and found many people reciting rote prayers without feeling or conviction. Many prayed so that others would see them, and some prayed to be victorious over others. I heard many prayers, but felt little heart. Just when I was about to give up I heard the tears of a little boy in a poor section of a big city. He was reciting, *A...B...C...'* and on through the alphabet. When I listened closer, I heard him pray, *'Dear God, I do not know how to read, and I cannot recite from the prayer book, but I love you with all my heart. Take these letters and form them into words that are pleasing to you.'"* The angel was given his wings.

It is not the form of our words or acts that brings us closer to heaven, but the sincerity of our intentions. Bring a pure heart to your prayers and deeds, and you will succeed.

Open my heart to true caring and pure love.
Let my words and deeds be motivated by sincerity and kindness.

My heart is God's heart.

Pass the Cream Cheese

I am content to be wherever He wishes, knowing He goes there with me.

— A Course in Miracles

When I began public speaking, I was invited to address a B'nai B'rith men's group, which met at a Jewish temple for a lecture, discussion, and buffet breakfast on a Sunday morning. As I began my talk, I was disappointed to see that the group was inattentive and seemed uninterested in my presentation. Some of the men smoked cigars as I spoke, others picked through their wallets, and during the guided meditation, several opened their eyes and scanned the bagel-and-cream cheese buffet. When I was finished, I was sorry I had come; it seemed that I had chosen the wrong crowd for my subject matter, and I felt as if my time had been wasted.

The following week, I received several telephone calls from organizations to which members of the B'nai B'rith group had recommended me. These callers wanted me to serve as a guest speaker and teach ongoing classes. Apparently a number of people in that group were impressed with my presentation and wanted to share it with their other affiliations.

We never really know what the effects of our service will be. Sometimes it appears that nothing is happening, or no good is coming, when behind the scenes, important changes are occurring, and progress is being made. This is why we must never judge the results of our service on surface appearances. Imagine that any good that you do, or intend to do, is being received by the right people at the right level for the right purpose.

Give me the faith to remember that Your hand is moving my life.

I act with confidence, knowing that Spirit is working through me for the benefit of all.

Build Your World

Make it a practice to judge persons and things in the most favorable light at all times, in all circumstances.

— Saint Vincent de Paul

A religious man learned that a prostitute was doing business in his neighborhood. He found her house, stood across the street, and watched men enter and leave her home. Every time he saw a customer walk out, he placed a stone in a little pile, symbolizing the weight and extent of her sins. Years later, the prostitute died, and soon afterward so did the man. When the man was shown to his heavenly abode, he was aghast to find but a heap of stones similar to the mound he had built to mark the prostitute's wrongdoing. On the other side of the gray pile, he saw a magnificent estate with rolling lawns and colorful gardens, where the prostitute strolled joyfully. "There must be some mistake!" he railed. "That woman was a prostitute, and I was a religious man."

"There is no mistake," a voice answered. "That prostitute hated her job, but it was the only way she knew to make money to support herself and her young daughter. Every time she was with a client, she inwardly prayed, 'Dear God, please get me out of this.' You, on the other hand, were fascinated only with her sins. While she was talking to God, you were talking to rocks. She got what she prayed for, and so did you."

Things are not what they appear to be. We never really know the motive or consciousness behind someone's actions. Any act can be a tool of the ego, or an avenue for the Holy Spirit. We inherit the world we build with our thoughts.

I pray to keep You in my mind today. Let me not wander into temptation to see less than love.

I build a world of beauty with my thoughts.

The Power of the Word

In the beginning was the word.

— John 1:1

A woman in relatively good health underwent dilation and curettage (D&C) surgery. After her operation, however, Sally was not recovering, and each day she sank deeper into the abyss. Medical professionals were at a loss, since all tests revealed she was physically healthy. Finally, someone suggested hypnosis. During her session, it was discovered that under surgery Sally had heard one of the members of the operating team ask her doctor, "Do you think she'll make it?"

The doctor answered, "No way—I give her a few days at the most." What Sally didn't realize was that the conversation was about another patient. Although Sally's conscious mind was asleep, her subconscious heard every word and, not knowing the bigger picture, she accepted the statement as true about herself and went on to manifest the picture her subconscious had adopted. Sally's hypnotic regression assisted her to realize this was not her prognosis, and she recovered.

The subconscious is the part of our mind that manufactures our experience. Psychologists tell us that *the subconscious cannot distinguish between imagination and reality*. If you hold an image in mind long enough and feel it as if it is real, you can manifest it. This is the essence of creative visualization, as well as self-fulfilling prophecy. If we think or worry about something enough, we may draw that experience to ourselves. We can use the same principle to bring us what we want. Hold in mind images of the life you desire, and refuse to feed thoughts of what you do not wish. Watch your words. Be careful what you say to little children (or the little child in adults), for children emotionally absorb ideas even if they are said in jest or the heat of an angry moment. Feed your mind and heart with the most positive, energetic, and enlivening ideas and feelings you can imagine. Then you will live not in the world that is cast upon you, but the one you choose.

Help me to feed myself and others with soul-nourishing thoughts and feelings.

I speak the word of love, and it is manifested.

This Too Shall Pass

All things must change to something new.
— Henry Wadsworth Longfellow

A king in an ancient land sought the counsel of a sage. "I am not a happy man," admitted the monarch. "My emotions are driving me crazy. When I win a battle, I am elated. When I lose, I am depressed. My happiness seems to come and go like a feather dancing on the wind. Can you help me?"

The advisor thought for a moment, and answered, "I will return with help in three days."

After that time, the sage came back with a ring he had forged for the king. When the king read its inscription, he found the peace that he sought. The ring reminded the king, *"This too shall pass."*

No matter what is happening, it will eventually give way to something else. Try to hold on to an experience, and you will lose it. Try to make it go, and it will cling to you. Allow it to be with you for its right time, and you will enjoy it or learn from it. Trust that you will have everything you need for the right amount of time. When it leaves, assume it is departing to make way for something better.

My friend Scott made a successful living as a car salesman. "The best piece of advice I ever received was from my boss at the dealership," Scott told me. "One day after I took a significant loss on a deal, I complained to him about it. 'Don't let it get you down,' he told me. 'It's all in the averages.' He was right. In the long run, the good deals offset the bad ones. You have to remember the big picture."

The next time you face a problem, remember: *"This too shall pass."* When you feel giddy, affirm: *"This too shall pass."* Only Spirit remains constant. With the right vision, we find comfort in the peace that remains behind all of life's changing forms.

Let me remember that Spirit is present, that I may enjoy my life as a colorful dance.

I trust the changes in my life, knowing that God alone is real.

Fame

Drop the idea of making a hit record,
and call in the energy of truth.
— Kenny Loggins

When someone asks me how to write a successful book, I tell them, "Come from your heart, tell the truth, and write for yourself. Do not write with the goal of pleasing people or becoming rich and famous. If you're true to yourself, the world will acknowledge and support you. If you seek fame and glory, your values are inside out, and you're setting yourself up for struggle, frustration, and pain. Seek to serve, and your happiness is ensured."

Kenny Loggins is one of the most beloved and successful musicians of our time; over 25 years, he has sold over 30 million albums. When I met Kenny, I found him to be one of the most sincere, genuine, and emotionally available people I have encountered. He lives in his heart and values relationship above glory. Kenny wrote one of his most popular albums, *Leap of Faith*, while he was going through a painful divorce. The songs on the album chronicle the emotions he wrestled with, as well as the vision of the new life he sought to live. Kenny was quite vulnerable about his process, and the album, a reflection of his turning point, has touched and changed many lives. I believe it is his best album because it is his most real.

Paul Simon went through a similar process. His career was sagging, and he was going through significant life changes. Ignited by the fire of transformation, he decided to chuck standard fare and follow his heart and play the music that turned him on the most. The result was his landmark *Rhythm of the Saints* album, which won a Grammy Award for Best Album of the Year and set him off on an international tour that broke down many walls of fear and prejudice as he brought musicians from different cultures together.

When I feel stuck, I remind myself of my true purpose. I am not here to gather accolades; I am here to remember who I am and express it without apology. Come from your heart, and the world will bless you with peace.

Help me remember that inner integrity is
far more important than worldly glory.

I dedicate myself to authenticity. As I live
what I am, I prosper in every way.

Divine Order Now

Now let the weeping cease; let no one mourn again.
These things are in the hand of God.

— Sophocles

"We regret to announce that Flight 317 has been canceled due to mechanical trouble. Please stay in the waiting room until we have a further advisory." A wave of groans and protests rose from the mass of disgruntled passengers. The stress level grew higher when the agent announced that the airline had found a replacement plane, but it was smaller than the original one; passengers for the new flight would be selected by lottery. Passenger Eric Butterworth reminded himself that divine order was in force, and if he was to be on that plane, he would be. He recognized that anxious stressing or complaining would not help anyone, and placed the whole affair in the hands of God. Dr. Butterworth saw that nearly everyone in the room was upset except for one man who seemed relaxed, taking it all in stride. Eric took a seat next to the fellow and struck up a conversation. Soon, the results of the lottery were announced. Can you guess which names were called first? That's right—Dr. Butterworth and his newfound friend.

Jesus reminded us, "Take no thought for tomorrow." Tomorrow means anything in the future. He asked, "Can any among you add one cubit to your height or one day to your life through anxious worry?" Of course not. The serenity prayer reminds us to ask: *God grant me the serenity to accept the things I cannot change, the courage to change the things I can, and the wisdom to know the difference.*

A Course in Miracles suggests that we affirm, *"I place the future in the hands of God."* Indeed we must, because the future *is* in the hands of God. We do not need to feverishly hustle to make sure everything will turn out right. We attract all that turns out right by being at peace.

Help me to not be distracted by appearances.
Let me remember that You are in charge, love is present,
and all is well.

Divine order is in force here, now, and always.

221

I'm Enough

The truth about you is so lofty that nothing unworthy of God is worthy of you.
— A Course in Miracles

While shopping one day, I met a woman whom I found very attractive. Before I left her store, I told her, "I think you're very pretty." Her response took me by surprise. Quickly, she answered, "I'm a twin."

As I walked away, I tried to understand why she would say that. I believe she was unable to receive the compliment fully. By pointing out that she had a twin, she was, in effect, saying, "Yes, but there are actually two of me, so I do not have to own the full responsibility of being pretty."

Many of us have difficulty accepting compliments because we subconsciously believe that we are not worthy of them. A compliment triggers our discomfort of believing that if the complimenters knew the truth about us, they would find the contrary. We do not recognize that the person who compliments us is closer to the truth than we are.

There are many ways in which we deflect love when it's offered. We say no to money when it's available, and we sabotage jobs. We deal similarly with relationships, running from quality people, acting in ways that we know will make them leave, or settling for less than we want and deserve. In sexuality, we may stop ourselves from receiving real pleasure or experiencing orgasm because we fear feeling vulnerable or being overwhelmed by the energy of the love. Then we go on living at half-steam and wonder why we are not happy.

We can cultivate our capacity to receive and enjoy love. Practice letting compliments in. Instead of firing off a polite "Thank you," take a breath and a moment to let the gift seep in; this will energize you and bless the giver. When offered money or support, gratefully accept. In relationships and sexuality, don't settle for half-fulfillment; cultivate being filled with the gifts your partner brings. Then we can all be wholly beautiful and lovable, no matter how many of us there are.

I pray to be able to fully receive the love that is offered me.

I honor God and myself by letting the love in.

Be the First

I walked up to an old monk and asked him,
"What is the audacity of humility?"
Do you know what his answer was?
"To be the first to say 'I love you.'"
— Father Theophane, *Tales of a Magic Monastery*

One of my favorite little-known movies is *Secret Admirer,* in which a teenage girl sends an unsigned love letter to a male friend she has a crush on. He guesses the letter is from another girl and sends a romantic reply to her. When the letter falls into his father's night-school accounting book, Dad surmises it was put there by his teacher, to whom he makes overtures. To retaliate, the boy's mom sets out to date the teacher's husband. You can imagine the web of convoluted relationships that unfurl in the wake of one unsigned note!

Finally, the girl who originally sent the letter despairs of ever receiving the boy's affection and sets off on an ocean voyage. Just as she's about to leave, the boy figures out the letter was from her and realizes he loves her, too. He speeds to the dock to try to stop her, only to find her ship making its way out of the harbor. At the top of his lungs, he shouts, "I love you!"

The girl shouts back, "I love you, too!" and each dives into the water to meet for a long-overdue kiss.

If we are unwilling to make a stand for our love, we create all kinds of aberrations and convolutions, until the universe forces us to tell the truth about who we are and what we feel. While it may seem safer to wait for someone else to say, "I love you," we empower ourselves and bestow a great gift when we're willing to be the first one to say it. I tell many people, "I love you"—not just romantic interests, but friends, teachers, co-workers, and people I have a sense of kinship with. If I feel it, I say it. "I love you" does not have to mean romance or sex. It may just mean, "I love you," the three words that everyone wants to hear but not everyone is willing to say first. Be true to your heart, and you will not want for love.

Give me the courage to be a great lover.

I am powerful in my love,
and I express it fearlessly.

The Lord in the Tree

Pray as if all depends on God,
and act as if all depends on you.
— George Washington Carver

Two men were walking in a field when a bull charged them. One man scampered up a tree while the other stood defiantly in the bull's path. "Get up here, you idiot!" called the man in the branches.

"The Lord will protect me!" retorted the other man.

The bull butted the man vehemently and went on his way triumphantly, leaving the obstinate fellow dazed and confused. The first man came down from the tree to help his bruised friend.

"I thought for sure the Lord would help me!" complained the injured man.

"He tried," answered his friend. "Didn't you hear Him calling you from the tree?"

A request for help from an unseen power often manifests itself through earthy channels. God's wonders are not restricted to supernatural miracles. Often miracles occur through people and tangible messages here on earth.

If you are looking for an answer to a question or problem, you may receive it through physical means. Someone may hand you a book, invite you to a lecture, or speak a phrase that resonates within you. You may feel a tingling in your spine, get goosebumps, or simply feel a sense of clarity or fulfillment. Be sensitive to your feelings and energies when such a sign is presented. The word *angel* means "messenger," and your message may come anytime through any means. Stay awake to listen!

Help me stay open to hear Your voice.
Let me receive Your answer and act upon it.

I act upon the messages Spirit sends me.

God Meant It for Good

Keep your faith in beautiful things;
in the sun when it is hidden, in the Spring when it is gone.
— Roy R. Gibson

The Bible tells of Joseph who, because he was his father's favorite son, incurred the jealousy of his brothers. To get rid of Joseph, they threw him in a desert pit and left him to die. But a caravan came along and took Joseph to Egypt where, because of his spiritual insight, he was elevated to the position of advisor to Pharaoh.

When famine fell upon Joseph's homeland, his brothers came to Egypt to ask for food, and they were sent to see none other than Joseph. Astounded to find him alive, and feeling guilty over their attempt to do away with him, they begged for forgiveness. "Not necessary," Joseph answered. "You meant it for evil, but God meant it for good."

Although Joseph's brothers did not recognize it, they were participating in his destiny for good. Similarly, when life hands us challenges or abuses, it may actually be moving us into a position where we gain greater good than if the incidents had not happened.

Instead of asking, "How could life be so cruel as to victimize me like this?" a more empowering question is, "How can I use this experience to grow in strength and become even more powerful to manifest what I truly want?"

In a Gallup Poll, 87 percent of those questioned stated that their most challenging experiences turned out to be among the most helpful. Consider the possibility that even though someone may seem to mean an act for evil, God means it for good.

I pray to use Your vision today. Remove any sense of smallness and victimization from my heart, and help me make my experiences work on my behalf.

I am the creator of my experience.
I take what I have and make what I want.

225

Don't Miss It

Carpe Diem! (Seize the Day!)

On my way to the San Francisco airport, I got caught in traffic on the Bay Bridge. Wondering how long I would be stuck, I began to worry about missing my plane. Just having come from a restful retreat in the mountains, suddenly I felt the stressful chemistry of anxiety encroach on my body. Then an inner voice spoke: *"It's one thing to miss the plane, but it's quite another to miss the moment."* Stunned, I recognized that I had just missed a moment of life. I took a few deep breaths, looked out at the springtime sun shimmering on the water, opened the window to feel the breeze, and turned on the radio to find some enjoyable music. Ah, that felt better. I could always catch another plane, but I could never catch another *this moment.*

All of life is right where you are. Never trade the peace of now for fear or worry. Because you carry the spark of God with you, you have the power to illuminate any time, any place.

Help me to be fully present.
Help me to find beauty where I am.

I claim the riches of the universe right where I am.

Prayer Conditioned

More things are wrought by prayer
than this world dreams of.

— Alfred, Lord Tennyson

At the orientation of a week-long spiritual conference at a Pennsylvania college, one of the 500 participants raised her hand and asked, "When are we going to get our dorm room keys?"

"We don't give out keys," the sponsor answered. "The entire campus is prayer conditioned. We have done conferences here for over ten years, we have never issued a key, and we have never had a theft or loss."

The consciousness we bring to any activity creates a psychic environment that protects or undermines what we do in that field. *Prayer works.* Holding an activity in prayer or a prayerful attitude will draw to it a wealth of support, energy, and protection. Scientific studies have shown that praying over food changes the food's chemical properties, and that hospital patients who receive prayer treatment recover faster than control groups.

In Russia, I visited a church where an icon of the Virgin Mary had been venerated during a plague. The plague took a grueling toll on the entire region except for the town that had prayed for intervention, which miraculously remained untouched.

When undertaking any significant enterprise or relationship, or when facing a challenge, make prayer your first line of support. It will help you far more than fear or worldly manipulation.

I place my trust in You. Though unseen to the human eye,
You are perfectly present.

God is my strength and my fortress.
Spirit never fails.

For, Not Against

Resist not evil, but overcome evil with good.

— Jesus Christ

In a restaurant, I noticed a woman wearing a white sweatshirt with the word *Pornography* splashed across the front in big red letters. Printed in tiny black letters below the red ones were the words, *"is not the will of God."* The latter phrase was written in such small type that I had to be quite near the shirt to read it. *"Pornography,"* however, was easily visible from across the street. While this woman was intending to campaign against pornography, she was actually advertising it. The moment I read the huge word on her sweatshirt, images of pornography came to my mind. She would have been more effective in her campaign if she wore a shirt advertising what she wanted to *create*, not destroy. She might have worn a shirt with an image depicting two people embracing lovingly, or some phrase that would have reminded onlookers of healthy sexuality.

The mind creates more of whatever it focuses on. For example, do not think about a pink elephant now. Whatever you do, you must not see a pink elephant in your mind. Of course, you are probably seeing a big pink elephant. The subconscious does not comprehend the meaning of *not*. Now think of your favorite elementary school teacher. Remember her face, name, and why you liked her. While you were thinking of the teacher, did you see the pink elephant? Probably not.

Jesus was a master metaphysician who understood that thoughts create. He advised, "Turn the other cheek," indicating that we must not give energy to what we *do not* want, but rather turn and look in the direction of what we *do* value. When Mother Teresa was invited to speak at an anti-war rally, she refused. "If you asked me to speak at a pro-peace rally, I would be there. I am not against anything. I am for love."

I pray to create heaven on earth by focusing on Your presence in all.

I bless the good and let all else go.

228

Make No Plans

Sitting quietly, doing nothing,
Spring comes and the grass grows by itself.
— Zen saying

"May I offer you three words of advice that could make all the difference in your vacation?" Fredrick asked me as he was about to drop me off at the airport.

"Sure."

He looked me in the eye carefully and told me: *"Make no plans."*

When I arrived in Bali for my two-week retreat, I rented a thatched-roof bungalow in the middle of a rice field near a mountain town, and I created each day as it came. I woke up not with an alarm clock, but when my eyes opened. Some mornings I meditated after awakening, other mornings I wrote, and on other days, I walked through the maze of rice paddies. When I was hungry, I walked into town, dined casually at a restaurant next to a lotus pool, and then strolled leisurely through the village. My entire time unfolded in magnificent perfection with a minimum of preparation. Occasionally I would hope to see one of my friends, and within a few hours or a day, they would show up at a house I was visiting. In spite of—or because of—minimal planning, I experienced more peace and freedom than I had in a long time.

In this world, we will not escape making some plans. Houses, meetings, and businesses call for blueprints. But we can escape planning anxiously. We do not need to set up our whole life before we reach it. Many of us plan, not out of necessity, but out of fear that if we had some unscheduled time on our hands, we would be lost. To the contrary, we would be found.

I turn my schedule over to You, trusting You
to arrange all meetings and events for me
far more effectively than I could arrange for myself.

God is my Day-Planner.

Breaker, Breaker

Stop!—in the name of love....
— from the song of the same name, by Eddie Holland

When the circuit breaker in my laundry room flipped off, I switched it back on. The dryer ran for a while, and again the breaker switched itself off. I turned it on again and did a few more laundry loads like this, discovering that I could get about 15 minutes of use before the circuit breaker would shut itself down. Finally, I called an electrician, who told me that he could come after the weekend. During that time, I did more laundry, working the system at 15-minute intervals.

When the electrician arrived, he opened up the electrical panel and showed me a charred wire going into the laundry circuit breaker. "You came this close to having a house fire," he informed me soberly. "These breakers are designed to be turned off and on maybe 15 or 20 times in their lifetime; after that they're useless—the resistance backs up into the wiring system and voilà, Kentucky Fried household." I shuddered to think that my home was so close to danger, and felt very grateful that he had caught the problem in time.

When something in our life is malfunctioning, we receive signs, warnings, hints, and tripped breakers. In an emergency, we can override the breaker and keep going for a bit, but before long we must take action. If I had been more tuned in, I would have realized that something was wrong with the system and that it was not wise to keep overriding the breaker. In life, too, we cannot afford to keep overriding the breakers. We must heed the breaker's warning and go to the source of the problem rather than simply treating the symptom. Instead of depending on aspirin to take away a headache, we need to face who or what is giving us a headache and deal with the problem at its source.

Keep your antennae up for signals: Take the grace and then take the action.

Show me what I need to do to live in integrity and wholeness.

I accept God's guidance through the messages of my life.

Honor the Angel

Allow children to be happy their own way;
for what better way will they ever find?
— Samuel Johnson

When a child is born in Bali, its feet are not allowed to touch the earth for the first 105 days of life. The Balinese regard their children as angels from heaven, and they do not want them to be shocked by contact with the heaviness of the world. Every Balinese child is constantly held until almost four months of age. Then, a colorful ceremony is held at which the child's feet are placed upon the earth, with prayers and blessings.

In our culture, we need to remember to honor our children as spiritual beings. We all come from heaven, and the transition to earth is not easy for anyone. We must give our children the opportunity to retain their spiritual identity for as long as possible.

Many children are extremely psychic and spiritual, as you may have been. They voice the wisdom of old and wise souls; some report memories of past lives, talk to invisible friends, play with nature spirits, have premonitions, and recount contact with departed relatives. Many are quite sensitive to the energies in their environment, feeling touched and healed by loving people and events, and jarred by violence in thought or deed.

We must give our children the best possible atmosphere in which to start their journey. Let them be spiritual beings for as long as they choose; do not force them to trade their heritage for our cultural idea of education. The best gift we can give our children is to draw forth that which they already are.

Help me to respect children as whole and wise beings.
Through them I will remember my own innocence.

I come from heaven to bestow
the gifts of God.

Because I Say So

The choice is yours to make between a sleeping death...or a happy waking and joy of life.
— *A Course in Miracles*

Walking out of the movie theater after seeing *Mr. Holland's Opus*, I felt exhilarated. In the midst of the parking lot, I stretched out my arms, looked up at the stars, and exclaimed, "Life is good!" I laughed and turned to my friend and asked her, "Do you know why? *Because I say so.*"

I recognized with perfect surety that I can live any life I choose. If I want to be happy, that's my choice. If others want to be miserable, that's up to them. I do not have to justify, explain, rationalize, apologize, or compromise my choice for joy. I create my own reality, just as you do. The universe is big enough to have all kinds of reality happening simultaneously, and none of us needs agreement from anyone to verify the world we choose to live in.

Do you remember when, as a child, your father laid down a rule, and when you asked him, "Why?" he answered, *"Because I say so."* He was affirming that he had the power to establish your reality, and you didn't get to question it. Now you have the power to establish your own reality, and no one else gets to question it.

When I worked with profoundly retarded people, most observers pitied them, but I respected them. They were some of the happiest and most loving people I have ever met. Their intellects were minimally developed, which allowed them to retain their childlike innocence throughout their lives. Perhaps on some cosmic dimension their souls decided they could learn a great deal about joy by living an entire life without thinking too much. Are they better or worse off than most people? That depends on the side of the telescope you're looking through.

What reality would you like to live in? Do you choose a world of love, abundance, and celebration, or one of fear, lack, and doom? The choice is yours—because you say so.

Bless me with the choice to live in a world that reflects Your loving presence.

I choose a reality of ever-expanding good.

Too Far to Turn Back Now

The march to freedom is irreversible.
— Nelson Mandela

When the new nation of Hebrews was liberated from slavery in Egypt, they found themselves dead-ended against the Red Sea with Pharaoh's army in hot pursuit. Facing the prospect of drowning, some of the Hebrews shouted, "Let's go back to Egypt; there we will be slaves, but at least we'll have homes and food." Others argued that anything would be better than slavery, and they would rather take their chances than return to a condition that they had fought so hard to relieve. The rabbinical commentary on the Old Testament tells that some of the Jews walked into the Red Sea up to their necks before the waters parted. It was on their faith, the rabbis asserted, that the seas opened.

Like the newborn Jewish nation, there is a part of us that is tempted to return to the old when we are frightened. As we face uncharted territory, our sense of insecurity bids us to take refuge in our past. But at such a moment of anxiety, we forget that the past did not work for us; that is precisely why we left it. It is but the voice of doubt and fear that urges us to be what we were rather than what we are growing to become.

There is more to life than material security, and more to safety than the known. The only true security is in Spirit, and the only real safety in freedom. We may have all kinds of material comforts, but if our spirit is not at peace, we are homeless. And we may have nothing in the outer world, but if our inner world is lit by love, we are unshakably secure.

Do not let fear tempt you to return to a condition you have outgrown. You have come too far to turn back now. Keep moving, step by step, day by day, and miracles will meet you to take you to the other side.

Give me the strength to keep moving ahead until I realize my goal.

I trust God to guide me to my new life and care for me always.

Let's Do Lunch

When a needy person stands at your door,
God Himself stands at his side.
— Hebrew proverb

"I had the most wonderful day today," DeAnn told me. "I took a beggar to lunch. As I was about to enter a restaurant, he stood at the door and asked me for a handout. I felt inspired to ask him, 'Would you care to join me for lunch?' His eyes nearly popped out of his head! Eagerly he answered, 'Sure.' We had a good talk, and I gained some insight into his life. He told me he didn't look forward to sleeping on the street in the middle of winter, so on my way home I dropped him at a motel and paid for his room. I can't remember the last time I felt so much peace."

While we may be prone to shy away from desperate or troubled people, a great treasure lies in serving them. Jesus said, "Whatever you do for the least of your brothers, you do for me." Many of us have high ideals for human service, but how many of us reach beyond our comfort zone to practice them? To care for the careless and house the homeless is to put love into action.

My teacher Hilda once asked me, "What would you like to stand for in this life?"

Immediately I answered, "Love."

"Can you love those who are unkind to you or different from you?" she asked.

I had to be honest. "Not always."

"Then you have not yet mastered love," she told me. "When you can love all equally, only then can you say you know how to love."

I was inspired by DeAnn's example. The next day, I tried to connect more with the people I met in public. I smiled and said "Hi" to the policeman directing traffic in a construction zone; I tried to catch the eyes of the man taking my order for tires; and I chatted with a cook about his vacation plans. Funny, in the midst of a busy day of errands, those moments are the ones I remember.

Give me the strength to go beyond judgment,
that I may meet everyone in the domain of the heart.

I behold the God in everyone and serve everyone as I would be loved.

Out of the Fishbowl

It's not trespassing when you cross your own boundaries.
— Anonymous

While cleaning her goldfish bowl, Mildred drew a few inches of water into her bathtub and placed her two fish in the tub. When she returned, Mildred found the fish swimming in a little circle the size of the bowl.

Just as these fish had a huge bathtub to swim in, so do we live in an unlimited universe. Yet, like the fish, if we have accepted limits from our past, when we have the opportunity to expand our horizons, we may not challenge our limits, so we stay confined to an old pattern.

We must constantly test our limits to see if they are real. If we have the courage to venture into uncharted territory, we will find treasures and freedom we would never have known if we didn't try. Buddha said, "To see what few have seen, you must go where few have gone."

The "laws" and limits of the world exist by agreement only. When we release small thinking, we inherit the kingdom founded on the laws of love. Which laws do you choose to agree with? Jesus challenged us, "Choose ye this day whom you will serve." The world you live in will be as grand as the thoughts upon which you found it.

Let me not rest content with a life less than
the one You offer me.
I pray to live in the grandest universe possible.

I move beyond my past
and claim a glorious future.
I manifest magnificent results because
I think unlimited thoughts.

The Power to Heal

The art of medicine consists of amusing the patient while nature cures the disease.

— Voltaire

A Band-Aid television ad suggests that the healing energy we need is already within us. Our job, the ad implies, is simply to cooperate with the universal healing force. All we need to do is protect ourselves while nature effects the cure. "Cuts and wounds," manufacturer Johnson & Johnson reminds us, "heal twice as quickly when they are covered with a Band-Aid." Their new slogan is "*The Power to Heal.*"

What a delight to see the world of pharmaceuticals coming closer to the truth! *A Course in Miracles* asks:

> *Who is the physician? Only the mind of the patient himself. The outcome is what he decides that it is. Special agents seem to be ministering to him, yet they but give form to his own choice....They are not actually needed at all. The patient could merely rise up without their aid and say, "I have no use for this." There is no form of sickness that would not be cured at once.*

While doctors can facilitate the healing process, the only true healer is God. Even the mending of a small cut is a miracle! What human being has the power to recreate it? To be healed, we do not need to add anything to who we are or what we have. We simply need to become still and allow nature to reinstate us to our rightful condition of well-being.

I open myself to be touched by Your healing power.
I lay aside all idols and invite the presence of love
to restore my true nature of wholeness.

Health is my natural state. I accept it now.

Don't Drop the Baby

The peace of God is my one goal.
— A Course In Miracles

Author Hugh Prather likens the peace of God to a tender infant. "If you were carrying a little baby," Hugh suggests, "you would make that child your first priority. If someone bumped into you on the street, you wouldn't just drop the baby to follow the person and yell at him. And if your car broke down, you wouldn't abandon the child as you walked to get help. In the same way, we cannot afford to put the peace of God aside for any worldly distraction. The peace of God is more valuable than anything the world has to offer, and we must protect it as consistently as a tender infant."

What have you placed before the peace of God? Money? Anger? Fear? Time? Possessions? Drama? Romance? Guilt? Sex? Work? If you've traded joy for any passing entity or experience, you've struck a poor bargain indeed.

Make an inner commitment to hold peace above all else for one day. It will be the most beautiful day of your life.

Beloved God, I want to know Your love fully.
Help me to remember You above all else.

The peace of God is my one goal.
My priorities are in order.

Whose Birthday?

Give to every other human being every right you claim for yourself.
— Robert G. Ingersoll

I took my eight-year-old goddaughter to the toy store to buy her a birthday present. When I told her, "Pick out anything you like," she ran to the display of Barbie dolls. "But you already have 32 Barbie Dolls!" I reminded her. "You have a blonde Barbie, a black Barbie, a cheerleader Barbie, and a beach Barbie, not to mention a Barbie house, a Barbie hot rod, and a Barbie executive office. Why don't you get something different?"

She clutched a new Barbie and answered, "But I want a Barbie." My first instinct was to tell her to put the doll back on the shelf, but then I realized something important: It was *her* birthday, not mine. I had told her to pick out whatever she wanted, and this was her choice. It was not my place to judge what made her happy. Even if she had 300 Barbies and this was her idea of a great birthday present, I had to honor her choice.

True service means surrendering our idea of what someone else should want, and supporting them in their vision of happiness. With the exception of helping someone do something that will hurt them, we love most genuinely by standing behind, not between, others and the choices they make. We must not impose our visions over theirs, but support them in manifesting their dreams.

Help me love and support my brothers and sisters for who and what they are, rather than what I would have them be.

I delight in affirming others on their path of joy.

A Few More Phone Calls

Everything he wanted to do was impossible.
Everything he did had never been done before.
— Said about *Muppets* creator Jim Henson

In the film *For Love or Money*, Michael J. Fox plays a conniving hotel concierge who wheels and deals to get his guests whatever they want. When he calls one of his sources to obtain some hard-to-get sports tickets, his contact tells him, "They are impossible to get."

"Nothing is impossible," Fox comes back, "'Impossible' just takes a few more phone calls."

If you're persistent enough, you can accomplish anything you choose. One morning I showed up at the airport at 8:00 A.M. to catch a 9 o'clock plane. When I handed the agent my frequent flyer award coupons to purchase the ticket, I was stunned to hear her tell me, "I'm sorry, sir, today is a blackout day for frequent flyer awards."

Well, that wouldn't quite do. I walked across the lobby to a telephone and called the airline reservation office. "No can do," I was told.

I called again. "Not today."

I called again. "Sorry, I can't help you."

I kept calling until finally I got an agent who told me, "I'll get you onto that flight." I knew that if I just kept asking, eventually someone would say yes. My intention to get on the flight was stronger than the airline's intention for me not to be on it. Soon after 9 o'clock, I sat back and enjoyed the view from the sky.

Every great invention or world transformation was once considered impossible. "Impossible" is a momentary and illusory belief in limitation. Expand your vision to see the big picture, and you will live in an infinite universe.

Help me to remember Your ability to manifest my good.
I say yes to love and welcome Your answer of yes to me.

All of God's power lives within me.
I am unlimited.

See Perfection

It is done unto you as you believe.

— Jesus Christ

Helen was very nearsighted for many years. The moment she woke up each day, she would reach for her eyeglasses; she would take them off only when she closed her eyes to sleep, and she became very uncomfortable when she was required to be without them for even a short time. Then Helen read a book on metaphysics in which she learned that physical challenges stem from inner decisions we make. Vision, Helen read, is related to our willingness (or resistance) to see what is happening in our life. Helen decided she would test the theory and shift her attitude to see all things as perfect. Whenever she was tempted to see a situation as faulty or victimizing, she reminded herself, *"I see perfection, and I see perfectly."* Before long, Helen's vision began to improve, and eventually she threw away her glasses. The vision of perfection manifested in perfect vision.

If you wear glasses, a powerful question to ask yourself is, "When I first began to need eyeglasses, what was happening in my life that I did not want to see?" When I ask this in my seminars, I hear some profound answers. Many people began to wear glasses when their parents were getting divorced, or they were feeling abused by family or friends, or they faced a life trauma. I began to wear eyeglasses when I was bullied by several boys in elementary school, and I felt unprotected.

Our physical body is always sending us messages about what is happening with our spirit. Just as we shut down on seeing or hearing when we don't want to see or hear what's happening in our physical world, we can restore our health by making a new decision to see and hear through God's eyes and ears.

Your will for me is perfect health and happiness.
I accept Your gifts and magnify Your love.

I see perfection as it is.

Acts of Friendship

A good friend who points out mistakes...is to be respected as if he revealed a secret of hidden treasure.

— Buddha

For years, I've loved visiting a local bookstore that is more of a healing center than a business. The energy in the store is always peaceful and welcoming, and the staff takes a personal interest in making each customer feel relaxed and important. When the store owner told me that she was hiring a local entrepreneur to manage the store, I winced. The fellow Rhonda chose was extremely caustic and had a reputation for alienating the people he worked with. I wrestled with the decision over whether to voice my objection, and realized that if I were in her position I would want to hear what I had to say.

I called Rhonda and gently told her how much I loved the store and that I did not believe this new manager would serve her interests. Rhonda became defensive and justified her position. I lovingly released my offering, knowing I had done what I had to do.

Several months later, Rhonda called to tell me that she had dismissed the manager because many of her customers had complained about his style. She admitted that she had first considered my feedback to be an attack, but now she recognized that it was an act of love, and she felt closer to me in our friendship.

A popular slogan reminds us, "Friends don't let friends drive drunk." Neither do friends sit back idly if their friends are about to drive over a cliff. If you are aware of a truth that you believe friends would benefit by knowing, it is your responsibility to tell them. You do not have to argue, justify yourself, or force your opinion. Simply state the situation as you see it, and then allow the individuals to do with it as they wish.

Honesty is not always comfortable, but it is always healing. Sometimes the truth hurts, but the only things it hurts are illusions.

Give me the confidence to speak the truth I see.
May my words serve.

I trust the truth to bless me and those who receive it.

A Little Bit of Heaven

In the middle of every difficulty lies an opportunity.
— Albert Einstein

In a documentary about the 1969 Woodstock Music Festival, a woman who had been there told how participants had to pull together to help each other in the midst of a city of 500,000 people that had formed overnight. People pushed each other's cars out of the mud, shared food, ministered to hippies on bad drug trips, and delivered a baby. "I guess there's a little bit of heaven in every disaster area," she noted.

Sometimes disasters set the stage for blessings that would otherwise go unnoticed or unappreciated. When Hurricane Iniki destroyed or damaged most of the dwellings on the Island of Kauai, residents had to pull together to take care of each other after the storm. One fellow told me, "It was the first time in many years that the aloha spirit returned to the island."

After the 1989 San Francisco earthquake, teams of massage therapists volunteered to treat firefighters who had worked nearly to exhaustion. Businessmen ate lunch next to homeless people in outdoor cafes while the damage was being repaired. Many heroes who would otherwise have remained anonymous came to the fore.

No event is entirely negative. Sometimes a hell can set a stage for an unexpected heaven.

Show me how to find the light in the darkness.
Help me be a light to others.

I have the power to create heaven wherever I am.

Where to Start

Can the world be saved if you are not?
— A Course in Miracles

"Daddy, will you play with me?" was the last thing Bill wanted to hear from his five-year-old son. He had just come home from work tired, and all he wanted to do was relax and read the evening paper. Suddenly, a scheme dawned on him. He took a picture of the earth out of the newspaper, tore it up into a hundred little pieces, and gave them to his son. "Here is a jigsaw puzzle, Scottie," Dad explained. "Take it to your room and put it together. When you're done, Daddy will play with you." Scottie enthusiastically ran off with the game, and Bill sat back smug and proud that he had bought himself some time.

To Bill's surprise, Scottie returned in just a short time with the entire page intact. "How did you do that?" asked Bill incredulously. "I couldn't have done that puzzle in three times the time you took."

"Well," answered Scottie innocently, "the picture of the earth you gave me was too complicated; there were so many pieces, and they were all the same. So I turned over one of the pieces and on it was the picture of a man's hand. I turned over another piece, and there was the picture of a foot. It was easier to put one man together than the whole earth. Then I discovered that when the man came together, so did the earth!"

Often, our need to save the world is a distraction from the real work of saving ourselves. In many cases, a crusade against world pollution conveniently shifts our attention from the psychic pollution of our own fears and upsets. Of course, world peace and environmental healing are extremely important, but it's even more crucial that we come to terms with the issues that undermine our own inner peace. It's hypocritical to try to end international war if you're ravaged by internal conflict. Personal integrity is the foundation of world transformation. Fill your spirit, and your service will be infinitely more effective.

Help me remember that my primary responsibility is the healing of my own mind and heart.

My own peace is my first contribution to world peace.

The Choice for Divinity

The spirit is smothered as it were, by ignorance,
but so soon as it is destroyed,
light shines forth like the sun when released from clouds.
— Shankara

I knew a man named Jessie who was an idiot savant, the technical name for someone who is partially retarded and partially a genius (like the character played by Dustin Hoffman in *Rainman)*. One day while I was sitting with Jessie, he casually asked me, "What day were you born?" When I told him the date and year, he blurted out, "That was a Tuesday." Astonished, I threw some more dates at him, and with equal swiftness, he rattled off the precise days of the week on which the events occurred. A few minutes later, Jessie was led onto a little yellow school bus because he was unable to find his own way home. He could not dress himself, drive a car, or handle money—but he could calculate long-gone dates as rapidly as a computer.

In a way, each of us embodies the characteristics of an idiot savant. We are sometimes inept at making common-sense decisions, yet moments later the wisdom of the ages shines within us, bubbling forth when we need it.

There was a time when I developed a huge physical desire for a certain woman. Every time I saw her, I was amazed by how quickly my mind and values would go to jelly. Then she asked me for a counseling session, and the most wonderful miracle happened. The moment she began to speak, I felt a sense of clarity and truth roll through me, and I was able to move beyond my primal attraction and be very helpful to her. My bodily desire gave way to a sense of service, which opened up an important channel to assist her. She walked away with a gift, and I walked away amazed.

At any moment, we can play the fool or the genius. If we happen to revert to madness for a moment, let us have compassion for our humanity; we are bound to make mistakes. At any moment, we can claim our spiritual power and bring the highest light and service to any task at hand; our results will proceed naturally from our intentions.

Let me be all I can be; I allow You to live through all of me.

I am a spiritual being going through a human experience.

One More Shot

When things go wrong, don't go with them.
— Anonymous

Frustrated and disheartened, the budding author threw his manuscript into the wastebasket. His latest rejection felt like the last straw, and he decided that his search for a publisher was fruitless. That night, his wife noticed the discarded manuscript, and she picked it out of the trash and cleaned it off. She believed in her husband and his work, and she was not about to see him give up. In the morning, she placed it before him at the breakfast table and told him, "Norman, don't quit now. You have a lot to offer; somehow you will get published."

The writer was Norman Vincent Peale, and the manuscript was *The Power of Positive Thinking*, which went on to become one of the most successful inspirational classics in history. The book has changed millions of lives, offering hope and motivation to people all over the world.

Sometimes the universe tests us with rejection; life asks us if we are confident enough in ourselves and our creations to keep going in the face of obstacles. Rejection is not always a statement about the quality of our material; it may simply be a reflection of the critic's consciousness. While we must be open to feedback, we must also hold a faith that supersedes the opinions of those who do not agree with us. If you believe in something enough, you will not be put off by obstacles or setbacks. Like the little *Pac-Man* icons, every time you gobble up a put-down, you gain power; the very thing that tried to devour you becomes your fuel.

No one and nothing in the world has the power to put you down; the only time you fail is when you agree with rejection. If you feel like giving up, remember Norman Vincent Peale. You may need just one more try to put you over the edge. Act with the confidence of a master, and you will find strength that you never knew you had.

Help me remember my worth and the importance of my creations.

I believe in myself as God believes in me.

The Matchmaker

Resign your destiny to higher powers.
— William James

Susan's friend Tanya insisted that she would be a good match for Gerald, a wealthy and successful New York executive. After she initially resisted, Susan took Gerald's phone number and contacted him when she was in New York several months later. Although he was surprised by Susan's call, Gerald made a date to meet her after work that day. While waiting for him, Susan called Tanya and left a message on her answering machine, letting her know she was about to meet the man Tanya had referred her to. Susan and Gerald met, sparks of romance flew, and the couple spent a delightful evening together. When Susan returned to her hotel room, she found 11 messages from Tanya, who frantically pleaded, *"Call me immediately!"*

Susan called her back to hear Tanya confess, "My suggestion to call Gerald was a joke; he was just a famous guy I heard of; I don't know him at all." Upon further investigation, Susan learned that Tanya was a pathological liar. This, however, did not preclude Susan and Gerald's marriage a year later.

The Cosmic Coincidence Control Center gets people together in any number of ways. Sometimes important meetings occur consciously, and often they occur through means that seem haphazard, chaotic, or downright ridiculous. Nevertheless, there is a wise and meaningful plan behind the appearances.

Even when we do something foolish or unkind, we may be participating in a plan that ultimately serves everyone involved. In retrospect, even those who tried to hurt us ultimately contributed to our healing. If we are better off after an adventure, we can thank everyone involved, no matter what part they played in the drama.

Trust that good things can come out of an apparent mistake. The big picture reveals that love is always present.

Help me to trust that I am serving You always.
I pray to have faith in the divine plan.

My life is guided by intelligent action.

True Offering

What the Holy Spirit does with gifts you give each other,
to whom He offers them
and where and when is up to Him.
— A Course in Miracles

In Bali I attended a service at a stately ancient temple on a high cliff overlooking the ocean. During the service, a large basket of fresh fruit was placed on the altar as an offering to the gods. After the ceremony, a group of monkeys emerged from the adjacent forest, made a beeline for the altar, ravaged the fruit, and cast banana peels on the floor. As I observed this destruction, I felt somehow violated. I found an old temple-keeper and pointed out to him, "The monkeys are eating the offering to the gods!"

He smiled and calmly answered, "Yes, they do that every day," and went on with his sweeping. Then I understood the whole point of an offering: If the people made an offering to the gods, and the gods decided to give it to the monkeys, who was I to try to boss the gods? The chances were slim that the bodiless gods would just strike the altar with lightning and consume the fruit by vaporizing it into thin air. No, physical meals end up in physical bodies; even if the monkeys did not get to the fruit first, it would be eaten by bugs or some other critters. Why not feed God's creatures?

True offering requires that we release the gift after we offer it; otherwise we're tainting the gift with our need to control its destiny. Then it is not a gift at all; it is a guilt bargain.

Communication is an offering. When you tell someone your truth, you must release your expectation of what the other person should do with it. They may thank you profusely, love you forever, argue with you, or ignore you. It doesn't matter. Of course we hope the gift will be received with appreciation and thanks. But if it isn't, we must not dictate. We've done our part, and we must trust the universe to do the rest.

I offer my truth without attachment to results.
I offer all my gifts to You, trusting You to use them in the highest way possible.

I give and let go.
I trust God to use my gifts wisely.

Simple Gifts

My advice is: Go outside...enjoy nature and the sunshine...and try to recapture the happiness in yourself and in God. Think of all the beauty that is still left in you and around you and be happy.

— Anne Frank

In the hotel lounge, a talented young pianist introduced a percussionist who would join him on the next selection with some impromptu drumming. The guest took out two drum brushes and began beating them on a thick Portland telephone book. Following some fine jazz improvisations, the drummer took an extraordinary solo. Afterward, the duo received a rousing wave of cheers from the small but enthusiastic audience. The drummer reported, "Over the course of my career, I must have bought at least $30,000 worth of sophisticated electronic drum equipment, but I must say that nothing I have ever played electronically compares with brushes and a phone book." I had to agree. The fellow had taken an inert object and made it sing.

Increasing the complexity of life does not always deepen its quality. To the contrary, when we make our world complicated, we lose the truth that was obvious when we began.

In a 1950s survey, about 60 percent of the population described themselves as happy. When a similar poll was conducted in the mid-1990s, about 60 percent said they were relatively happy. During the 40 years between the two studies, technology advanced immeasurably. But people are not necessarily happier. That is because happiness comes from inside, not out.

I pray to find beauty in the world as You created it.
Help me to be satisfied with simple gifts.

My life is enough because I am enough.

How Big Is Your Wheelbarrow?

Your reasoning is excellent;
it's just that your premise is all wrong.
— Ashleigh Brilliant

When a laborer in a hardware factory asked the company president for a promotion, the CEO gruffly told him that he didn't have enough business savvy to be a manager. The laborer answered, "I'll bet you I can make it appear as if I'm bringing the company business, but I'll be robbing the organization blind without you knowing how. If I can pull this off, will you give me the promotion?" The president, a sportsman at heart, could not resist such a challenge.

The next day at 5:00 P.M., the laborer showed up at the cash register of the factory store with a wheelbarrow full of items for purchase. One by one, the checkout clerk rang up each article, which the laborer paid for and took home. The next day he did the same, and the next, and the next. The president, watchful for the laborer's deception, gave strict orders to be sure that every item in the wheelbarrow was paid for, and that the laborer was searched for concealed articles. After a few weeks, the company showed a loss in profits, and by the end of the quarter, it was in the red. Finally, the president called the laborer into his office and conceded the bet. "Now you must tell me how you've gotten away with your plot under such scrutiny. What have you been stealing?"

A sneaky grin grew on the laborer's face as he answered, "Wheelbarrows."

You can work profusely to make cosmetic changes in your life, but unless you address the foundation of your belief system, no real change will occur. Our consciousness is the wheelbarrow that carries all of our activities, and if our container is faulty, everything in it is liable to leak. Do you believe in a universe of abundance, love, and support, or do you think in terms of lack, loss, and separation? It will do you no good to make a change in the outer world unless you first change your consciousness. Change your mind about the nature of life, and accept the presence of God in it, and everything else will change automatically.

Be in my thoughts today.
With You at my center, all must go well.

I build my world on the reality of Spirit.

249

Tell Me Why

The only meaningful contribution the healer can make is to present an example of one whose direction has been changed for him, and who no longer believes in nightmares of any kind.

— A Course in Miracles

My friends Cheeah and Fairoh are a lovely couple who have dedicated themselves to peaceful living, and they make a real effort to walk their talk. As a result, they exude a quietness that is inspiring; to simply be in their presence is a delight. While giving a talk on creative writing at a community college, they opened the floor to questions. "Something about you is different," one student noted sincerely. "What is it?" The young woman had been touched by the gentleness of the couple's presence, which was a welcome contrast to the sharpness of many teachers she had known.

To walk with the peace of God in your heart is to transform the world by your presence. When love is your keynote, there is nothing in particular you need do; your gift is your being. Many people seek to change the world by getting everyone to join their religion or organization, use their product, agree with their philosophy, or replicate their experience. But real transformation does not come from manipulating people or events; it proceeds naturally from inner awakening and then living the light.

Often our attempts to create social change are a distraction from the real work of changing ourselves. Ram Dass observed angry bickering on the board of an organization dedicated to bringing health care to Third World countries. "What's the use of working for world peace," Ram Dass asked, "if you cannot even get along with the person working at your side?"

Jesus suggested that we be *in* the world, but not *of* it. Let us move through our daily activities with the peace of God in our hearts, and thus establish love on the planet.

Lord, make me an instrument of Your peace.
Help me give healing by my being.

I am the light of the world.
I live the truth I know.

Miracles, Nonetheless

Miracles arise from a mind that is ready for them.
— A Course in Miracles

There is a debate among Biblical scholars as to whether God actually parted the Red Sea for Moses and the Israelites, or if it just happened to be low tide when they arrived. Was the occurrence natural or supernatural?

It doesn't really matter—it was a miracle, nonetheless. If you showed up at the Red Sea with Pharaoh and his army in hot pursuit, and you were able to get across by the hand of God, low tide, or the Staten Island Ferry, you would be elated to escape, and you'd thank God for the gift of freedom, no matter how it manifested itself.

While many miracles occur through inexplicable, supernatural means, many come about through seemingly mundane "coincidences." It is not so important *how* miracles happen, but that they *do* happen. Meeting the right person at the right time for the right purpose is just as valuable as if God plunked the person in front of you. While the reasoning mind wants to analyze and question, the childlike heart accepts blessings as gifts. When we habitually doubt, we paint ourselves into a corner and miss out on the greatest joys of life.

A Course in Miracles suggests that each day be devoted to miracles. Keep your mind, heart, and eyes open for events that override the expectations of the fearful mind and demonstrate that we are loved. The more we look, the more we will find.

Help me to be miracle-minded. Give me a childlike heart, that I may recognize You in all.

I create miracles because I look for them.

Experience, Not Opinion

Stay at home in your mind. Don't recite the opinions of others.
— Ralph Waldo Emerson

Vinny was a fellow with whom I enjoyed working. He was always very kind to me, and he followed through on his business agreements. When I spoke to others about Vinny, I heard quite a different story. I was astounded by the number of people he had managed to alienate, all of whom complained about his lack of integrity. When one of Vinny's competitors invited me to break my association with Vinny and work with him instead, I had to dig into my soul to determine my truth. While it was obvious that Vinny had created poor business relationships with nearly everyone else, that was not my experience with him. For whatever reason, he had shown me only kindness and fairness. I realized I would be out of integrity if I jumped ship because other people had had a bad experience with him. I told the other fellow that I was satisfied working with Vinny, and until I had an experience to the contrary, I would stay with him.

No matter what experiences other people create, we have only our own to go by. Looking back, I see that it would have been cruel and unkind of me to leave Vinny because other people did not like him. My relationship with him was what it was, and it did not depend on what other people thought of him.

In the film *A Man for All Seasons*, Thomas More was an English nobleman who faced extreme pressure to side with a criminal king. More was brought before a kangaroo court of his peers and urged to sign an oath of allegiance "for the sake of camaraderie." More's response: "When you go to heaven for following your conscience, and I go to hell for not following mine, will you join me there 'for the sake of camaraderie'?"

Honor your friends by being true to your own experience.

Help me be confident in my own truth, and live it.

I create according to my own consciousness.

Ripcord Grandma

Try to keep your soul young and quivering right up to old age, and to imagine right up to the brink of death that life is only beginning.

— George Sand

When 98-year-old Hildegarde Ferrara's friend offered to pay for a skydive for Hildegarde's next birthday, she was joking. When Hildegarde answered, "I'd be delighted!" she was not. The offer was right in line with Hildegarde's life of endless adventure. At the age of 93, she had her naked body slathered with mud by the Mud Men of New Guinea, and was flattered that one Mud Man offered 500 pigs—10 times the going rate—for her hand in marriage. She has dined with headhunters, slept in King Ludwig's Neuschwanstein Castle, and savored termites and eggs for breakfast. Her flare for individuality erupted in 1917 when she was suspended from an all-girls Catholic high school for posing for a photo in which she brazenly exposed her shoulders. There are only a few places on earth Hildegarde has not visited, and she advises, "Go out and see the world before it's too late." Apparently for Hildegarde, it's never too late.

Hildegarde is not an exception to life, but an example of its possibilities. She has not fallen prey to the notion that age determines our abilities or activities; she chooses to live from joy, and life supports her in manifesting her dreams.

There is a Hildegarde in each of us. We may not desire to see all the world, but we do yearn to be all that we can be. What have you been holding off doing because you are too old, sick, poor, inexperienced, uneducated, unqualified, tired, or unhappy? What if none of these conditions had any power to stop you from being what you want to be? What if, at this very moment, you could take action to mobilize the visions you have had on the shelf? What would you do if I dared you to put down this book right now and take a step toward one of your hidden dreams?

Now is the moment you have been waiting for. Live it to the fullest.

I pray to live my life in brilliant joy. Turn up my flame.

I can do anything I choose. I am unlimited. I am free.

Again!

When your heart is in your dreams,
no request is too extreme.
— from the song, "When You Wish Upon a Star,"
by Ned Washington

The film *Wild Hearts Can't Be Broken* is based upon the true story of Sonora Webster, a girl whose deepest dream was to ride the diving horse in the famous act on the boardwalk in Atlantic City. Sonora found the man who trained the horses for the act and, in spite of rejection after rejection, she convinced him to teach her to mount a running horse. In her first attempt, Sonora fell flat on her face, leaving the trainer laughing.

"Again!" Sonora shouted, and again she fell, hurting herself. "Again!" she repeated, over and over, until after many painful falls, this courageous girl mastered the mount and eventually went on to become a very famous diver. Sonora lost her eyesight later in her career, and she continued to dive blind.

It is said that "the only time we fail is the last time we try." Errors or setbacks are nothing to be ashamed of. Keep trying, and eventually mastery will be yours.

Give me the strength not to give up. Help me walk past discouragement. I will live in You as You live in me.

I can do all things through God who strengthens me.

Turn on Everything

You can have it all.[10]

— Arnold Patent

After I built a sauna at my home, I began to have electrical outages. I discovered that when the sauna was on at the same time as the hot tub, the house's main breaker would trip off. I concluded that the power required by the sauna and spa was too much for the house's electrical capacity, so I made a rule that the sauna and hot tub could not be used at the same time. When my electrician friend Gil came by, I told him about the problem, and he instructed me, "Turn on everything in the house."

"Won't that blow the circuit?" I asked him.

"There's no way it should. Your electrical capacity is great enough to handle everything you have and more." I went around the property and turned on the sauna, spa, oven, washer, dryer, and other major appliances (inwardly praying that Gil knew what he was doing). As everything was humming along, Gil opened up the electrical box and called, "Aha! I think I see your problem." He called me over and showed me, "This screw is loose. When you have a loose screw, the circuit heats up and trips the breaker." He tightened the screw and told me, "This should solve the problem. Now you can run anything you want at any time."

I couldn't have asked for a better lesson on abundance. I had been thinking in terms of a limited universe: "There's just so much available, so I better start choosing between things that I want because there's not enough to go around." Gil, on the other hand, held a huge consciousness that there's enough supply for everything I needed. I was thinking small, and he was thinking big.

If you feel you must compromise what you want or need because there's not enough to go around, reconsider your belief system. The circuit may be much bigger than you thought, and your problem might not be that your supply is limited, but that one little screw is loose. Don't curse the source; tighten the screw.

Help me to remember that I live in a universe of abundant supply.

I can have everything I need to be happy.

The Choice for Happiness

Everyone is about as happy as
they make up their mind to be.
— Abraham Lincoln

Connie's mother-in-law was a very unhappy person. Among her many complaints, she griped that she hadn't been on a vacation in years. So Connie and her husband decided to give Mrs. Fraser a luxurious Caribbean cruise. "Perhaps this will give her a lift and let her know that she is loved!" the couple hoped. After Mrs. Fraser received the notice of the gift in the mail, the couple was surprised to receive a phone call from her turning down their offer. The present did not include a flight to Miami, where the cruise originated, and Mrs. Fraser did not want to have to pay the fare from South Carolina.

If someone is intent on being unhappy, you cannot make them happy. A negative mind will seize on any excuse to find fault; it will find the 1/50th of the glass that is empty, overlooking the other 49 parts.

It is not within your power to choose happiness for another person, nor is it your right or purpose. If you could, you would violate their free will; perhaps they chose this situation to help them reconsider how they are living, and ultimately choose a more rewarding path. You cannot afford to make your happiness dependent on another's. You can love, bless, nurture, suggest, support, give, and honor, but in the long run the only way the other person will be happy is if they choose to do so.

If you offer love or gifts to someone, and they are not received in the spirit of love, do not take it personally. The rejection is a statement of the person's pain, not your inadequacy. If you have tried for a long time to make certain people happy and have not succeeded, then just give love. Assume that they are where they need to be for a reason, and someday they will make another choice. In the meantime, be happy yourself.

I place my loved ones in Your care. I pray for their happiness, and I release them to choose.

I give happiness by nurturing peace within my own heart.

The Diet That Always Works

The one thing we can never get enough of is love.
And the one thing we never give enough is love.
— Henry Miller

I heard about a woman who is performing miracles with anorexic and bulimic patients. She takes emaciated 50-pound women out of the hospital and brings them to her home, where she holds them, cradles them, looks into their tired eyes, and tells them, *"I love you...I want you to live...I believe in you."* She has had a remarkable success rate, far beyond any medical or psychotherapeutic modality. She has cut past all intellectual models and belief systems, and has gone to the core of our existence: the giving and receiving of love.

A Course in Miracles tells us that every act we do is either an expression of love or a call for it. Love is the only diet, therapy, or activity that always works. When we cut past all our facades, many of our actions stem from our need to know we are lovable. To love ourselves and each other as we are, is to become utterly Godlike.

The next time people become upset with you, give them love. And the next time you lose your peace, give yourself love. We are here to love; nothing else will satisfy us.

I pray to love as You love.
Show me how to live from my heart.

I live to love, and I love to live.

Destiny by Choice

Chance plays no part in God's plan.
— A Course in Miracles

In the film *Mr. Destiny*, James Belushi plays a man who wishes that his life were otherwise. For many years, Larry agonizes over striking out in a crucial situation while playing high school baseball under observation by major league scouts. He knows that if he had gotten a hit, he would have landed a professional baseball contract, generated a huge income, and married a woman as enticing as his boss's wife. Then Larry meets a shaman who shows him what his life would have been like if he had taken the glamour road. While Larry is initially in bliss, the demands placed upon a rich and famous person soon catch up with him, and he realizes that he created a hell, not a heaven. Finally, he prays to return to his regular life, which, although mediocre, is joyful for him. The caption on the movie poster asks, *"Would you trade everything you have for everything you want?"*

While it may be tempting to fantasize about how it all might have been different if a key decision from your past had turned out another way, trust that it actually turned out in your best interests. On a deep level, our soul knows what will best serve our destiny, and the situations we manifest are in harmony with where we need to be for a particular purpose. Where else could you be but where you are, and who else could you be but who you are?

Don't waste a moment regretting past mistakes or wishing it were otherwise. Ask yourself how you would like it to be now, and invest your energy in building the life you believe in. Then your life will reflect your choices, not your fears.

Help me trust that the decisions
You make through and around me are perfect.

I am in my right place on my right path.
I cannot lose because God is with me.

What a Job Is Worth

Get happiness out of your work,
or you may never know what happiness is.
— Elbert Hubbard

In a classic Woody Allen scene in the movie *What's New, Pussycat?* Woody meets a friend on a Paris street and tells him he has just gotten a new job helping the lovely dancers of the Folies Bergère to get dressed before their performances. "How much is the pay?" asks his friend.

"Twenty *sous* per week," answers Allen.

"Twenty *sous* per week? That's next to nothing!" the friend chides him.

"I know," Woody answers. "But it was all I could afford."

You know you are in your right job when you have a sneaky feeling you should be paying someone for the opportunity to do it. While this does not mean you need to pay to do it (indeed, the universe will pay you to be in your right place), it points to the truth that right livelihood blesses the giver of a service as much as the receiver.

If you're searching for your right livelihood or evaluating your current work in light of your vision, a good question to ask is, "What would I be doing even if I weren't getting paid for it?" What turns you on so much that you would do it for sheer delight? That is the arrow to follow toward work that will bring you joy as well as prosperity.

Prosperity is not a level of income; it is a consciousness. If you are happy, productive, and giving service in a profession, you are living in the abundance consciousness. This attitude will move you to produce quality work and draw to you plentiful good in the form of money or other material support. When you do what you do not love, you affirm that the universe cannot provide you with joyful livelihood, and that compromise is required of a divine being. The universe will also mirror this attitude if you hold it.

I receive as much from writing and teaching as do the readers or students. Even if no one ever reads what I write, it would still be entirely worth writing it. Work from your heart, and the universe will work for you.

Help me to serve in a way that brings me joy,
as well as others.

The universe supports me
as I follow my bliss.

Bought the T-Shirt

To see what few have seen,
you must go where few have gone.

— Buddha

When opera star Beverly Sills retired from the stage to become a director, she was constantly asked, "How could you give up such a glorious and lucrative career?" Finally, Beverly had a little gold pendant made displaying the letters *"I.A.D.T."* When someone at a party would question Beverly about leaving the stage, she would hold up the pendant and recite, *"I already did that."*

Just because something has worked for a long time, that does not mean you must do it forever. If you still feel enlivened and emotionally rewarded in it, carry on. But if the juice is gone, you must ask yourself where your heart really calls you, and move in a new direction.

To keep rubber-stamping an old activity is not a career; it is hiding. Some writers, musicians, or artists produce a dearth of works that are but variations on an old formula or theme. The products sell, but on the inside, these souls are dying artistically. What is required is not more of the same, but a leap of faith to do something new and different.

If you can say, *"Been there, done that, and bought the T-shirt,"* it's time to venture onward. To live is to explore, reach out, and risk. The only real security lies in adventure.

Give me the courage to try something new.
I want each day to be more alive than the last.

I launch into uncharted territory,
trusting that Spirit is guiding me.

The Whole Truth

The truth shall set you free.

— Jesus Christ

A married man is interested in me," Marilyn told me. "But I don't feel attracted to him."

"What did you tell him?" I asked.

"I told him that I do not date married men."

When I heard Marilyn's response, something did not sit well with me. "You did not tell him the whole truth," I ventured.

"What do you mean?"

"The bottom line is that you are not interested in a relationship with this man. The fact that he is married is secondary. What would you do if he got divorced, showed up at your door with flowers, and announced, 'Here I am—not married anymore'?"

"I guess I would tell him I was not interested in creating a relationship with him."

"That's the other half of the truth you need to tell now."

Life is a series of lessons in discovering the truth and living it. Whenever we hedge, compromise, withhold, deny, or camouflage what is really happening, sooner or later we will have to retrace our steps to the point where we diverted from the whole truth, and tell it. Speak up now, and avoid the rush later.

Take a moment to consider any areas of your life in which you have not told the whole truth. This is not to make you guilty, but to liberate you. Whenever we set aside what is happening and pretend, our "stash" robs our energy from being fully present. Consider what you would say if you had the courage to put your cards on the table. Although the prospect may be challenging, it is a lot less work than carrying a lie and then having to come back and say what you wanted to say in the first place.

Help me be aware of the truth and have the courage to live it.

The truth is my strength and my friend.

261

Holy Loafing

To do great work a man must be very idle as well as very industrious.

— Samuel Butler

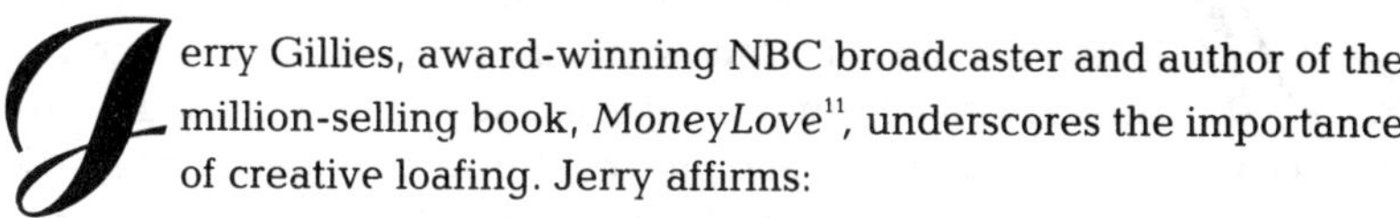

Jerry Gillies, award-winning NBC broadcaster and author of the million-selling book, *MoneyLove*[11], underscores the importance of creative loafing. Jerry affirms:

> *Self-reflection is one of the most productive things you can do with your creative imagination...When I was the director of the Biofeedback Institute, I demonstrated to some of the top executives of major corporations that by slowing down they'd be able to tap into deeper levels of their subconscious and come up with more valuable ideas. One publishing executive started taking Wednesdays off to relax and meditate. He reported back to me that he had gotten much more work accomplished in the remaining four days than he had ever gotten done in five!*

Rest, relaxation, play, imagination, and daydreaming are as vital to the creative process as hard work. A good graphic or interior designer will attest that the white space on a page or open areas of a room are as important as the words or objects that border the space. While *doing* is important, so is *being*; a balance of the two is the secret of success.

The next time you feel overwhelmed, tired, jammed, or uncreative, stop and refresh your spirit. Renew yourself by doing something entirely unrelated to your work. Go to a movie, dance, walk in nature, listen to music, or immerse yourself in your favorite hobby. During your recreation time, you may receive important insights, and when you return, you will be far ahead of where you would have been if you worked without ceasing.

Help me remember to take care of my heart.
Teach me how to play, that I may serve You better.

I love myself enough to rest, play, and renew.

Just Keep Driving

The dogs bark, and the caravan moves on.

— Persian maxim

As I was driving around a bend on a country road, a huge dog jumped at the car window and started barking vehemently. After my initial surprise and a moment of fear, I took a breath and realized I was entirely safe and protected. The dog stayed quite close to the car for a while, but I just kept driving calmly. Soon he could not keep up with the car, and he retired from his chase.

I saw our encounter as a metaphor for the way troubles jump at us in life. Suddenly, unexpected beasts seem to lurch at us from out of nowhere, and we may be tempted to become afraid and run or counter-attack. The answer, however, is usually very simple: just keep driving. Who you are (a spiritual being) and where you live (deep within yourself) is entirely protected from any passing event. We fuel the upsets of life by getting into the ring and battling them. If you just keep moving toward your chosen destiny, any worldly difficulty will eventually drop away. You are bigger than anything that bothers you.

I love the story in the film *Tucker: The Man and his Dream*. In 1947 Preston Tucker developed an automobile that was many years ahead of its time, with a range of features that have since become standard equipment. Because his invention posed a threat to other auto manufacturers, he was squashed and falsely accused of crimes. As his trial was being conducted, Tucker doodled. Eventually, Tucker was acquitted, and he showed his sketches to his wife—schematic plans for a new kind of refrigerator with the potential to revolutionize the industry. Tucker wasted none of his precious time. Why bother with a trial when you can be creating things that will change the world?

Pay as little attention as possible to your troubles, and as much attention as possible to your dreams. You will receive more of whatever you invest your energy in. You are bigger than any dogs that bark as you pass.

I pray to keep my vision high.
Help me to be true to my dreams.

Steadfast in truth,
I march on to my destiny.

Gold In, Gold Out

All limitations are self-imposed.
— Oliver Wendell Holmes

Clad in coveralls and galoshes, 61-year-old Cliff Young, a farmer from Australia's outback, seemed an anomaly in the grueling 400-kilometer marathon. As the younger athletes mentally psyched themselves to run 18 hours a day and sleep 6 hours a night, they wondered if old Cliff would survive the first day. But then an amazing event occurred. A full day-and-a-half before the lead runners were expected to finish, a 61-year-old foot in rubber galoshes crossed the finish line. Cliff Young completed the race in record-breaking time, 36 hours before men 40 years his junior. No one, you see, had told Cliff that he was supposed to sleep. While the younger men were snoozing, Cliff Young was cruising.

Ignorance is bliss when the thing we are ignorant of is limitation. Our mind establishes the reality in which we will live, as well as our subsequent physical experience. We live as large as we think.

The next year of the race, several runners broke Cliff Young's record. They adopted his method of running without sleep and gave up their belief system that one had to sleep six hours a night to win the race.

When you make up your mind, you make up your life. Be sure that the building blocks of your belief system are the ones you want to be reflected in your experience. In the computer world, the term "G.I.G.O." means *Garbage In, Garbage Out*. If you program a computer with faulty information, you will receive faulty results. We may also affirm, *"Gold In, Gold Out."* Feed your mind golden ideas, and your life will be golden.

I accept only those ideas that lead me to freedom.

I create the life I choose with my sacred thoughts.

Rock Formations

Do not return evil for evil, but return evil with good.
— Jesus Christ

The driveway to a retreat center I visit in Hawaii is meticulously landscaped with a garden in which a group of large rocks spell out the word *Aloha,* the Hawaiian greeting of love. One day as I entered the grounds, I was surprised to see that some local vandals had reconfigured the rocks to spell "*Fags,*" as a slur against several gay men who manage the resort. When I pointed this out to one of the managers, he told me, "Some of the locals do that every couple of months." The next day, the rocks were beautifully rearranged into *Aloha* again.

This episode symbolizes how we can deal with negativity when it comes our way. We may take the time and care to make a statement of love and kindness, and then someone may take our gift and try to use it to hurt us. Then we have a choice: We can either retaliate and try to hurt them, or we can reaffirm our stand of kindness. The managers chose not to fight the vandals, but to simply rearrange the rocks with love.

Every day, we have many opportunities to rearrange our rocks and decide what message we wish to offer. Even if someone keeps perverting our message, we can keep affirming the truth we wish to establish. Aloha is always more powerful than prejudice. When all else falls away, it is the aloha we will remember.

Give me the strength to answer evil with love.

I found my actions on the power of love.

Abundant Universe

There is room at the top for everyone.
— Anonymous

I remember the Saturday afternoon long ago when the ticket-taker at a movie theater handed me a petition to sign against the establishment of cable television. At that time, cable was just an idea, and movie owners feared that if people were able to watch movies at home, they would lose interest in attending the theater. Now cable has become almost as common as telephone, and both theaters and cable (with hundreds of available channels) are booming. In addition, home video is a mega-business, and Pay-Per-View satellite screening is a thriving enterprise. Contrary to the early sense of threat that theater owners felt, cable did not detract from movie business, but enhanced it. The two forms of media were not in competition at all; ultimately, they empowered one another.

The notion of competition is fear based and has little value in a creative world. There is room in the world for many good ideas. The element that determines your success in a venture is not what the person around the corner is doing, but what *you* are doing. Invest your work with integrity, caring, creativity, and service, and you are sure to succeed.

Eliminate from your mind the notion that someone else can take away your good. You are the source of your life and experience, and everything that comes to you or goes from you is a result of your consciousness. It is quite literally possible for everyone on the planet to succeed gloriously at whatever their heart calls them to do.

I pray to think with You, God. Help me remember that
I create my life with my consciousness,
and support me to live from truth.

I can have it all because I am it all.

Letters from God

Dreams are like letters from God.
Isn't it time you answered your mail?

— Marie Louise von Franz

Dreams carry some of the most important messages of our lives. When we sleep at night, the static of the conscious mind is stilled, and Spirit is able to speak to us through symbols, imparting what we are unable to access during our daily activities. An entire world of blessing is available to us in our dreams.

There are at least four levels and types of dreams, all of which offer us healing. Some dreams work out unresolved issues from our day. If you underwent a traumatic situation such as an argument or near-miss auto accident, and you did not take time to process it, your subconscious will perform that unraveling for you. Other dreams are prophetic; Universal Mind is giving you a vision of a situation that will or could happen if you stay on your current course. Other dreams allow us to make contact with people we love or need to meet on the inner plane. If there is someone in your life who has passed on, or from whom you have been separated physically, the world of spirit can give you easy access to communicate with them even more deeply than if you had met them physically. Other dreams are inspirational; directly or through a messenger, God brings you love, guidance, and confidence. If you wake up with a feeling of deep peace in your heart, you have been touched by Spirit on the inner plane.

Before going to sleep, prepare yourself to receive the richest gifts in your dream world. Do not eat a heavy meal, watch negative television shows, argue, or stir up your thinking mind with office work. Instead. read uplifting material, listen to gentle music, or meditate before retiring. As you close your eyes, ask the Holy Spirit and your guides to come to you during your sleep time and bless you with rest, healing, and any information or visions that will help you spiritually. Thank God for your day and the night to come. Happy dreams!

Father, be with me tonight.
Speak to me through my visions.

I am open and receptive to
God's guidance and healing.

Enough Is Better

Who is a happy man? He who is content with his lot.
— The Talmud

My friend Matt owns a small but successful vegetarian restaurant in Maui. Although *The Vegan* is small and inexpensively decorated, the humble eatery has earned a vast reputation for its quality food prepared with love. When I asked Matt if he had ever thought of expanding, he told me, "A famous movie star who loves my cooking offered to set me up in Hollywood with mega-bucks backing; he was sure this could become the next trendy L.A. restaurant. I told him, 'No thanks, I like it here. I know my customers, I step outside to enjoy the sunset, and my kids do their homework here and play with their friends next door. I make enough to get by; I have no need to move.'"

Matt reminded me that more is not always better. Sometimes enough is better.

In our materialistic society, many of us labor under the illusion that if we only had more stuff, we would be happier. But sometimes more stuff would only make us more unhappy. If you are not happy with what you have, more stuff is probably not going to fulfill you. The outer world can do no more for you than you are willing to do for yourself through your own attitude.

Since becoming a homeowner, I have learned a lot about stuff. Buying something is not the end of getting it—it is the beginning. If you have something, you have to take care of it, keep it clean, use it, protect it, fix it, and replace it. To own a car, house, or any item is to enter into a committed relationship. If you expect it to be there for you, you have to be there for it. If you are willing to make the commitment, dive in. If not, you may choose to just be happy with what you have.

If it is right for your material world to expand, the universe will arrange it joyfully. If not, you may discover that the sunset is just as beautiful from your backyard as it would be from Hollywood.

Help me to live lightly, use wisely, and remember that spirit is more important than matter.

I have enough because I am enough.

Breathe

In the name of God, stop a moment, close your work, look around you.

— Leo Tolstoy

I placed my baby parrot on my desk while I typed, and when I looked over at her I beheld a sight that moved me deeply. I had set her tiny body on a greeting card envelope with a silver foil on the inside of the exposed rear flap. On the foil I could see the condensation from her wispy breath, forming and dissolving as she inhaled and exhaled. The sight touched me so deeply that I stopped and uttered a prayer of thanks.

The infant bird's breath reminded me that the breath of God moves through all creation. Every living creature draws life from the universe and gives it back. Metaphysically, breath symbolizes the spirit that animates every creature, from the tiniest insect to the great whales to the whole of the cosmos.

Right now, take a few deep breaths. With each inhalation, draw into yourself the wealth of love, and with each outbreath, radiate your life-force back to the universe.

If you feel upset or uptight, stop and breathe deeply. Allow the breath to purify you.

Today, let your breath remind you that you are loved and that you have a purpose. Receive all that life has to offer, and return it magnified.

I accept Your love in the form of inspiration, and give it to the world through my creations.

God lives and breathes through me.
I am very holy.

Enjoy the Journey

There must be more to life than increasing its speed.

— Gandhi

Years ago, a profound commercial depicted a young black boy in a city ghetto. The now-famous caption reminded viewers, *"A mind is a terrible thing to waste."* After dealing with my own mind for many years, I would offer this advice: *"A mind is a terrible thing to race."*

The purpose of the mind is to discover and reflect the truth; it is a sacred tool given to illuminate and expand divine wisdom. If we keep our mind cluttered or racing, we miss the beauty that the mind was intended to reveal.

Stephen Backart poetically described the way many of us have attempted to get things done: *"He flung himself upon his horse and ran madly off in all directions."* What is the use of running in any direction unless the journey is in harmony with the destination? I have fantasized about producing a bumper sticker proclaiming, *"Going nowhere faster will not get you somewhere."*

One day after I had moved to Hawaii, I found myself rushing to get to the bank before it closed. Driving along a mountain road, I glanced to my left, where I beheld the entire central isthmus of the island, green with sugar cane and bounded by azure oceans on two sides and a verdant mountain range on the other. An inner voice asked, *"Is it really worth missing this for the bank?"* No, it wasn't worth missing this for *anything*. One of the most majestic sights on the planet was before me. I could have it all, if I was but willing to breathe long enough to take it in.

The beauty of life is right where you are. Remember to enjoy the journey.

Help me to be alive to this moment and keep peace in my heart.

I walk in balance, ever aware of the presence of love.

My Other Whole

True friendship can occur only among equals.
— Plato

While waiting to be seated at a restaurant, I overheard a customer tell the maître d', "My other half will be here in just a minute." It seems to me that we diminish ourselves by defining ourselves as "a half" when we are in relationship. Perhaps that is why so many of us have had difficulty maintaining our whole self in a relationship; how can we remember who we are when we trade our wholeness for halfness?

Relationships are multiplicative, not additive. If you believe that you are less than whole and you look for someone else to make you whole, you will only lose, for your premise is faulty. One-half times one-half makes one-quarter, and you end up being even less than when you started. If you bring yourself as a whole person to another whole person, one times one is still one, and you both remain whole as individuals and as a couple.

Most popular songs in our culture keep us small and needy. Nearly every "love" song bemoans our loneliness, wrings our hands over lost love, or celebrates finding the person who finally completes us. Rarely do we hear about whole persons who join with other whole persons to celebrate the riches we already own.

Good relationships are built on two individuals walking side by side to the light. The other person is not the object of our happiness, but a partner in adventure. We do not need these other people, but we can certainly enjoy them. They do not have the power to give or take away our good, but they can add depth, color, beauty, reward, and delight to our life. We love them not because they rescue us from the abomination we are, but because they remind us of how beautiful we are. In such a golden consciousness, it would constitute blasphemy to define either of us as half, and sacred to acknowledge both of us as reflections of a complete God.

Help me to remember and honor my wholeness and that of my partner.

True love makes me stronger as I share it.

Real Authority

You have no power except what is given you by my heavenly Father.
— Jesus Christ, to Pontius Pilate

I had a landlord in whose presence I felt intimidated. Whenever we interacted, I felt small, defensive, and apologetic. My roommate observed, "Whenever you talk to Martin, you become a little boy; you give your power away to him." Stunned by this accurate assessment, I began to consciously hold my peace and power in Martin's presence. Eventually, I even enjoyed him.

We hurt ourselves when we ascribe undue power to another human being. While landlords, police officers, doctors, and attorneys have the authority of their roles, they do not have authority over your spirit. Although we occupy worldly positions, we are all equal spiritually.

The words *authority* and *authentic* are derived from the same root word. When you are authentic, you proceed from the deepest place of empowerment within you, and your words and actions bear the most effective results. When you do not act authentically, you are not effective because you are moving from a place of fear or emptiness.

The Bible tells us that the people respected Jesus because "he spoke with authority." When we tap into our divinity, the true author, God, authorizes us to be authentic and, thus, we bear the highest and only authority.

Let me not hide my true power under a cloak of smallness or unworthiness.

Everyone is my equal in divine strength.

Lighten Up

Life is too important to be taken seriously.

— Oscar Wilde

The crowd was packed into the huge lecture hall, eagerly awaiting the arrival of the renowned guru, Swami Satchidananda[13]. His saffron-robed devotees and the secular onlookers maintained a sense of reverence and expectancy. Suddenly, the rear door of the auditorium opened, and there appeared the dark-skinned sage with sparkling eyes and a long white beard. All rose, his disciples bowed, and the yogi was ushered to his plush chair onstage, surrounded by many flowers. The swami took his place, folded his legs into lotus position, closed his eyes, and meditated for a few minutes. Then he opened his eyes and began to speak the long-awaited pearls of wisdom. "This microphone looks like a big cigar in my mouth!" he uttered, and the audience broke into peels of laughter.

The surest signs of enlightenment are joy and laughter. While many of us have approached the spiritual path with great sobriety, it is more accurately a path of play and celebration.

A Course in Miracles tells us that "the separation occurred when the son of God [all of us] forgot to laugh." If you cannot laugh about something, you are not healed with that experience. Psychologists note that one of the clearest symptoms of psychosis is an absence of a sense of humor; when we lose our ability to laugh, we go a little crazy.

Cultivate laughter as a way of life. To see the humor in a situation is to find a divine viewing point. Laugh often and deeply; it's the best therapy.

Help me to keep my sense of humor;
let me remember that nothing is too important.

I laugh at life and at myself. I lighten my life with celebration and play.

Hot and Cold

A man's heart deviseth the way,
but the Lord directeth his steps.
— Proverbs 41:9

Do you remember the children's game of "Hot and Cold?" In the game, a player would step out of a room while others hid an object. Then the player returned and tried to find the hidden item. As he or she searched, the others would call out, *"Getting warmer"* when the seeker approached the object, and *"Getting colder"* when the seeker moved away from it, until the object was found.

In the game of life, joy and enthusiasm are the voice of Spirit letting you know that you are "getting warmer." Boredom and fatigue are the universe's clues that you are "getting colder." We are led to our good by the energy of delight.

If you are accustomed to relying only on your mind to make decisions, you will become confused and bewildered. The mind is but one component of successful decision making. The other is the heart. One can go only so far using the mind as a tool; eventually the heart must be honored as a source of wisdom and insight.

The next time you have to make a decision, ask yourself how you feel about any given alternative. If the direction warms, delights, stimulates, or interests you, it is a sign to step toward it. If the possibility leaves you cold or flat, do not pursue it. The universe will warm or cool you as you move toward, or away from, your objective. Trust the voice of Spirit; it will speak if you will listen.

Thank You for speaking to me through the voice of joy.

The loving voice of God
guides me to my Good.

274

Supermarket Saints

We must not, in trying to think about how we can make a big difference, ignore the small daily differences we can make which, over time, add up to big differences that we often cannot foresee.

— Marion Wright Edelman

Down the road from my house lives a saint. He does not lecture, issue cosmic prophecies, or solicit disciples. He dons not a white robe, but a green, hooded sweatshirt. This master gives blessings not from a pulpit, but from a wheelchair. Paralyzed after a stroke, Raymond sits at the end of his driveway, grinning and waving to every car that passes. He can move only his arm, and he uses it to bless. His daily communion begins when the school buses pass in the morning, and concludes when the buses take the children home in the afternoon. All the kids know Raymond and wave back.

When I pass Raymond, I am usually on my way to an appointment, and my mind is immersed in the busy-ness of life. When I see him, I feel happy; he reminds me that the real business of life is love. It has occurred to me that this man is making a paramount contribution to planetary healing. In his own simple way, he is transforming the world by bringing joy to everyone who passes before him. What greater ministry could one have?

Our spiritual life is founded on the spirit in which we act. When evaluating any activity, check in with your heart. How much peace or reward do you feel? Do you carry the spirit of joy through your day? Do you greet the security guard with respect and appreciation? Can you offer a gentle touch to the child who bumps into you in the supermarket? Can you laugh in the face of a business delay? In the end, you will count your good based on the depth of love you generated, not on the amount of time you spent in the office. In the movie *Ghost,* as Patrick Swayze's character is about to go into the light at the end of his life, he exclaims, *"It's amazing—you take all the love with you."*

I shall not wait for the afterlife to find heaven.
I pray to bring the richest spirit to all that I do.

I use every moment to magnify love.

Ask for the Rolls

It is not more difficult to create a castle than a button. Most of you have more buttons than castles, however, because they're easier to expect.

— Abraham[14]

God was giving a tour of heaven to a man who had passed on. After observing various rooms, the two passed a closed door. "What's in that room?" asked the man.

"It would make you very sad to see what is in that room," answered God.

"I want to see it anyway," insisted the man.

God opened the door to reveal a chamber of vast treasures. Luxurious jewels, sophisticated electronic toys, and sports cars filled the floor. "Wow!" exclaimed the man, "what a cache! Why would this make me sad?"

"These are the gifts I offer people," God explained, "but if they are not willing to accept them, I must take them back and keep them here."

"That's incredible!" exclaimed the man. "Isn't that a Rolls Royce over there?" He went to sit in the Rolls, and he was astounded to find his name on it. "This was the car I always wanted!" the man confessed."Every night I prayed to you for a car—how come I never got this one?"

"Because you prayed for a Ford," God answered.

Instead of asking for what he really wanted, the man asked for what he thought he could get, and so he manifested not according to his possibilities, but according to his expectations. The universe is happy to fulfill our grandest visions, but we must have the confidence to ask for them. Do not be shy when praying to God or communicating to people. Aim high, and you may be surprised by how the universe responds.

Abundant Universe, I claim my kingdom. Take from me any unworthiness, and replace it with the knowledge of my true deservingness.

I open to receive all the good that life has to offer me. I ask for and accept the best in every situation.

When Your Heart Is Strong

Throw your heart over the fence and the rest will follow.
— Norman Vincent Peale

On the threshold of recording her blockbuster album *Unforgettable*, Natalie Cole wrestled with her soul. The notion of electronically marrying segments of her dad's famous 1951 song with her voice in response was a bold and unprecedented experiment in the music industry. But in spite of potential criticism, there was something inside Natalie that kept pushing her to go ahead with the project. Subsequently, the recording became a top-selling album, and the singer won numerous Grammy awards for it.

Natalie looked back and summarized the process: *"When your heart is really strong about something, there comes a point at which you just close your eyes and go for it."*

All the figuring, planning, and reasoning in the world will do you no good unless you are willing to follow your instincts. All healing occurs outside the safety zone. Sometimes all you have to work with is a compelling urge, and sometimes that is enough. It is said that "the heart has reasons that reason knows not of."

Practice acting on your intuition. Faith is like a muscle—the more you use it, the stronger it becomes, and the greater your capacity to use it. If a particular venture keeps knocking at the door of your consciousness, it is likely that this is your direction. Ask yourself, "Can I *not* do it?" If you cannot *not* do it, your path is obvious.

Speak to me through my heart.
Compel me to do the will of love.

Empowered by joy, I follow my path with courage and confidence.

Greater Than Starfish

Behold the lilies of the field. They do not toil and neither do they spin. Yet even Solomon in all his glory was not arrayed like one of these. If God cares for the grass, which is here one day and cast into the fire the next, how much more shall He care for you, His beloved child?

— Jesus Christ

In the Virgin Islands, I saw a lizard being chased by a cat who swiped off its tail. A local fellow laughed and told me, "In a short time, the tail will grow again." The regenerative power of nature is miraculous. If an earthworm is cut in half, it will regrow itself to completion. If a starfish loses a limb, it will be renewed.

If such rudimentary creatures as worms and starfish can regenerate lost body parts, so can we. Surely we are at least as evolved as an earthworm!

I know a man who regrew a part of his thumb after losing a section in a construction accident. I met a woman who, after having a lung removed, regenerated it. These people are not exceptions to the laws of nature; they are reminders of our potential.

Let us open our minds to manifest the blueprint of our perfection. Created in the image and likeness of an all-powerful God, we have the capacity to be whole at all times.

Help me manifest the magnificence with which You created me.

My birthright is perfect wholeness. I claim my destiny to live in strength and health.

Agree on What?

Let not littleness lead God's Son into temptation.
— A Course in Miracles

I saw a television news story about a priest who had covertly molested many children in his Catholic elementary school. When he was reported after many years, scores of children came forth to corroborate his crimes. The priest was deposed and became the object of considerable legal motions. In viewing a meeting of an ad hoc group of the now-grown adults who had been abused, I felt disturbed by the mob energy generated. These people were severely angry, and the primary intention of the group was to punish the priest. While they were performing a great service to get him out of his position so that he could do no further damage, I observed a cry for vengeance that debilitated those who voiced it. Their gathering reinforced the message, "We are victims, and we want blood."

It occurred to me that the members of this group would help themselves most by dealing with their pain and rage. What they needed was not retribution, but to become free of the wrath they were embroiled in. By focusing on punishing their perpetrator, they were not growing beyond their experience, but merely reinforcing it.

We must be careful about what we get together to agree on. Agreement is powerful, and it can be misused. Jesus said, "Wherever two or more are gathered in my name, there am I," indicating that a shared acceptance of Spirit brings healing. It may also be said that wherever two or more are gathered in the name of fear, only more darkness ensues.

My teacher Hilda explained that the worst use of a marriage or friendship is to agree on shared victimhood. When we band together to define ourselves as small, we become only smaller. When we join to affirm our power to love and heal, we become infinitely powerful. Take care to agree that you are great and not wounded.

Help me to align with those who empower me to be great in strength and not small in weakness.

I agree with those who affirm my wholeness and perfection.

Embrace Yourself

I dreamed I had a child, and even in the dream I saw that it was my life, and it was an idiot, and I ran away. But it always crept into my lap again, clutched at my clothes. Until I thought, if I could kiss it, whatever in it was my own, perhaps I could sleep. And I bent over the broken face, and it was horrible...but I kissed it. I think that one must finally take one's life into one's arms.

— from *After the Fall,* by Arthur Miller

At a conference, I met a psychotherapist named Leonard who told me, "I try to get my patients to accept and appreciate all of their feelings. I teach them that there is no such thing as a bad feeling. Anger, fear, and sadness all bring us valuable opportunities to awaken and grow. We must embrace all that we are and experience."

Later, I overheard another man telling someone about Leonard's work: "I heard a therapist this morning who says we should tolerate ourselves."

But Leonard hadn't said anything about *tolerating* ourselves. He suggested that we *celebrate* ourselves. In that distinction lies the entire key to our healing. To tolerate is to put up with something that is obnoxious or abhorrent, and hope that it goes away soon. To celebrate is to find the beauty, honor it, expand it, and live in the glory of a precious treasure.

True healing begins with self-acceptance. We must embrace ourselves, rejoice in what we are, and magnify it to the highest degree.

Help me see myself through Your eyes.
Bestow upon me the vision of my own perfection,
that I may honor it.

I am a miracle of love.
I am perfect as God created me.

Life and Details

You can't do anything about the length of your life,
but you can do something about its width and depth.

— Evan Esar

In an airport, I saw a man wearing a baseball cap and a sweatshirt proclaiming, *"Baseball is Life—Everything Else is Details."*

Each of us chooses what we will value as important, and everything else becomes details. The question is not, "Will I make something important?" It is *"What have I made important?"*

Jesus explained, "A man cannot serve two masters; he will love the one and hate the other, or he will honor one and despise the other." The law of consciousness is that we will live in the world ruled by whatever we make important.

Because we are spiritual beings, the only world that will ever fulfill us is the realm of spirit. On an airplane, I sat next to a well-respected cardiologist who confessed, "I have all manner of material wealth—several luxurious homes, a Porsche, and a Ferrari. One day my 11-year-old son tearfully told me, 'Dad, I don't know you. I don't see you. When will you have time for me?' That moment I realized that I had placed my values in all the wrong places. Now I spend quality time with my son, and that has made all the difference."

Found your life on that which truly gives life, and leave the details to the universe.

Help me keep my sights on heaven. Today I place love first.

Established in Spirit,
I live my deepest values.

Frame of Mind

We must strengthen, defend, preserve, and comfort each other. We must love one another. We must bear one another's burdens. We must rejoice together, mourn together...

— Puritan John Winthrop

Amidst a busy day of errands, I stopped at the local picture-framing store. Steve, the clerk, was an amiable fellow who seemed comfortable telling me about himself. After a few minutes of chit-chat, Steve told me that he was wrestling with the decision to call a friend whose husband had died unexpectedly. "I have been putting it off because I feel so uncomfortable about it," he confessed. "I am afraid that I may say something stupid and be embarrassed. I guess I'm really afraid of death, and I don't want to face it."

I was stunned and moved by Steve's candor. A moment earlier, we were discussing picture frames, and suddenly he was exposing his pain and fear to me. I caught Steve's eyes, and for a moment I could really see him. I saw behind his job and his rap and his fear, and I saw the person that he was. I thanked him for his honesty.

That moment was worth everything to me. It stood out in contrast to a day of unconscious business like a delicate flower growing in a pile of rubble. In that moment, I remembered what friendship and human relations are really about. They are not about stuff and talk and presentation; they are about people joining in the place where we are one.

I once heard that we are most alike in our vulnerability. In that moment, I felt very close to Steve. I hardly knew him, and yet I *knew* him. While I went into the store for a new picture frame, it was a new frame of mind that I found.

I pray to be open to the tender moments of life.
Let me not miss an opportunity to connect
with the heart of a brother or sister.

I am one with everyone I meet.
I let my heart be touched.

Just Changed Addresses

There is no death.
— A Course in Miracles

For a long time, my mother asked me to put up a *mezuzah* on her doorpost. In the Jewish religion, a *mezuzah* is a small box that contains a parchment from the Bible. It is placed by the door as a reminder that God is present in the house, and serves as a blessing to those who enter and leave. I put up the *mezuzah,* but it kept falling off, and because I was not motivated, it ended up in my mother's kitchen drawer until she passed away. Six months after my mom's passing, I received a call from my clairvoyant friend, Carla. "Have you received the present from your mom yet?" Carla asked in a matter-of-fact way.

Her question threw me for a loop. "No, I don't recall anything with the postmark, 'Heaven.'"

"You will receive a gift from her soon; I sent it to you. I was in a gift shop in St. Louis, and as I was looking at a certain item, your mom whispered in my ear and told me to get it for you. I don't know what it is, but you will." Several days later, I received Carla's package. When I opened it, I was stunned to find a *mezuzah.* I put it up quickly and made sure it stayed!

I believe that my mom spoke to Carla from the other side of life to give me a sign that she is still very much alive and present. Although she had passed from my visible sight, she was still my mom, she still loved me, and she was still with me.

When a friend of mine told me that he had just come back from his father's funeral, I told him I was sorry to hear that. "It's okay," he answered. "He just changed addresses."

Life never dies; it just changes forms.

Help me to know that life is eternal.
Banish thoughts of death, that I may know the truth of life.

God is alive everywhere.
My loved ones are always with me.

Get Off Your Buts

If you sit in the middle of the road,
you will get hit by traffic from both directions.
— Bryce Courtenay

After spending a day with a small group of friends in New York City, we were deciding whether to go to a movie or go home. As we drove along, each person gave their input. "I'll go with the flow," said the first person.

"I'm not attached," offered the second.

"I'll do whatever the group wants," added a third.

"I'm just happy," reported a fourth.

The driver pulled off the road, turned to face the others, and half-irritated, half-humorously, announced, "That's enough! Can't you guys come up with anything but new age platitudes? I need to know what direction to drive this car; this is one of those situations in which everyone is just going to have to be honest. Now, let me ask each of you again. What would you like to do?"

As it turned out, no one wanted to attend the movie, so we all just went home—but not before I learned an important lesson in taking a stand.

When you're honest about where you are, you and others have something to work with. If you're vague or withhold your truth for the sake of pleasing others, it's hard to get anywhere. Even if you're upset or feeling unclear, you serve by reporting where you are. Often simply speaking up moves the energy to the next level.

Sometimes all we have to offer is our current experience, and that is enough. Even if we're not in touch with the ultimate truth of the universe, or if our position changes, we do well to give the driver a direction before he has to pull off the road to ask.

I pray to be clear with myself and others.
Give me the confidence to know that
where I am is good enough.

I make a stand for who and what I am.

With the Energy

If your morals make you dreary, depend upon it, they are wrong. I do not say give them up, for they may be all you have, but conceal them like a vice lest they should spoil the lives of better and simpler people.

— Robert Louis Stevenson

As I was about to step up to the podium to speak at a church dedication in Virginia, it occurred to me that the service was probably on a strict schedule, and I did not want to exceed my time allotment. I turned to the minister and asked her, "How long would you like my talk to be?"

She smiled and answered, "Just go with the energy." I was touched and surprised that she trusted me and Spirit so implicitly.

I have spoken at churches where ministers and board members cautioned me with dire seriousness not to exceed 20 minutes, since some church members complain if the service goes 5 minutes over schedule. I wonder why such people would go to church; is it out of joy and love, or are they simply paying their dues?

Structure and rules help life function more peacefully, but the spirit of an activity is more important than the form. In Hawaii, the colloquial name for Caucasians is *Haole,* which translates to "without breath." One explanation for the term goes back to the time when white missionaries first conducted church services in the Hawaiian islands. The native Hawaiians observed that the missionaries' practice of prayer was in sharp contrast to the Hawaiians'. While the Hawaiians prayed with song, dance, color, and laughter, the missionary services were somber, rote, muttered and, as far as the Hawaiians could tell, lifeless and "breathless."

The word *spiritual* implies spirit and aliveness. If we are not bringing vitality and joy to our spiritual path, we are missing its essence. Fear shuts down life, and joy opens it. Move with the energy; things go better when we let life flow.

I pray to make my spiritual practices come alive with joy and celebration. No longer will I worship at the altar of fear. From this day on, I live from the heart.

My deep trust in life is rewarded with continual miracles.

Don't Wait for Worth

Think not you lack a special value here.
— A Course in Miracles

In all his lifetime, Vincent Van Gogh sold a single painting for a pittance. At a recent auction, one of Van Gogh's paintings sold for $82.5 million—an all-time high for a piece of artwork. Currently four of his paintings are among the ten highest-priced paintings ever sold.

It's ironic that Van Gogh was not acknowledged during his lifetime, and posthumously has become the highest-valued painter in history. This tells me that the immediate reaction or acknowledgment of the world is not always an indication of true quality. Quite often great artists and geniuses are overlooked in the early stages of their careers or during their lifetime.

When setting out to create art, music, or literature, to invent an object or method of service, or to choose a career, consult your own heart rather than the world. If you build your creations around the opinions of others, you will give your power away rather than draw it from within. As you allow your creations to spring from your inner vision, you will be a master of your own destiny and ultimately render great service.

Anyone can plug numbers into a formula. Many movie, television, novel, and song writers play on stock storylines that are sure to sell to the masses; some successful writers crank out plot after plot that simply dress old puppets in new clothing. True art, on the other hand, moves beyond what has been, and invites viewers to look at life from a grander perspective. Here is where originality, spirituality, and vision are called for. Such inventors must play on the cutting edge of their own creativity and call the masses to be bigger than they were.

Allow your genius to come forth uniquely—it is your greatest hope to live your destiny.

I pray to be a channel for fresh and wonderful ideas that bring healing and empowerment.

The mind of God within me creates beauty, service, enlightenment, and success.

Honesty and Truth

Ah, love, let us be true to one another!

— Matthew Arnold

Do you know the difference between honesty and truth? *Honesty* means that your words and deeds are consistent with your experience. *Truth* means that your expressions are consistent with reality.

EST founder Werner Erhard did an experiment in which he gathered together various groups of people who knew each other and asked one person to sit in the center of each group. The people in the circle were asked to express their feelings and reactions to the person in the center. The group members spoke in turn, over and over until they had each communicated all of their deepest and most personal feelings.

Werner discovered a consistent pattern—the initial responses were usually negative communications: "I am upset about this," and "I don't like when you do that." At a certain point after each person had exhausted expressing their upsets, they began to spontaneously express their appreciation for the subject. Finally, nearly every person, without any coaching, spontaneously communicated, "I love you."

This experiment tells me that at the core of our being we really love each other and we seek to express that love. Our fears and upsets cover the love at the center. When we honestly bring our upsets into the light, we unveil the love that was hidden. When these group members told of their angers and irritations, they were honest. When they declared their love, they were telling the truth.

We must be honest before we can be truthful. You cannot express the truth of love if you are harboring major areas of unspoken pain or upset. Be unafraid to speak of your upsets. If you hold your communications with the intention of healing and awakening, they will bring you to the love that is the truth.

Show me the truth of my love.

I speak from my heart and illuminate the truth.

The Mirror's Gift

We think in secret and it comes to pass;
Environment is our looking glass.
— James Allen

One day while living in a farming community, I sat on a porch and watched Pete the duck quack at several people on their way to lunch. As the first lady, a singer, passed Pete, she exclaimed, "Why Pete, how nice of you to sing me a morning song!"

The next person was somewhat overweight. When Pete quacked at her, she retorted, "Always quacking for more food, Pete—it's about time you got serious about your diet!"

The final person to pass was a cerebral intellectual. When Pete quacked at him, he responded, "Questions, Pete, always questions! How about some answers for a change?"

Meanwhile, Pete just went on quacking.

Each of us sees the world not as it is, but as we are. The world we experience is a direct result of the vision we are using. If we see a cruel and threatening world, we are filtering it through cruel and threatening thoughts. If we look upon a world of beauty and delight, we must hold those thoughts to create that perception.

At any moment, we can choose which vision we will employ and which world we will live in. Even if we have chosen dark or painful thoughts, we can shift our vision and immediately transform our experience. The world we see reflects the thoughts with which we build it.

Show me the beauty, goodness, and purity
that reflects my true self.

My vision is God's. My beautiful thoughts create a beautiful world.

Connect with Source

Anyone who is too busy to pray is too busy.
—Anonymous

Imagine a deep-sea diver in a diving suit with a long lifeline connected to his boat at the surface of the ocean. As the diver walks the ocean floor exploring the marvels of the deep, his life-support tube delivers a steady flow of vital oxygen to him. If his air tube becomes clogged or cut off, the diver will be unable to function; he will probably panic, flail, try to return to the surface, or expire.

We are like divers in earth suits, exploring the wonders of life on this planet. The earth is not our home; we are visitors here. Our true nature is not physical, but spiritual. We, too, have a life-support tube, and that is prayer, meditation, or any other form of communion with our Source. If our supply of spirit is cut off, we will not live well or long. Our connection to God is as important to our soul as the diver's supply of air to his body.

Each day, take time to feed your soul. Make your first priority any activity that nourishes your inner being. Pray or meditate, practice tai chi or yoga, walk in nature, play music, dance, read uplifting words, or share meaningful talks with friends. Any activity that renews your spirit is a form of prayer.

Commit to your spiritual practice first. Devote the beginning of your day to self-renewal. Your day will go better, and the time that you invest will pay for itself a thousandfold. Again, before you close your eyes to go to sleep, be with God. Feed your soul; it is your most important meal of the day.

You are my first priority. Knowing You makes all the difference in my life and my world. Knowing You is knowing myself. Be with me today, that I may be with You always.

Nourished by the spirit of love, my heart is whole.

Not Funny Anymore

If you believe, it means you've got imagination...
you don't face facts. If you believe, then you hang on—
what can stop you? If I don't make it today,
I'll come in tomorrow.

— Ruth Gordon

In 1995, two underdog baseball teams made it to the American League Championship Series. For the first time in 40 years, the Cleveland Indians registered a league-leading season, pitted against the long-suffering Seattle Mariners. During the series, the television announcers showed an old clip from the TV sitcom *Family Ties*, in which Michael J. Fox's character announced to a group of friends that he had two tickets to a baseball game. "Who's playing?" asked one of his buddies.

"Cleveland and Seattle."

Instantly, his friends rolled with boisterous laughter and told him, "We don't think so."

The video clip represented a world of contrast against the respect these two teams had earned and the excitement the series generated. In 1995, tickets were no laughing matter; they were at a premium.

What once seemed to be a joke can eventually emerge triumphant. Most great ideas and inventions were laughed at before they were appreciated. Just because someone laughs at your idea or rejects it does not mean it is a bad idea. It may just mean that your audience has limited vision.

Hold the faith in your vision. If you believe it is good and you receive internal signals that you should continue, refuse to be put off by the opinions of the world. Do it not for others, but for yourself. Someday the tickets will be at a premium.

Guide me to the highest service and give me the faith to pursue my visions with diligence.

I believe in what I am and what I do.
I value truth over opinion.

Eggs

Anyone can count the number of seeds in an apple,
but only God can count the number of apples in a seed.
— Anonymous

While watching a public television program on the process of human birth, I learned an astounding fact: When a female child is born, her body contains all the eggs she will ever produce as a woman.

This fact bears tremendous symbolic import: When we arrive on earth, we contain all the potential for everything we will ever accomplish. No matter how long we are here or what we do, we cannot add to our potential. The question is not, "How much potential do you have?" It is, "*How much potential will you live?*"

The word *education* is derived from the Latin *educare*, meaning "to draw forth from within." True learning is not accomplished by pounding something new into our psyche; it is allowing our innate wisdom to come forth. Much of what we call education is not a drawing forth, but rather an indoctrination or regimentation. Real education spotlights a child's uniqueness and stimulates her to discover and act on her natural talents.

What would you be doing differently if you knew that the seeds of greatness were already with you? Everything you need to succeed has been given to you.

"What you are is God's gift to you. What you make of yourself is your gift to God."

You made me what I am. Help me to live it.

I have all that I need to succeed. I put my gifts into action and draw success to me.

Sensitive Souls

Great geniuses have the shortest biographies. Their cousins can tell you nothing about them.

— James Thurber

In a college psychology class, I was required to read a book subtitled *The Mental Institution as a Last Resort.* The book's thesis was that many people in mental institutions are not crazy, but just more sensitive than most people in the society. The authors suggested that many mental patents are simply too finely strung to fit into the mainstream, and an institution is a safe place—similar to an ashram or monastery—where they can be who they are without having to adapt to a society that is in many ways more insane than they are.

Hilda Charlton noted that souls who are particularly fine-tuned emotionally, artistically, or spiritually are often unable to cope with the heaviness of the world, and so they turn to various addictions to escape. Alcoholics, drug addicts, and many mental patients are highly evolved souls who cannot find comfort, acceptance, or a forum for expression in their worldly circles, so they sedate their sense of homelessness with chemicals or insanity. Indeed, many great artists, musicians, thinkers, inventors, and visionaries have sought to take refuge in addiction or illusion.

A Course in Miracles confirms that we do need to escape from the world we see, for it is not a place of truth or Godliness. But, the *Course* asserts, we will not find refuge if we follow the promptings of fear; if you must escape, then escape into truth.

In the Hindu culture, holy men and women are revered and cared for by the society. Saints and mystics are not tested, prodded, poked, cross-examined, rationalized, written off, and shunned as they are in the West. In that culture, genuine visionaries are supported to do their spiritual work while people care for their worldly needs and responsibilities.

Let us honor our sensitivity and create a supportive space for talented souls to express our true self.

I pray to create a world in which the gifts of God are respected and empowered.

I express my artistic nature with courage and confidence.

As Much As the Valet

Every decision you make indicates
what you believe you are worth.
— *A Course in Miracles*

We pulled up to the Beverly Hills Hotel behind a line of luxury cars. My partner Charley handed the valet a $5 tip, and we went in for breakfast. The menu, like many *haut cuisine* restaurants, had no prices printed. Charley placed his order and then asked the waiter, "How much would a side order of bacon cost?"

"Five dollars," answered the man.

Charley thought for a moment, and then answered, "I guess I'll pass."

After the waiter left, I could see that Charley really wanted the bacon. "Go ahead, get the bacon!" I encouraged him.

"You're right," he answered, and called the waiter to make the order. Then a stunned look washed over Charley's face as he told me, "I just realized something very profound: I thought nothing of giving the valet a $5 tip—that's just what is done here. But when it came to feeding myself some food I enjoy, I had a hard time doing it. I wasn't even loving myself as much as the car attendant."

The next time you're faced with a choice about taking care of yourself, ask yourself, "Would I give this gift to another person if I could?" Most likely, you would feel very blessed and joyful to nurture someone in a way they would love. Then go ahead and bestow yourself with the same blessing. God rejoices just as much when you give to yourself as when you give to another.

It's not selfish to love or pamper yourself—it's a holy opportunity to celebrate what you truly deserve. Open your heart to yourself as much as you would to others, and you will find the meaning of true love.

Show me how to love myself as You love me.

I give myself all the good I can imagine.

All in the Timing

To know how to wait is the great secret of success.
— De Maistre

Do you ever have days or weeks when nothing seems to come together? The people you are looking for are out of town, the product you ordered is delayed, and you get everyone's answering machine. Finally, you throw your hands up and declare, "I give up—I'm going to a movie!"

That may indeed be the best strategy, for the universe is giving you a message that this is not the right time to try to make anything happen. It may be the perfect time for you to step back and nurture your spirit. If you pay attention to the cycles of your experience, you can make them work for you, rather than letting them overwhelm you.

Periods of nothing coming together are often followed by periods of everything coming together. After a week or month of frustrating attempts to make things happen, suddenly everything clicks; everyone calls back the same day, business deals that were on hold fall into place, and everything that was broken gets fixed. It's as if the universe was laying back to build up momentum for a huge leap forward. Don't be discouraged. If you've done all you can to make something happen, and nothing seems to be coming of it, get the hint. Let go. Turn it over to God. Do something else more rewarding or fun. It's all in the timing.

Help me attune to Your divine rhythm.
Let me find Your will in time.

I dance with life, stretching and resting in rhythm with the universe.

The Inside Story

The only true measure of success is happiness.
— Anonymous

One of the most difficult things I have ever had to do was to walk into the college class that I was co-teaching and inform the students that our senior instructor had committed suicide. My task was especially onerous in light of the fact that the course was a self-improvement class for adults who were seeking motivation to get back into the job market. Dr. Doughty was a brilliant, personable, and vital man who had won the respect and appreciation of many; no one had any clue that he was so unhappy that he would take his own life.

The face that many successful people present to the world is a facade. Behind the smiles, charm, and bravado of many famous and admired people, there lies great emptiness and pain. It is only when there is a tragedy such as a suicide, a violent crime, or a painful divorce that their inner life becomes obvious to the world.

Do not be fooled by appearances. The presentations of the world are deceptive. Many people in my seminars have described the glamorous lives they lived as successful business people or entertainers, followed by horror stories of how they were dying inside.

If you are smiling at the world but crying inside, you must begin to tell the truth about your experience. Share your real feelings with a friend or counselor, and make a commitment that you will not settle for a double life. Pray to be released from any activities that dishonor your spirit or your integrity.

Seek the company of people who are genuinely happy. The happiest are those who have nothing to prove or protect. I thoroughly enjoy "what you see is what you get" people. God created each of us in magnificent beauty. Every human being has enormous gifts to share and bless the world, if we will only be who we are instead of who we are supposed to be. Just be yourself.

I want to live from my heart.
Help me to be me, without hiding or protection.

What I am is good enough.

Drive It

There is nothing you need to do first to be enlightened.
— Thadeus Golas

On a billboard, I saw a marvelous *Lexus* advertisement: *Don't pursue perfection—Drive it.* Now there is a powerful affirmation for mastering life! Many of us have gotten caught up in the game of seeking. We attend seminars, read books, sit at the feet of gurus, get psychic readings, and do all manner of therapies, processes, and initiations, all the while identifying ourselves as students on the path of truth. But we get more of whatever we identify with. As long as we see ourselves as students, that is all we shall be.

There comes a point at which we must identify with our wholeness rather than the part that is striving. Learning and growth will always occur, but behind all of the external unfoldment, we are full.

Imagine that all of your trying, seeking, and striving has been completed. Imagine that you have within you all the awareness and tools you need to live a life of joy, creativity, success, and love. Imagine that you don't have to pass any more tests or prove anything to anyone. Imagine that you don't have to earn the love or favor of God. Imagine that you have the abilities and credentials to offer healing and support to others. These imaginings are much closer to the truth than the imaginings that you are broken, wounded, or needy. Jesus said, "I am the way, the truth, and the life." If you recognize who you are, you can make this statement with equal authority.

Practice being enlightened. It is the truth about you.

I am ready to live my wholeness. Shine through me that I may bless myself and the world.

I am the light of the world.
I let it radiate in full splendor.

Guaranteed Overnight Delivery

Healing is available to you now, unless you believe the will of God takes time.

— A Course in Miracles

One evening when I was teaching creative visualization in adult school, I guided a strong meditation on abundance. "Know that we live in a rich and abundant universe," I told the students. "All the good you seek is available and on its way to you; just open your mind and heart and let it flow." The energy of the meditation was especially poignant, and I felt something click in my own heart. The next morning I went to my mailbox to see if anyone had registered for one of my first retreats, and I was astounded to find 12 checks. My internal acceptance of abundance was mirrored by external manifestation.

A trucking company on the East Coast has huge letters painted on the sides of its trailers: G.O.D.: *Guaranteed Overnight Delivery*. Indeed, God is capable of Guaranteed Overnight Delivery, in far more miraculous ways than any worldly enterprise.

When the results we seek do not come about, it is not because the universe is incapable of delivering them; we may not be ready or willing to receive them. We may harbor doubts about our worthiness; we may have bought into the limitation thoughts of others; we may fear that our life will change if we succeed; or we may hold some subconscious belief that we need to suffer to be happy. *None of these notions are true*, and we must rid them from our consciousness to make way for the success we desire.

Another way we separate ourselves from our good is with the belief that the will of God takes time. *It does not.* You can manifest your good now if your heart is open to receive it. An apple falls from the tree when it is ripe; there is no way it can continue to stay on the branch. In the same way, there is no way your blessings can be separated from you if you affirm in your gut, "Yes, I accept."

Show me that love is here now. Help me be open to receive all You would give me.

I accept the love of God and all my good into my life now.

Closer Than You Think

When you come to the end of your rope,
tie a knot and hang on.
— Attributed to Franklin D. Roosevelt

In *The African Queen,* Humphrey Bogart and Katharine Hepburn are exhausted after a long and grueling adventure down a troublesome river. After overcoming terrible obstacles, their boat is stranded on a dry river bed, inestimably far from the ocean they have fought so hard to reach. Spent, and knowing that they can do no more on their own behalf, the couple falls into deep sleep, prepared to surrender to death. As their eyes close, the camera slowly pulls to an aerial view that reveals that the ocean they have sought lies just beyond the next bend, but a few hundred yards away. Then a miracle happens. While the couple sleeps, rain comes, and in a short time the river begins to flow again. By the time they awaken, the boat has floated to the ocean they believed was many miles away. They were closer than they thought.

You, too, may be just inches from your goal—not the miles you believe. If you have done everything that you can possibly do, it may be time for you to surrender and accept help from above. Self-made millionaire and insurance mogul A.L. Williams called his book *All You Can Do Is All You Can Do But All You Can Do Is Enough.*[15] We are asked to do only what we can; beyond that the universe is in charge.

Consider any projects or goals you have been struggling over or about which you feel are fruitless. Write them down on a piece of paper, and place it on an altar. Make a statement of surrender in which you let go of your efforts to make something happen, and entrust the entire process to the hands of a loving God. Like the *African Queen* travelers who made their best efforts and then surrendered, you may find that the ocean is just around the next bend.

I have done all I can. Help me to find the peace I seek.

I turn my intention over to God,
trusting that love will care for me.

The Sigh

It is our hearts that He asks of us.
— François Fénelon

A cobbler told his rabbi, "Most of my customers are men who work every day and drop their boots off to me at night for repair. I often stay up all night to get their boots ready for them in the morning. Sometimes I am so tired that I do not say the morning prayer. Other times I just say it quickly so I will have time to work. Other times my heart just sighs, 'How I wish I had the time and energy to say my prayer.'"

The rabbi answered, "If I were God, I would value that sigh more than the prayer."

Our love of God is not measured by the rituals we do or the forms we create, but by the intentions of our heart. We may lead a busy lifestyle, but if our soul is connected with Spirit, our daily activities become our communions. By contrast, there are people who go through rote prayers and rituals, but their minds and hearts are elsewhere.

The great illusion of the world is that we are what we do. The great truth of Spirit is that we live from our heart or we do not live at all. Here is a benchmark by which you can assess the quality of your actions and make important decisions: *What is your intention?* If you truly seek to serve and give love, you cannot fail.

Throughout your day, say hello to God occasionally. Lovers call each other several times a day just to say hello. I used to call a girlfriend who had a pager. I would punch in the numbers equivalent to the letters, "I love you," or other romantic phrases she would decipher. Those brief messages were the highlights of our days when we were apart. Give God a heartfelt call every now and then, and your love affair with Spirit will bloom in the most wonderful ways.

I pray to keep my heart open to You
in the midst of all my activities.

I am always connected with the God I love.

Clear Away What Isn't

Nothing real can be threatened. Nothing unreal exists.
Herein lies the peace of God.
— *A Course in Miracles*

Michelangelo was asked how he sculpted the magnificent classic statue of David. "I looked into the stone and saw David. Then I simply cleared away everything that wasn't David."

Our work in life is exactly the same. We do not have to create who we are; indeed, we have been created in utter perfection. We just need to discover what about our life is not who we are, and let it go.

The great Indian sage Ramana Maharshi offered one straightforward path to enlightenment: Continually ask, *"Who am I?"* Sincere, consistent inquiry into this most important question will eventually reveal that many of the things we identify with, are not who we are. When all of our illusions are peeled away, only divinity remains.

Who are you? You are not your name, which could change. You are not a husband or wife only; your identity goes far beyond your relationship. You are not your bank account, which rises and falls. You are not your house, from which you come and go. You are not your job, which is temporary. You are not your emotions, which wax and wane. You are not your religion, which is a mutable belief system. You are not your body; some people have body parts removed, and they are still a whole person. You are not even your thoughts, which vacillate and turn in all directions. If you are not any of these things that you commonly identify with, who are you?

We are spiritual beings, and any other identity detracts from the majesty of our true essence. Let go of false beliefs about yourself, that the true you may shine in all its splendor.

Teach me who I truly am, that I may
live my highest potential.

I am Spirit. I am whole.

About Time

Get over it.
— from the song, "Get Over It," by *The Eagles*

Ben Cohen and Shoshana Hadad had a rude awakening when the State of Israel told them their marriage was not legal because Shoshana's noble ancestor married a peasant—in 580 B.C. That's a 2,500-year punishment!

Have you been punishing yourself or someone else for something that happened a long time ago? Any payoff you perceive for holding a grudge is an illusion; there is no value, only a weighty price. A friend of mine in chiropractic school showed me a diagram of what happens to a human body in the throes of anger or rage. All kinds of chemicals are released into the system that exact a heavy toll on our health and vitality.

A Course in Miracles tells us that true forgiveness is "selective forgetting." Our pain comes not from what happened to us in the past, but from holding on to painful memories. It is within our power to release the thoughts that trouble us. The *Course* also reminds us, *"I can elect to change thoughts that hurt."*

Jesus was asked, "How many times should we forgive—seven?" Jesus's answer was clear: "Seventy times seven," meaning just keep on letting go. We must remember that forgiveness is more of a gift to ourselves than to the person we are forgiving.

Today, declare liberation day. Open the prison door, and let the war of fear end.

Give me the willingness to let go.
Let me perceive no value in holding hurtful thoughts.
I want to be free.

I release the past and get on with my life.

No Mistake

Doubt whom you will, but never yourself.
— Christine Bovee

When I walked into the hotel room, my jaw dropped, and my eyes opened to saucer size. The room looked straight out of the Palace of Versailles—thick padded gold wallpaper, gold-leaf French colonial furniture, a separate sitting room, and ultra-plush decor. "There must be some mistake," I thought, looking at my key.

When I called my sponsor to double-check if her organization had selected such an elegant room for me, she answered, "Of course it's for you! We appreciate you and want you to be comfortable." Okay, I can live with this, I thought.

If we believe we are unworthy, we will question or doubt our good when it comes to us. We will believe there is some hidden motive or catch, or we may fear that it will be snatched away as easily as it came.

If we know our worth, we will attract and accept our blessings in a spirit of joy and celebration. We will see our experience as an affirmation that we live in an abundant universe, and delight in passing generosity along at our next opportunity.

Today I will walk in the dignity in which You created me.
Thank you, God, for all of Your treasures and blessings.

I accept love in all forms.
I allow an abundant universe to
shower its gifts upon me.

Walking the Talk

The louder he talked of his honor
the faster we counted out spoons.
— Ralph Waldo Emerson

At a spiritual conference, a sum of money was stolen from the table of one of the vendors. The fellow became angry and sought to lay blame. When the theft was announced to find out if anyone in the large audience had any information, silence ruled. Then a speaker named Carolyn raised her hand and suggested, "I would be willing to auction off a counseling appointment and donate the money to the man who lost his income. Who will make the first bid?" By the time the bidding was done, the auction yielded an income of more than twice the woman's regular fee, which equaled the amount the vendor had lost.

I was inspired by Carolyn's willingness to help; it showed me that she is willing to live what she teaches. Such integrity is a magnificent demonstration that the spiritual path is only as real as we are willing to live it.

Many of us talk a good game, but how many of us put it into action? Lao-Tse noted, "He who says, does not know. He who knows, does not say." We do not need to talk a lot about what we are doing; we just need to do it. When we talk too much, we dissipate the energy we could be putting into action.

Words, although potentially powerful, are the least reliable index of who we are and what we believe. Emerson noted, "What you are speaks to me so powerfully that I can hardly hear what you are saying." We can lie with words, but not with our being. We can fool ourselves and others with rhetoric, but only actions reveal who and what we really are.

I pray to live what I believe.
Help my action match my words.

My deeds reflect my soul's truth.
I am integrated in thought, word, and action.

Spit It Out

Truth is always straightforward.

— Sophocles

Ben sat his eight-year-old daughter down to tell her that he and her mommy were getting divorced. He stammered and hedged for a few minutes, until the little girl finally blurted out, "Come on, Daddy, what are you—chicken? Why don't you just spit it out?"

Children usually know the truth before we tell them. In their innocence and openness, their antennae are up, and they see things we believe we can keep concealed. Children exemplify a faculty we all have. Everyone is psychic, and everyone always knows what is going on. In your conscious mind, you may be asleep, but subconsciously you know the truth. There is a book entitled *To Be Alive Is to Be Psychic.* Many of us were quite psychic as children, but when our parents reprimanded us for talking about our intuitions, premonitions, or invisible playmates, we quickly learned to shut down and play dumb.

Lies are perpetuated only when both parties agree to the lie. If someone lies to you, a place in you knows that what you have heard is untrue. If you do not confront the lie, it is because you have some investment in keeping the lie going. If more of us would own our ability to know the truth and tell it, the world would be quickly transformed.

Practice telling the truth and calling others to tell the truth. If you see something that is not in integrity, shine the light on it. If you have something to say, imagine that the person you are going to address already knows it on some level. So do we come closer to living our true nature as omniscient beings.

Give me the courage to speak the truth I know.
Support me as I claim my higher knowing.

The truth is my friend.
Integrity empowers me to succeed.

Fast Forward

If it walks out of the refrigerator by itself, let it go.

— Anonymous

A woman in a seminar confessed, "Everything I have to let go of, I leave claw marks on."

How do you respond when life asks you to let go of something you have valued? We are living in a time of incredibly rapid change. Many of us go through several marriages, careers, living situations, spiritual paths, and belief systems in a lifetime. We may feel guilty that we did not stay with one partner forever, or believe that there is something wrong with us because we change so much. But perhaps what you thought was wrong with you, is what is *right* with you. Perhaps *in wisdom* you chose to go through many experiences so you could master a host of lessons in one lifetime.

If you lived a hundred years ago, your life would have been more stable. You would have been married to one partner for a lifetime, lived in one town, practiced one profession, and attended one church. You would not have questioned the beliefs handed to you and them; you would have passed them on to your children. The lessons of life came more slowly, and so did personal growth. Now, never before in history have so many chosen to learn so much in such a short time. Rather than requiring an entire lifetime to learn from a marriage or profession, we may move through the lessons in a number of years.

When Barbara De Angelis[16], the well-known author who has written several books on relationships, was interviewed on a television news magazine show, the reporter rudely confronted her: "You've been married four times. How can you pass yourself off as a relationship expert when you're a four-time loser?"

Barbara responded coolly, "I don't see myself as a four-time loser; I consider myself a four-time *learner*. Although those marriages didn't last, I gained valuable insights and strengths that helped me bring more depth and presence to the relationships that followed."

If you feel like you're a loser because you've often changed relationships or jobs, re-identify yourself as a learner; if you've gained wisdom, the experience was a success. Rather than criticize yourself, honor your courage for being willing to grow through rapid change.

Help me to bless my lessons as gifts.

I value every experience as a lesson on love.
I am better for what I have learned.

Out of the Closet

You must look upon your illusions and not
keep them hidden...
Illusions have no place where love abides, protecting
you from everything that is not true.

— *A Course in Miracles*

In our fascination with the monsters of Halloween, we forget that the holiday began as a celebration of purification. "Halloween" is short for "All Hallows (Holy) Evening," the night that precedes November 1st, All Saints' Day. The lore tells that the presence of great spiritual light on All Saints' Day calls forth all the unhealed spirits so they can be blessed and released. The process is similar to cleaning laundry in a washing machine. When the soap and water touch the garments, the grime is loosened, and it rises to the surface. To look into a washing machine during the agitation cycle, you would be repulsed and think that the clothes are getting dirtier. But they are actually getting cleaner. The muck must be extracted before it can be discarded.

While our culture has forgotten the spiritual origin of Halloween, you can make use of it. Are there any monsters lurking in the closet of your consciousness? Are you carrying any hidden fears, resentments, or grotesque memories that stalk you in the night? Are you annoyed by any emotional goblins that undermine your relationships? If so, open the door and let them fly away. Call forth the energy of love and healing, and ask God to free you of anything that stands between you and your good.

Monsters are dangerous only when we run from them. No bogeyman has any power over us unless we feed it with fear and denial. Face your demons, and you will see that they are illusions. Shine the light of truth on your ba[illegible], and you will have a whole new room to play in.

Give me the courage to move beyond my fears and be free.

I release the darkness to make way for the light.

306

President of the Inner States

Confront the dark parts of yourself, and work to banish them with illumination and forgiveness. Your willingness to wrestle with your demons will cause your angels to sing.

— August Wilson

"I am angry at myself because I failed in my goal of becoming President of the United States by 1996," Jerry stated. "It was my lifelong ambition, and I am ashamed that I have not completed my mission."

"What would you do if you were President?" I asked.

"I would free the country of oppression," Jerry answered vehemently.

"It sounds as if you have been oppressing yourself by beating yourself for not attaining your goal," I suggested. "Perhaps you could begin to free the country of oppression by releasing yourself. If you quit beating yourself up emotionally, you might not need to be President; maybe your aspiration for the office was a reflection of your desire for your own freedom."

Jesus instructed, "Before you attempt to remove a speck from the eye of another, take the log out of your own eye." Masterful psychology and metaphysics! When we feel driven to fix the outer world, it is really our inner world we are seeking to improve. While it is tempting to project our need onto others, it is really inner transformation we seek.

It is useless to try to change another person unless we have first changed ourselves. *A Course in Miracles* asks us, "Can the world be saved if you are not?" Our primary responsibility is the healing of our own mind. With our own self purified, we are in a perfect position to see how we can truly be of service.

Help me to heal my own mind so that I may be a pure channel of blessing.
Help me to awaken, and let me not be seduced by projecting my needs onto others.

I look within for truth and improve the world by transforming my own consciousness.

Unforeseen Circumstances

Never make forecasts, especially about the future.
— Samuel Goldwyn

I was taken aback to read a newspaper article about a convention of psychics that had been canceled "due to unforeseen circumstances." If we can't depend on a group of professional psychics to know their own future, who can we look to? Is the future knowable? Can anyone truly predict what will happen?

A psychic, seer, or prophet can look down the road and see likely outcomes of actions and attitudes that are currently in motion. But at any moment, a human being can make a new decision and alter the course of events. A good psychic always leaves room for free will. Because we are imbued by God with the power to create, we can re-create our life at any time.

Experts in worldly sciences, too, make predictions based on history and trends. A doctor may tell you your chances of recovery, an economist may forecast market cycles, and an astrologer may indicate fortuitous times to act. But all of these predictions are based on you and others continuing what has always been done. If you choose a different course, you will create a different destiny. "Terminal cancer," for example, is a very dishonest term. A long time ago, I read that more persons have survived cancer than make up the population of Los Angeles. I am certain that that number has increased immensely by now. I know of support groups for "former terminal cancer patients"—now *there* is a beautiful oxymoron!

You have the power to create unforeseen circumstances. You were not born to be a statistic; you were born to be ecstatic. Choose your own destiny, and live by your own rules, not the world's.

Help me to live by the laws of love and create the future I choose.

I step forward into the world I create by my choice.

A New Face in the Mirror

Behold, I make all things new.

— Revelation 21:5

A television newsmagazine reported on a group of cosmetic surgeons who are donating their services to women whose faces have been disfigured from battering and abuse. I was astounded to behold bruised, beaten, and scarred faces restored to smoothness and softness through skillful surgery. Even more amazing was the energetic transformation these women exuded when they looked in the mirror and for the first time in many years saw a countenance of beauty. Each of them laughed and shed tears of joy and appreciation; they never thought they would see a whole face again.

On some level, each of us has felt beaten or battered by the world. And on some level, each of us has feared to look in the mirror, terrified that the scars we see will remind us of the pain we have accepted or inflicted on ourselves.

Grace is available, and our life can be made new at any time. No matter how disfigured we appear or how grotesque we feel, we can become reformed and renewed. We do not have to see a cosmetic surgeon. The most skillful surgery takes place when we open our minds and hearts to become new and allow Spirit to shine through us.

Let me see a new face in the mirror.
Let me open my eyes and heart to
the beauty I have forgotten.
Renew my life by renewing my mind and my vision.

I create a new life by thinking
new thoughts.
My life is changed because I am.

309

Follow Your Star

On the whole, as this wondrous planet, Earth, is journeying with its fellows through infinite space, so are the wondrous destinies embarked on it journeying through infinite Time, under a higher guidance than ours.

— Thomas Carlyle

Every winter, the magnificent humpback whales come to Maui. In a basin about 30 miles in diameter, these gentle giants play, mate, sing their haunting songs, and give birth. In April, the humpbacks return to the north Pacific, where they feed until they return the following December. Astonishingly, the same whales return to precisely the same place every year. Although they traverse three or four thousand miles in each direction, they pinpoint the same tiny basin in the middle of a huge ocean.

To me, this is compelling proof that the Great Spirit has imbued all creatures with the wisdom to be in their right place at the right time. The blueprint of our destiny is etched deep into our psyche, along with the guidance to achieve it. As spiritual beings, we have the capacity to find the place in life where we feel most at home. Each of us has a right living situation, relationship, career, and spiritual path that our internal guidance system will show us if we relax and cooperate. We don't have to add any intelligence; we just need to let go of all thoughts and activities that obscure our innate knowledge.

Should you doubt your ability to fulfill your destiny, remember the whales. Consider dogs and cats who find their way home after being lost many miles away, and remember the birds who fly south for the winter and return to the same backyard in the north. If God cares so carefully for the birds, surely we are known and loved, and our way shall be made clear.

I place my life in Your hands,
trusting that You always lead me to my right place and my highest good.

I give my life to God to guide me today.

Whose Business?

It's not enough to be busy
The question is: What are we busy about?
— Henry David Thoreau

When Jesus was young, his parents took him to Jerusalem. In the midst of their errands, they discovered that he had wandered off. After searching, they found him on the steps of the great temple, lecturing to learned men. When they asked Jesus why he had gone off on his own, he answered, "I am about my Father's business."

Whose business are you about? Do you remember your purpose as a divine being, here to give and receive love, discover great truths, and celebrate life? Or, have you become so caught up in the busy-ness of everyday life that you have all but stifled the voice of peace that calls to you from deep within your heart?

My teacher Hilda gave a lecture in which she affirmed, *"If you take care of God's business, God will take care of yours."* After her program, someone asked me for a ride home to an area out of my way. At the time, there was a gas shortage, and only a few stations were open at night. Remembering Hilda's lesson, I trusted Spirit to care for me, and I gave the fellow a ride. After dropping him off, I had just a little fuel, and I had to go onto a freeway on which there were no services. On the last corner before the freeway, there was a gas station open at midnight—a practically unheard-of situation at that time!

Remember your purpose as a spiritual being, and all of your needs will be taken care of, sometimes in miraculous ways.

I pray to keep my priorities in order. My business is love.

I live from my heart and trust that all my needs will be met.

Give Me a Sign

Ask, and you shall receive. Seek, and you shall find.
Knock, and it shall be opened unto you.

— Jesus Christ

Marvin was confused about whether to leave his job in St. Louis and take a more lucrative position in Washington, D.C. After wrestling with the dilemma for a long time, he decided to turn the decision over to Spirit. "Just give me a sign!" Marvin prayed. Late that night when he went home, Marvin was stunned to find a "For Sale" sign on his lawn. "Well, there's my sign," he concluded.

The next morning when Marvin asked his wife about the sign, she did not know what he was talking about. Marvin took her out to show her, and the sign was gone. But as far as Marvin was concerned, the move was a done deal—he had his sign. He accepted the position, which proved to be very fulfilling.

Although all prayers for signs are not answered so dramatically, the universe will prompt us in a direction. A friend may utter a key phrase, we may notice a particular book on a coffee table, or we may see a symbol in a dream. In compassion, God is willing to point us in a direction if we ask sincerely and keep our antennae up for a signal.

Show me what I am to do for the highest good of all concerned.

I walk the way appointed by the hand of love.

You Get Paid for This?

Find out what you like doing best,
and get someone to pay you for doing it.
— Katherine Whitehorn

As I paged through Frank Levinson's *Adventures on Horseback* guest book, I occasionally glanced out the picture window from his ranch, overlooking meadows, palm trees, and ocean panorama. Amid the many enthusiastic comments, one caught my eye: *"And you get paid for this?—I'm sending you my résumé!"* The writer was referring to the fact that Frank is living his dream and being supported for it. Frank has taken what many people consider *vacation*, and turned it into *vocation*.

Here are some points to consider when trying to assess whether or not you are in your right job: *You know you are in your right place if you feel you should be paying people to let you do what they are already paying you to do. And you know you are in your wrong place if you are laboring in a position that is made worthwhile only by the money.*

Some other good diagnostic questions for right livelihood are: Do you get up in the morning with a sense of enthusiasm, looking forward to what is before you? Do you feel creative and inspired to expand? Do you have more energy at the end of your work session than when you began? Do people thank you for making their life easier or more beautiful? Do you feel that Spirit is working through you to deliver results that you could not have manifested on your own? Would you want your child to create a profession with the attitude you hold toward yours?

You deserve to be paid for doing what you love. You deserve to be uplifted by what you do. You deserve to live your personal destiny through your vocation. Don't waste any more time in an unfulfilling job; begin now to create the life your heart yearns to live. Someday someone will write in your guest book, *"And you get paid for this?"*

Help me to find peace and fulfillment in my work.

I am richly rewarded for following my dreams.

I Have a Chance

Trust your hopes, not your fears.
— David Mahoney

In the film *Dumb and Dumber,* Jim Carrey finally gets a date with his ideal woman and tells her he is in love with her. Then he asks her, "What do you think are my chances—one out of ten?"

After barely a moment's thought, she bluntly answers, "More like one in a million."

Carrey grows very serious, and then a huge smile breaks out on his face. "Wow!" he exclaims ecstatically. "I have a chance!"

For once at least, this character's simplemindedness works in his favor. He is the eternal optimist, acknowledging the one-millionth of the glass that is full, rather than the rest that is empty. His attitude is more prone to create success than someone who would be turned away by initial rejection. Many great people were rejected before they became celebrities. Einstein failed mathematics; Beethoven's violin teacher called him hopeless as a composer; the sculptor Rodin failed three times to gain admission to art school; eighteen publishers turned down Richard Bach's *Jonathan Livingston Seagull* before it became a sensation; Walt Disney was fired by a newspaper editor for lack of ideas; several record companies rejected the Beatles before they made their first album, and one producer commented that their music was passé.

Remember that your destiny is determined not by chance, but by choice. No matter what chances you are quoted by statistics, you have the ability to make your own statistic. Sometimes all you need is that one chance in a million. If you capitalize on it, it is all worth it.

Give me the confidence to believe in myself.
Help me to see the light rather than the darkness.

I make every experience work for me.
Everything that happens to me is an
opportunity to further my success.

It Takes Two

You are your brother's savior.
— *A Course in Miracles*

When she performed weddings, my teacher Hilda gave one marriage vow: "*Don't fight on the same day.*" She suggested, "You can be mad on Monday, and then your turn is on Tuesday. As long as at least one of you keeps your head at any given time, you will be all right."

When I first heard Hilda's advice, I laughed and thought her idea was a cute joke. As I went on to explore my own relationships, I realized that her suggestion was profound and had the potential to save much pain. *A Course in Miracles* echoes that relationships are safe as long as one person remains sane at any moment.

Anger, upset, and blame are forms of temporary insanity. When two people lose their clarity simultaneously, the issue to which the insanity is applied seems real. If one person can hold his or her awareness of the light, while the other has slipped in the darkness, the light-holder will have the leverage to lift the other out. Two people in the dark have a much harder time finding the light.

If your partner goes insane momentarily, hold your peace. Your upset will pass much more quickly if you do not agree to match it or fight it. Once my partner was quite upset, and she vented for about half an hour. I simply remained still and listened. Finally, she relaxed and said, "Thank you for listening—that is just what I needed."

If you temporarily lose your sanity, do not try to drag your partner to the netherworld with you. If they can keep their peace, do not be offended; you are blessed. Clarity is the greatest gift we can offer one another.

I pray to remain sane when others lose their clarity, and that they do the same for me.

Peace is my most powerful response.

Truth and Consequences

The essence of communication is intention.
— Werner Erhard

While speaking with a woman whose partner had just left their relationship to marry another woman, she asked me, "Did you know that Walter was once in jail for embezzling?" No, I hadn't known that. "I just thought you should know the truth about him," she added. Her comments struck me as harsh and out of context. Reflecting on her position, I understood that she felt wounded by this man, and this was her way of retaliating or justifying her loss. But it was not truth that she was seeking to offer; it was injury.

Many a disservice has been rendered in the name of "telling the truth." What use is telling the truth if our intention is to cause pain? The truth, like a knife, can be used to perform life-saving surgery or to maim. It is a power that must be used with consciousness, forethought, and service.

To make a rule that we must always tell all facts, thoughts, and feeling, is to open the door to unnecessary pain. Higher than any factual truth is the truth that we are loving beings, here to support one another in healing and awakening. If someone is not ready to hear a truth, or it would hurt them emotionally or damage them socially to speak it, we must yield to service rather than a rote rule.

Before speaking truth to someone, ask yourself some important questions: What is my intention in offering this? How would I prefer to hear such a truth spoken to me? Am I truly seeking to communicate, or am I "dumping" to relieve myself of upset or guilt? What do I want to come of this situation? How can I best serve everyone involved?

Consult your heart; it will guide you to offer truth in the highest way possible.

Guide me to speak healing words,
that I may be closer to my brothers and sisters.

I use the truth to heal and bring peace.

Direct Is Better

Let every man do according as he is disposed in his heart; not grudgingly, or of necessity.

— Anonymous

I had an assistant named Joel who did not know how to say no. He would say yes to everything and then not do the things he did not want to do. Psychologists call this "passive-aggressive behavior." Once I asked Joel to go into town to pick up a computer part. He assured me that he would, and then delayed and delayed doing it. Finally, he made the trip one afternoon, and when I asked him about the part the next morning, he told me he could not find the shop. I gave Joel explicit instructions, and he went back into town the next afternoon. I received a call from him asking, "What was the name of that company?" After several attempts he finally got the part, but in retrospect, I wish he had told me outright that he did not wish to do the job. It would have been a lot easier to get someone else to do it.

I have a simple definition of integrity: Say *yes* when you mean *yes, no* when you mean *no, maybe* when you mean *maybe*, and *I don't know* when you mean *I don't know*. We get into trouble and confuse others when we say *yes* when we mean *no, maybe* when we mean *I don't know*, and on and on through all the permutations. You are in integrity when what you're doing in the outer world matches what is real in your heart.

In college I read a book by Sidney Jourard called *The Transparent Self*. The title speaks for itself. We usually do much better to let people know what is going on inside of us than to play a presentation game that is out of synch with our inner truth.

When my friend told her teenage son that she did not like him hanging out with the working-class kids in school, he told her, "I like these kids because they'll tell you exactly who they are and what is going on with them."

If you tell your truth with your actions but not your words, you're going to have to come back and admit where you are. Save yourself and others trouble by being direct at the outset: honesty always serves best.

Give me the courage to tell my truth in word and deed.

I trust who I am, I speak what I believe, and I live what I know.

Select, Don't Settle

It is not what you ask for that is appalling;
what is appalling is what you settle for.
— Alan Cohen

As a teenager, I regularly heard a radio jingle for a men's clothing store in New York City: *"Select, Don't Settle, at Barney's."* Although I did not realize it at the time, the message was offering a profound instruction for life.

How much of how you live your life is your preference, and how much are you settling for? On a piece of paper make two columns: *I Select* and *I Settle.* Then consider your activities in the course of a day, week, month, or year, and honestly record what you're doing that comes from your heart and what you're doing that comes from fear, obligation, or accommodation.

Every time we settle, we die a little bit inside. When we accept something that we would not choose, we affirm that we do not deserve to be happy and that the universe cannot support us in living our vision. When we make a stand for our goal, we affirm that we are worthy to live in a loving and abundant universe.

After a lecture, I was invited to the sponsor's office to unwind. "What kind of tea would you like?" Melodie asked.

"Peppermint," I told her.

"I'm not sure if we have peppermint," she noted as she rummaged through the shelf.

Quickly I responded, "That's okay—I'll take whatever you have."

Melodie turned and glared at me playfully, "Didn't I just hear you give a lecture on not settling?" Oops. (It's always annoying when your students or children use your truth against you.) She searched again and announced, "Peppermint!"

A humbling lesson, but a good one. Ask for what you want, and as long as there is a chance of getting it, keep asking.

I pray to live at choice. Give me the strength to
claim my highest good
and not stop until my dreams come true.

I deserve the kingdom.
I choose my life with self-respect.

Gladden Yourself

Have you really considered how many opportunities you have had to gladden yourself, and how many of them you have refused?

— A Course in Miracles

I met a man who has found a way to be happy. Dr. Christian Almyrac, also known as "Dr. Happiness," uses a simple technique to reframe situations that seem negative.

"Ask yourself, 'What is the happiest thought I can think about this situation?'" suggests Dr. Almyrac, "and then assume and act as if that is the truth about it."

I have been practicing the method, and it works. If, for example, you are faced with the end of a relationship, and you have a whole range of thoughts about it, including, "Everything I do ends in failure," and "This just proves that men are turkeys," and "Here is my opportunity to learn to love myself without needing a man," imagine that the last thought— the most empowering—is the truth. You will succeed because the truth is always the thought that brings us the most life. Conversely, if something brings you down to think it, it cannot be the final truth.

A friend was agonizing over which of two job offers she would accept. Although both jobs were attractive to her, choosing either one would give her certain benefits she would miss if she chose the other. "I feel like I'm damned if I do and damned if I don't," Sharon recounted. I was surprised to hear that, since both jobs sounded like good ones.

"It seems to me that you actually have a pleasant dilemma here," I told her. "You're choosing between two good things. I would say that you're blessed if you do and blessed if you don't."

There are two ways that we can gladden ourselves: first, by asking for what we want and being willing to receive it when it is offered; and second, by shifting our attitude about what we have, so that we see the gift rather than the problem. The truth brings happiness.

I pray to see and receive the blessings You bring me.
Help me see my life through the eyes of love
rather than fear.

My birthright is joy. I choose it now.

Must Be Some Mistake

Miracles are examples of right thinking, aligning your perception with truth as God created it.
— A Course in Miracles

Kathi returned to her hotel room to spruce up before her evening meeting. As she stood in the bathroom brushing her teeth, she was shocked to see a tall burly man standing in her shower. Before she could say a word, he grabbed her and started to wrestle her to the floor. "Suddenly the whole scene went into slow motion, and I became an observer," Kathi told me. "I started to scream, but it was as if I was watching myself from a distance. Then something came over me. I ceased to see myself as a victim of an attack, and my heart became filled with only love and compassion. All I could think was, 'There must be some mistake here. This man is my brother; there is no reason for him to do this.' All this happened in a flash, and in spite of the outer struggle that ensued, inside I felt at peace. Then something truly miraculous happened. Suddenly the man stopped and said, 'There must be some mistake here; I'm in the wrong room. I have to go. I'm sorry.' He ran out the door, and that quickly it was all over."

A Course in Miracles reminds us that "miracles are natural. When they do not occur, something has gone wrong." The laws of miracles reverse the laws of the world, which tell us that it is natural for life not to work, and when it does, it is an exception. But the universe was designed to work, and in spite of appearances, it does. All of life, from the tiniest amoeba to the trillions of stars, planets, and galaxies, operates with clockwork precision. Surely there is an intelligent force with an unfathomably creative mind and loving heart behind such magnificent perfection!

Success, harmony, and happiness are not mistakes; they are our natural state. When we remember that love is who we are, miracles occur *continuously*.

Help me remember that there is only love.
Let me always be aware of Your comforting presence.

I am safe because love is the only reality.

Firewalking

Feel the fear and do it anyway.[17]

— Dr. Susan Jeffers

Do you know the difference between courage and fearlessness? When you're fearless, you're not frightened by the task at hand, and you simply go ahead and do it. When you're courageous, however, you feel afraid and walk ahead in spite of it.

In this world, courage is far more important than fearlessness. One of our missions in life is to discover what holds us back from being ourselves and dismantle our illusions.

If we do not face our fears, we cannot heal them. Someone who is not afraid of snakes may walk into a snake pit and impress everyone who sees him; such an act is of little value, though, as there is no risk, stretch, or growth; he is doing something that is easy for him. If, however, he harbors a fear of public speaking, he would accomplish more by joining Toastmasters than walking through a snakepit.

Fear is not real, for if it were, everyone would be afraid of the same things. The word *real* implies constancy. If you're afraid of spiders and I'm not, and if I fear enclosed spaces and you do not, we demonstrate that there is nothing inherently fear-inducing about spiders or closed spaces. The next time you face a fear, think of someone you know who is not afraid of that thing, and visualize the ease and peace with which they would handle that experience.

Make a list of your responses to the open-ended statement, *"If I were not afraid, I would..."* Include only those responses that you would make if fear were not a block. Then just do them. One by one, walk through your fears, and you will discover that none of them has any power whatsoever.

Help me to be bigger than fear.
I can do all things with the strength You give me.

My nature is love and strength.
I overcome all fear with the power of peace.

More Inside

Abundance is a blessing to the wise;
the use of riches in discretion lies.
— Richard Cumberland

"When I entered the Peace Corps, I believed that if all the poor people in America had more money, their problems would be solved," Annie told me. "Then, after living in the New York City ghetto for a year, I realized that what these people needed was not more money, but more consciousness. They needed to learn to handle the money they had; many of them would spend any additional funds they received on liquor, gambling, or things that would only hurt them more. Money is not the answer; the answer is wisdom, understanding, self-respect, and richer values."

There is a theory that if all the money in the world were redistributed equally among every person on the planet, within six months all the money (or absence of it) would be exactly where it was before the redistribution. This is because each of us manifests not according to external conditions, but according to our consciousness. At every given moment, we are creating according to what we believe; if we wish to change our external circumstances, we must first change our awareness.

I read about a philanthropic program in which two wealthy women were offering seed funds to Third World women. Applicants would submit a basic business proposal to the organization, and if approved, they would receive several thousand dollars (a large sum by their standards) to start a business of their choice. If the business was doing well a year later, the applicants would receive another stipend. This system struck me as a wise use of green energy, for it encouraged users to make the most of their initial gifts and offered them the responsibility to expand their own world.

The answer to problems is not to get more of something from somewhere else; it is to gain more inner awareness so you have the power to attract more of everything forever.

Give me the wisdom to use Your gifts properly.

I live in an abundant universe.
My good proceeds from inside me.

May I Believe for You?

Miracles are performed by those who temporarily have more for those who temporarily have less.
— A Course in Miracles

When Rev. Mary Morrissey asked her mentor Rev. Jack Boland to support her in prayer for an expansion for her church, he asked her, "Would you allow me to believe for you?" Jack was asking Mary if she would be willing to have the project manifested on the strength of his faith. His offer was an invitation to Mary to extend her faith to allow the dream to come true through a mind that temporarily envisioned greater possibilities than she could see. Since that time, the Living Enrichment Center[18] in Wilsonville, Oregon, has become one of the most successful new thought centers in the world, with a huge facility serving many thousands of students of truth.

If you find it difficult to believe in something you desire, ask someone to believe for you. Such an invitation requires humility and magnitude: you must be humble enough to admit that you don't feel you can swing it on your own, and confident enough to believe that it can be done with help.

When selecting a prayer partner, choose someone who has manifested good in the area you are seeking to edify. If, for example, you have manifested financial abundance and wish to create a rewarding relationship, invite someone who has a good relationship to pray for you while you hold the vision of their abundance.

A Course in Miracles tells us that a little willingness is all that is required to set a miracle in motion. When you declare that you are willing to have your dream come true, no matter by whose hand it is manifested, you signify that willingness.

We have the capacity to open the door to miracles for one another. When you cannot believe for yourself, let someone else believe for you.

Help me accept Your gifts with a little help from my friends.

I am willing to receive support to make my dreams come true.

323

Scan Your Lines

Through your holy relationships, reborn and blessed...thousands will rise to heaven with You.
— A Course in Miracles

Every night while you sleep, the telephone company is examining your circuitry. The phone company runs a massive diagnostic scan of every phone line in its system to see if there are any faulty connections. If they discover a bad line, they will repair it at the company or come out to your house to fix it.

In the same way, we need to scan our relationships daily and see if there are any that need attention. Each day, sit in meditative prayer for a few minutes and feel if any of your relationships are out of harmony. Are you harboring any irritations you have not dealt with? Do you have any long-standing grudges? Is there someone you want to appreciate and acknowledge, but have not? Have you made any commitments you need to follow through on? Has someone made a commitment to you that you need to remind him or her to complete? Do you need to make any changes you are delaying acting on? Have you pushed anyone out of your heart? Is there someone you can serve better? Ask God to show you if you can bring any of your relationships into greater love and integrity. You don't need to labor over the process; just relax your mind and see who pops into your awareness. If someone does, you are being called to bring that relationship into greater peace.

Jesus taught, "Before you bring your gift to the altar, settle with your brother." We cannot be present with God if we are unhealed with our neighbor. Years ago, I had a conflict with someone and did not see him for a long time. Every time someone would talk about forgiveness, his face would pop into my mind. Finally, after 11 years, I wrote him a letter. The moment I dropped it in the mailbox, I felt free.

Our relationships were meant to bring us joy and empowerment. If any one is not, Spirit is calling you to heal it. Then you can wake up in the morning and have all of your lines available.

Help me to heal my heart and be at peace with my brothers and sisters.

I enjoy harmony with all my relations.

Sharks or Goldfish?

They can do all because they think they can.

—Virgil

"How big will this shark get?" asked Richard, an aquarium enthusiast.

"That depends on the size of your aquarium," answered the pet salesman. "Keep him in this little area, and he'll stay seven inches; give him an entire ocean, and he'll get big enough to eat you."

Sharks, like goldfish, will grow in proportion to the size of the environment offered them. And so will thoughts. Give your positive or negative thoughts some space and food, and they will shape your life.

Behold the power of potential and attention. We can make anything we want out of our lives; we have the raw material to do it all. But we must choose what we want to make, or else we will be subject to the downward pull of mass thinking. If you don't use your mind, someone else will.

An Indian came to a medicine man and told him, "In my mind there are two dogs fighting all the time; one is beautiful and one is ugly."

"The beautiful one will win," answered the shaman.

"Why is that?" asked the brave.

"Because you will feed the beautiful one."

Give me the wisdom and strength to nourish the good, the beautiful, and the true.

I am free to build the life I choose.

325

Light on the Shadow

If I keep busy, I won't have to look at what is frightening me.

— Anonymous

One night Nasrudin's neighbor Jalami found Nasrudin on his hands and knees under a streetlamp, searching for his house key. Wanting to be of service, Jalami joined Nasrudin on the ground and together poked around in the grass. After 20 minutes, Jalami asked Nasrudin, "Do you remember where you were standing when you dropped the key?"

"Yes," answered Nasrudin, "over there," pointing to a tree 30 feet from the lamp where the two men were searching.

"Then why are you looking for the key here?" Jalami had to ask.

"Because there is more light over here."

It is tempting to look in easy places for answers, instead of confronting our inner thoughts and beliefs about ourselves. One of the techniques we use to distract ourselves from facing our fears is to create endless errands, projects, meetings, emergencies, dramas, crises, upsets, and intellectual dances that keep us so occupied that we have little or no time left to be with ourselves. But simply taking a few quiet moments to honestly face what is troubling us may be exactly what we need to heal the insanity we create in our outer circumstances.

Enlightenment is an inside job. Doing more in the outer world will not result in more peace; only *being* more will get us what we want. Peace is attained by letting go of everything that distracts us from it.

Step back from your busy-ness and look within, where you will find everything you have ever sought in the outer world, and more.

All I really want is to know You. Help me to stay on purpose. Give me the inspiration to look within for my answers. Help me take the time to be with myself and find the peace I seek.

In quiet I look within and discover the light I am.

Divine Alchemy

In each holy relationship is the ability to communicate instead of separate reborn.

— A Course in Miracles

I am fascinated by the explosive development of the Internet, one of the most exciting and profound evolutionary leaps in history. Now, anyone with a computer and phone line can communicate with any other like person on the planet instantly and almost for free. A vast library of knowledge is available at the touch of a finger. Significantly, no institution or government can restrict or inhibit this communication. I asked a computer expert, "Is there some central office for the Internet? If someone pulled out the plug in St. Louis, would the whole system fall apart?"

"No," she answered, "and that's the beauty of the net. If any one nexus goes down, any communication will find its way through another path. The net has a life of its own, beyond the control of any person or organization. It's as if the planet has just grown its own electronic nervous system."

The Internet was originally designed by the military. The Defense Department wanted a communication system that would be impervious to destruction by a nuclear attack in one central headquarters. So they developed this system that is now bringing billions of people closer together through unlimited communication.

The way we keep prejudice, ignorance, and fear alive is by not looking at our enemies. The moment we being to communicate, we realize that our interests are joined. The more we see and know about one another around the planet, the closer we are to wisdom and peace.

The Holy Spirit can use anything for healing. An elaborate defense system can be transformed into a sophisticated healing tool. This is divine alchemy, taking the lead of life and turning it into gold. Nothing is beyond God's ability to use for healing.

Take the lead of my life and turn it into gold. Take my pain and turn it into strength. Let my tears become a cleansing stream. Replace my fear with faith.
Let me find Your hand everywhere.

Heaven comes alive with the master's touch.

Don't Even Try It

Let not the cloud sit upon your brow.
Look up, laugh, love, talk big, keep the colors in
your cheek and the fire in your eye.

— William Hazlett

While reviewing the sales records of one of my early books, *Joy Is My Compass,* I saw that it was selling rather sluggishly. Perhaps, I thought, it's time to let it go out of print. A short time later, I was presenting a lecture when a woman in the audience rose and stated, "I just want to thank you for writing *Joy Is My Compass.* That book inspired me so much that I decided to follow my bliss and I founded an AIDS hospice. Thanks to your influence, a significant number of people with AIDS are dying with dignity in the presence of love and compassion."

I was stunned. While I had judged the value of the book based on sales, this woman was applying its principles to render a high and holy service. I recognized that even if no one else ever read the book, it would have been worth writing and publishing for that one purpose.

At times, I have felt guilty for not being out on the front lines of relieving human suffering. "While people are ministering to dying paupers on the streets of Calcutta, feeding hungry children in Africa, and changing the bandages of lepers on Molokai, I'm just writing books," I berated myself. But of late, I have come to peace with the understanding that I am in my perfect position to serve best. If I were to be a missionary, Spirit would put the inspiration in my heart to do so. Instead, words come to me that inspire others to do what they do best.

Know that God is using you in the highest way by instilling you with joy to do what you love best.

I will not attempt to judge against Your will of joy for me. I surrender to what I love, trusting that You are serving through me.

I follow my heart and trust God to run the universe.

Fido Was Right

Resolve to be thyself, and know that he who finds himself loses his misery.

— Matthew Arnold

At the conclusion of a radio program I was on, the interviewer signed off with a priceless piece of advice: *"Be the person your dog knows you to be."*

Many people report that their relationship with their dog is among the most supportive and unconditionally loving in a lifetime. What is it that we receive from canines that we miss with people? Dogs love us for who we are. They do not have a lot of complicated expectations or demands. They are happy to see us, and show it. They express their affection without restraint and appreciate even a little pat on the head. They are honest, dedicated, and they live joyfully in the moment.

By contrast, we believe things about ourselves that are less than loving and accepting. We judge, criticize, berate, undermine, put ourselves down, and have little patience for our errors. It is no wonder we love our dogs—they love us more than we love ourselves!

I studied with a teacher who consistently saw the good in me and reminded me of my worth and beauty. For many years I came to her with fear, guilt, and unworthiness, and she answered with support, forgiveness, and blessing. Ultimately, I realized that our visions of who I was were so radically different that one of us had to be wrong. I decided I would rather have her be right.

You, too, can be the person your dog knows you to be; Fido may see you more clearly than you see yourself.[19]

Help me know how lovable I am, that I may shine forgiveness into the world.

I accept God's vision of my innocence.

Talk to Mrs. Jones

If you want to gather honey,
don't knock over the beehive.
— Dale Carnegie

"Many of you speak more rudely to your mate than you would to a person on the street," my teacher Hilda noted. "But you should extend *more*, not less, courtesy to someone you are building a life with. The next time you are tempted to mouth off to your partner, stop for a moment and ask yourself, How would I speak to Mrs. Jones at the bank? Then give your mate the same respect."

Somewhere in our cultural programming, many of us picked up the idea that we have license to speak rudely to our partner, family, or those close to us. Even a little examination will show how self-defeating and destructive such a belief is. Our relationships are our primary means of emotional support; we join and bond to empower each other to be strong, powerful, and great. Our primary relationship is the place where we need to give and receive the *most* nourishment and respect. To insult or tear each other down in the family is to undermine the foundation upon which we are cultivating our dreams.

Of course, in an intimate relationship, we must be honest, direct and, when necessary, confrontational. It is possible to communicate anything, including our upsets, without attacking our partner. Report your experience objectively with the intention to heal: "These are the things that I am feeling, and I would like your support in returning to peace." If you harbor any other intention, the communication will fail because it belittles the other person and yourself rather than honoring both of you.

Make your primary relationship a refuge where you can come to be healed and nourished. Use words that invite your partner to join with you, and not separate. When you build your partner up, she or he will do the same for you, and you will live not in a state of fear, but blessing.

Show me how to make a temple of my relationships.
Give me the strength to support my beloved ones with
kindness, and help me to receive the same.

I delight in supporting my loved ones,
and they delight in supporting me.

Thankslіving

Praise the bridge that carried you over.
— George Colman, the Younger

As I look back over my life, I recognize that everything that has ever happened to me has contributed to the person I am now. While I have gone through different professions, living situations, travels, and relationships, I see that each of them bestowed me with a gift. Even the painful or difficult times taught me lessons that make me a better person now. All of it has been a blessing.

It is important that we hold our past in a sense of reverence, along with the people we have known. If we resent our former spouse, employer, or friends, we are tied to the pain and unable to move forward. The hardship of the past will stay with us until we find a way to make it a gift; then it will empower us to move ahead.

Make a list of significant past events and relationships, and next to each entry note the gifts you received from that person or experience. If you are willing to find the good, you will. Assume that everyone who shows up in your life is here to bless you in some way. The other person may not know their role in your awakening, and they may serve you in ways quite unrelated to the reason you thought you interacted with them. Spirit's intentions go far beyond human planning.

Then write a note or letter of gratitude to each person on your list. Thank them for the gifts they brought to your life, and specifically describe how you have grown and improved your life as a result of your interaction with them. Be sure to include those who challenged you. While this writing is for your own illumination, you may send letters to the people when appropriate. By the time you finish your writing, you will be bursting with so much peace and joy that you will wonder how you could have ever thought anyone was your enemy.

Gratitude is the key to happiness; apply it to your past, and you will find friends you never knew you had.

Show me the gifts I have overlooked, and fill my heart with gratitude for all my blessings.

Everyone and everything in my life is a gift from God.

I Am Good Fortune

*I do not seek good fortune. I **am** good fortune.*
— Walt Whitman

On an episode of *Northern Exposure,* the character Shelly received a chain letter telling her that if she mailed the letter on to a friend within three days, she would enjoy unprecedented good luck. Believing the prophecy, she copied the letter and mailed it at the local post office. To Shelly's delight, all manner of good things befell her, and many blessings she desired came true; she felt deeply grateful that the good fortune of the chain letter came her way. A week later when Shelly returned to the post office, the clerk held up her letter and informed her that he did not mail it because she needed more postage. Shelly's jaw dropped when she realized that the letter was not the source of her good luck. She admitted, "I guess we *are* in charge of our own lives."

There is no force outside of you that can determine what happens to you. But there is a very potent force *inside* you that sets the stage for every event you experience. Enlightenment is an inside job. Luck is not a capricious gift that whimsically falls into our lap; it is a force we activate with our thoughts, feelings, attitude, words, and actions.

If you are waiting for your ship to come in, get into the captain's seat and pilot it yourself. If you are waiting for a particular person to come along and make your life wonderful, that person is you. The more you love yourself, the greater your power to draw quality companions. At this very moment, you have everything you need to set into motion a chain of events that will change your life forever.

I claim my power to generate my good.
Thank you, God, for allowing me to co-create miracles with you.

I call all of my good to me now.
It is done unto me as I believe.

Percentages

You can't expect to get the jackpot if you don't put a few nickels in the machine.

— Flip Wilson

"Would you like to sleep with me?" the man in the elevator asked Nancy.

"Excuse me?"

"Would you like to go to bed with me tonight?"

"What makes you think I would want to go to bed with you? I don't even know you!"

"I just thought I'd ask; one out of ten women says yes."

Regardless of the apparent gap in this fellow's integrity, he is onto an important principle: If you keep asking, sooner or later someone is bound to say yes. While this man is apt to hurt himself and others with his use of percentages, you and I can take the same principle and make it work toward the valuable goals that our hearts desire.

If you have a strong and sincere intuition or guidance to accomplish a certain task, somewhere in the universe there is someone who is seeking to help you fulfill it. Many people would come to Hilda's prayer class with intentions of finding homes, jobs, and mates. Hilda would always remind them, "Your need is connected to someone else's; at this very moment someone wants to offer the very thing you seek. Know that the divine connection system is always operating." As a humorous application of this principle, one night Hilda asked everyone who wanted to lose weight to stand up. Then she asked everyone who wanted to gain weight to rise. Then she prayed, "May all the weight these people want to release go to those people who need it."

Growth, change, and achievement take nerve and action. Your vision can and will be accomplished if you keep asking.

I pray for the perseverance to accomplish my goals.
I trust in Your power to provide matching resources to serve my visions as well as others.

My dreams are good, and the universe supports me in attaining them.

Press Out

I want to tell you not to move into that world where you're alone with your self and your mantra and your fitness program or whatever it is that you might use to try to control the world by closing it out...I'm just telling you to live in it, to look at it, to witness it....Take chances, make your own work, take pride in it. Seize the moment.

— Joan Didion, giving a commencement address

While working out at a health club, I was fascinated by how deeply the patrons insulated themselves with buffers to social interaction. One woman was riding an exercise bicycle, listening to a Walkman through earphones, and reading a magazine. In another section, the music was so loud that it was difficult to carry on a normal conversation, and everywhere, television sets were blaring news at a high volume. There was very little incentive, invitation, or possibility to reach out to connect or communicate with others.

While health and fitness are worthy endeavors, we must be careful not to use them to escape from life. Do you medicate your pain with a particular habit? If so, what is it?

In one of my seminars, the participants generated a long list of ways we attempt to escape from our challenges, including drinking, using drugs, smoking, anxious eating, unconscious sex, workaholism, busy-ness, relationship dramas, exercise, watching TV, whirlwind social activities, computer obsession, sports fanaticism, soap operas, romance novels, and religious fanaticism. While many of these activities are innocent when used for joy or play, they can hurt us if we hide in them at the expense of dealing with the issues that we face.

Begin to tell the truth about where you are hurting, and confront your pain. You will gain so much energy, strength, and peace through your fearless quest that you will become a true master. You will find that the discomfort you attempted to escape contains the key to your healing when you face it.

Give me the strength to bring forth my true aliveness.

I am empowered by life.
I master challenges by facing them with love and courage.

The Faithkeeper

Keep your faith in all beautiful things; in the sun when it is hidden, in the Spring when it is gone.

— Roy R. Gilson

I saw Bill Moyers interview Oren Lyon, a Native American whose role in the tribe was "The Faithkeeper." Eloquent, centered, and purposeful, Oren Lyon explained the importance of having one person in the tribe who consistently holds the higher vision. He was designated to be the voice of hope, an inspiration to remember the bigger picture when others forget it.

Each of us needs to be a Faithkeeper. When others around us go into fear or confusion, we serve best by remembering the light and holding peace.

I went to a hospital to visit an infant who had been born with some serious health challenges. As I stood outside the nursery with the child's relatives looking at the baby laden with tubes and bandages, I sensed great worry, fear, and pessimism from the infant's family. In that moment, I realized that my purpose there was to simply remain peaceful; the greatest service I could offer would be to stay calm while others were losing their cool. Without saying a word, I meditated inwardly and affirmed the presence of God, knowing that the child was loved, cared for, and protected by an unseen hand.

I know a woman who was invited to sit meditatively in the room where Middle East peace negotiations were being held. Her role was to pray and hold the vision of unity and healing. We hire people to be responsible for all aspects of important projects. Why not designate someone to fulfill the most important aspect—the remembrance of the presence of God.

The next time someone around you loses their cool, remember to be the Faithkeeper. As long as you remain sane, the situation is assured of healing.

I pray to be a force for faith.

I magnify the presence of God wherever I am, and bring peace to the world.

335

Watch Your Bags

When it comes time to do your own life,
you either perpetuate your childhood or you stand on it and
finally kick it out from under.

— Rosellen Brown

While peering over the edge of the airline counter, I noticed on the agent's keypad a long strip of paper displaying a question in bold letters: **"Are you carrying anything given to you by a stranger?"** The notice reminded the agent to ask each passenger this question, in compliance with stricter federal aviation measures to protect airplanes from terrorism.

As the agent processed my ticket, I realized that the question is a good one for all of us: *Are you carrying anything given to you by a stranger?* Are you unconsciously holding any ideas, beliefs, opinions, morals, judgments, intentions, or world views that you have adopted from others? Learning values from others is natural, but unless they serve you, they are dangerous.

While our parents, teachers, and ministers taught us many valuable lessons, they also passed to us various forms of fear and prejudice. My sixth-grade teacher lived in fear of Communism. When the Russians placed their Sputnik into orbit, Mr. Kraftchick inflicted a long diatribe on our class about how the Soviets could now place nuclear bombs in their satellites and drop them all over America. Since Mr. K. was a wise teacher who ostensibly knew so much more than I did, I accepted his fearful projections, and I became terrified. Although this man was a good teacher in many ways, he did a great disservice to us little children by frightening us with his own insecurity. I adopted his nightmare and began to live in terror of nuclear war. When I later visited Russia, I found warm and openhearted people who had grown up fearing that people like me would drop bombs on them.

If you are in pain or fear, or have difficulty with dysfunctional patterns in a relationship or in financial areas, you may be carrying a bomb in your luggage. While you were unaware at the time you accepted it, you now have the wisdom and power to remove it.

Help me to undo illusions from my mind and heart.
I pray to live in the real world of love.

I believe in the truth of God's presence,
and let all else go.

Don't Take It Personally

I am not a victim of the world I see.
— A Course in Miracles

When I walked into my aviary to feed the parrots one morning, Yogi made mean faces at me and tried to bite me. My heart sank; my first reaction was, "I must have done something wrong to make him dislike me." Yogi kept up this behavior over a period of weeks until I discovered that he had taken up courtship with one of the other birds, and he had gone into a protective mode stemming from his mating instincts. When I realized this, I felt relieved; it was just a genetically dictated "bird thing" and had nothing to do with me.

When someone is unkind or abusive toward you, don't take it personally. Anger is more about the giver than the recipient. If you accept their attack as a statement about you, you will not see clearly, and the situation will be even more muddied. Do not accept their "gift," and you will help them face their own issues.

Cultures, genders, and belief systems have unique properties that are statements about the giver, not the receiver. Just as my bird's aggressive behavior was a bird thing, there are ethnic things, man things, woman things, and religion things. Do not confuse a programmed behavior with a statement about your own value or the person who is speaking.

My friend who had emigrated from Russia was very aggressive, and I often felt intimidated by her. Then I went to Russia and stood in a crowd at a department store. The only way I was able to catch the attention of the clerk was to literally push my way to the front of the mob. That experience gave me an important insight into my friend's programming, and I was able to understand her behavior. No one is mean on purpose. Since love is our nature, anything unlike love is a statement of an individual's history of pain. Unkindness is not an attack, but a call for love.

I pray to see myself as innocent,
along with my brothers and sisters.

Through the eyes of love
I behold only love.

Terminal Improvements

Stop improving yourself and start living.[20]

— Roberta Jean Bryant

As I approached the departure area of an airport undergoing remodeling, I saw a sign that grabbed my attention: *Terminal Improvements.* Although the sign referred to the construction, I was tickled by its double meaning.

Endless self-fixing is a detour from the spiritual path. We can become so obsessed with personal growth that we lose sight of the truth that everything we need is within us and we are good enough just as we are. The path to enlightenment is not one of self-improvement, but *self-discovery.* When we recognize that we are whole, the game shifts from getting something from outside of us, to releasing the splendor within us.

Seminars, books, psychic and astrological readings, trainings, techniques, and practices can be extremely helpful, but they can also be a means to hide from living life where you are. At some point, we must admit that we have amassed all the data we need, and get on with applying what we have learned.

Gandhi affirmed, "My life is my message," and we must aspire to this ideal. First, we talk the talk; then we talk the walk; then we walk the talk; then we walk the walk. Reflect the highest truth simply by living what you know and being what you are.

I am ready to get on with living my destiny.
Help me go beyond words and
teach love through action.

I live the truth I know.

The Man Who Wrote the Book

He that is in me is greater than he that is in the world.
— Jesus Christ

As I was about to present a full-day seminar, I felt quite weary. I had been on a long lecture tour and did not know where I would get the energy to deliver this intensive program. As I entered the seminar room, a man approached me, took my hand, and tearfully told me, "Your book has touched and changed my life. I drove several hundred miles today to meet the man who wrote the book." I was deeply moved by the fellow's sincere appreciation; immediately I felt a wave of energy surge through me, and my fatigue dissolved. Suddenly, the puny, tired person with whom I had identified myself seemed unreal, and the strong and illumined person the fellow referred to came forth. In that moment, I had a choice: I could either be the tired guy or the healer. Fueled by his vision, I chose to identify with my magnificence, and I went on to present a powerful program.

Every moment we are choosing who we will be. No matter how discouraged or lost you feel, within you is the man or woman who wrote the book, or sang the song, or cared for the child, or who embodied your highest potential. Choose in favor of your genius, and you will discover that it is your reality.

Let me remember who I really am,
that I may be at peace with myself and my purpose.

Today I choose to be my highest self and live my magnificence.

Nature Bats Last

Let us permit nature to have its way; she understands her business better than we do.

— Michel de Montaigne

I saw an abandoned tennis court that had been nearly entirely dislodged by grass that had grown through cracks in the surfacing. Of all the demonstrations of the power of nature, I find it most compelling to consider how a tiny blade of grass can undo an entire humanmade structure. Given the slightest opening, nature will work its way out from under oppression and reassert itself.

At every moment, nature is seeking to restore balance and harmony where it has been upset. This is the essence of healing. No matter how we may violate the given order, nature will restore the way it was intended to be. Even though humanity may defile and disrespect the planet, eventually the earth will grow green again. If we are wise, we will cooperate with this process.

It is important that we know what our true nature is, that we may align and be bolstered by it. On the deepest level, we are spiritual beings; that is why nothing material can satisfy us completely. We may have all manner of material comfort and beauty around us, but unless our spiritual self is fed, we remain hungry. Our true nature is wholeness; we cannot be broken into parts and treated as a commodity; we are more than we appear to be. Our true nature is kindness and love; we cannot act or identify with cruelty and feel at peace or have life work.

The Taoist religion is one of the simplest paths to God. It advises, "Just be what you are. You do not need to change yourself to be divine. You are created of spirit, and to be powerful and happy, simply let nature take its course."

Help me remember that I am divine.
Return my birthright of peace to me.

My nature is godly.
I am healed as I express my true self.

Make a Stand

Life is a great big canvas—throw on it all the paint you can.
— Danny Kaye

At a seminar, a man confessed, "I was afraid to tell my friends no, because I feared they would not like me if I did, but then I realized I didn't have any friends because no one knew who I was."

For a long time, I was afraid to tell the truth, for I feared I would be rejected if I did. Then I discovered that I had paid the dear price of intimacy. In my fear that I would be unlovable if people knew who I was, I found that I was unreachable because I was unknown.

No matter what you say or do, there will be people who agree and disagree, those who like you and don't like you. It's unrealistic to expect that everyone is always going to approve of you. The only person whose approval really counts is your own.

I once sent out a newsletter mailing with the tongue-in-cheek return address of "Immaculate *Cohen*ceptions." To my surprise, I received several angry letters, including one from a convent, complaining that I had insulted Catholicism. Since my intention was harmless, I felt unnerved by this reaction, and I voiced my concern at a retreat I was conducting.

A man named Scott offered this comment: "Alan, one of the things I love most about you is your sense of humor; I have found it to be very healing. If you shut down on your creativity because you're afraid of a few reactions, then I must tell you that I will be disappointed in you, probably along with a bunch of other folks."

Suddenly I realized that there is no way I'm going to please everyone. I might as well just be who and what I am, and trust that the universe will support me for my authenticity. As an old tombstone in Texas reads, "*Be what you is, 'cuz if you is what you ain't, you ain't what you is.*"

I pray to know and trust that You created me in wisdom and goodness.

I live from my heart.
Sincerity is my key to success.

Golden Words

The world is divided into two classes of people: the few who make good on their promises and the many who don't; get in Column A and stay there. You'll be valuable wherever you go.

— Robert Townsend

In the film, *Holy Matrimony*, Patricia Arquette plays a huckster named Sonora who follows her husband in order to hide from the law in a Mennonite community. When her husband dies, Sonora is required by religious law to marry his 12-year-old brother, Jeb. Despite his tender age, Jeb has strong values, and he is a wiser man than his brother ever was. After Sonora sneaks off to have an affair with an older man, Jeb challenges her choice, asking her if this man has any integrity. He asks Sonora, "Is his word golden?"

The act of keeping our word is an immeasurable gift. To be in a marital or working relationship with someone whose words you can trust is a precious blessing. And to be such a person is to give your friends the greatest gift of all.

Because we have the power to co-create with God, the words we utter have enormous import. Our words make our life if we speak them with conviction, and they can break us if we let our tongue be guided by foolishness or fear. Take care to speak only what you want to see manifested.

Take care, too, to do what you say you are going to do. To make a promise to others, even to meet them at a particular time, is a sacred act. If you do not keep your promises, you become untrustworthy, and your loved ones will be confused about who you are and what you will do. Do not make promises that you are not sure you can keep. If you've made a promise that you're unable to fulfill, go to the other person quickly and seek to find a new way that will work for both of you.

Be at peace with yourself by being at peace with the words you speak. A golden life begins with golden words.

Your word is perfect, comforting, and trustworthy. May my words be the same.

I empower myself and others by living the words I speak.

Flesh and Spirit

What is born of flesh is flesh,
and what is born of spirit is spirit.
— Jesus Christ

Many on the spiritual path have a difficult time with their family of origin. Nearly all of us grew up with some (or a great deal) of dysfunction, and as we advance on the spiritual path we may feel that our family relationships hold us back from being who we are and living the life we choose. I have seen many different reactions to stifling family-of-origin relationships—from total denial, to numbness, to fearful clinging, to hurt separation, to passive-aggressive hostility, to ongoing conflict. None of these responses work, for they all create only more pain and separation. How, then, are we to deal with our blood families?

Love them, give them the respect they deserve, and live the life you choose. Our primary pain comes not from the life our family lives but from compromising our life to meet their expectations. If you are true to yourself and you live in integrity with your ideals, you will see your family clearly and know how to deal with them.

Our real family is our spiritual family—the people with whom we feel safe, supported, and free to be ourselves. Sometimes our blood family matches our spiritual family, and that is a great blessing. If your spiritual family is elsewhere, then you must be where your true nature is honored. Meanwhile, do your best to bring your family-of-origin relationships into harmony. Pray for your family members, tell them the truth, love and support them where they are without requiring they be otherwise, and do not compromise your well-being for the sake of dysfunction. Honor your family's path, but not at the expense of your own.

Family healings are the most rewarding for, as *A Course in Miracles* tells us, *"the holiest place on earth is where an ancient hatred has become a present love."* Remember that forgiveness is the greatest gift we can give, and continue on your path to the light.

Help me find peace with my family.

I live the life I choose, and I bless my family as they live theirs.

All Taken Care Of

The Lord is my shepherd, I shall not want.
— Psalm 23

In their inspiring book, *The Peace of God Is My One Goal,* Barbara and Robert Varley recounted many experiences in which they put *A Course in Miracles* into action and proved that faith works.

While traveling across the country offering seminars, the couple needed a new van. They went into a local auto dealership and found a vehicle they liked, but the salesman quoted a price beyond what they felt they could afford. When the Varleys meditated on it, however, their guidance was to buy the van and not even bargain with the salesman. They agreed to the asking price, and the salesman began to weep. "It has been a very slow season, and I did not know how I would provide for my family for Christmas," he told them. "This sale will enable me to buy my children some decent presents." Over the next few months, the income from the Varleys' seminars, on a donation basis, swelled significantly, and the van was paid off in short time. Then their income subsided to its previous level.

The universe provides for all our needs if we trust it. We do not have to fight for our good or struggle with others over a seemingly limited supply. The God that created countless stars and fathomless seas is able to create abundance for us to the extent we require it. Our job is to listen to our guidance and trust.

Search your mind for thoughts of lack, and offset them with thoughts of abundance. Practice living as if you always have enough of what you need, and you will manifest great supply. Some people have bank checks printed with the motto, *"God is my source."* Turn to the invisible hand of grace, and you shall see it made visible.

Help me to remember that
You are the source of all my good.

I allow God to provide me with an abundant life.

Withholding Tax

When we're hungry, love will keep us alive.
— from the song, "Love Will Keep Us Alive," by *The Eagles*

Would you like more love in your life? Do you long to be closer to other people? Is your heart yearning for more intimacy and safety? If so, here is a practice that will ensure all of these goals if you put its principles into action.

Begin to notice the ways you are withholding love from others. Such an introspection requires courage and honesty, for we are prone to avoid facing or admitting our resistance to love. If you can do it, you will be rewarded far beyond any fear you have to walk through in order to get there.

Withholding love is made visible through the symbols we attach to love. Are you withholding money from anyone, refusing to pay them, diminishing the amount you will pay, or delaying payment to get back at them for something they did that hurt you? Usually divorce-settlement fights over children or assets have nothing to do with the objects, which become pawns in the ego's game to withhold love to punish. Do you withhold sex from your partner? Do you withhold the completion of your part of an agreement? Do you withhold your presence by making yourself so busy that you cannot be there in quality relationships? Are you consistently late? Do you withhold sharing your feelings for fear of being hurt? Do you withhold generous words of praise when someone deserves them?

While the ego perceives that withholding these things is protecting us, it only hurts us. Whenever you withhold love, you are the one who loses. In our efforts to punish another, we punish ourselves. In attempting to maintain worldly security, we lose our spiritual security. Only giving love can keep us secure. Love is the real food of our soul; the way we get more is by giving it away. Begin to discover where you are holding back from giving what would heal you; there you will find the doorway to the peace you seek.

Show me where and how I can love more.

I give all the love I would receive.
The more I love, the happier I am.

Just Sit There

All that is necessary to break the spell of inertia and frustration is this: Act as if it were impossible to fail. That is the talisman, the formula, the command of right-about-face which turns us from failure toward success.
— Dorothea Brande

Rev. Diane Winter has established a unique prison ministry in which she spends most of her time teaching spiritual classes, counseling, and assisting inmates before and after their release. When I asked Diane how she got started, she told me, "It wasn't easy. I went to the administrator's office and told him that I wanted to teach a class on spiritual growth. He told me I had to go to another city two hours away and get permission from his three supervisors. Then he told me, 'I will think about it.' I knew he was just trying to put me off, and I made an appointment to meet with him again. Then he forgot about me and never showed up. But I wasn't about to quit. His secretary refused to make another appointment for me, so I decided I would just go to his office and sit there until I could see him. If I had to sit there every day, all day, I would. But I didn't have to; that day he saw me and gave me permission. I later learned that he and the other administrators made bets on how long I would last; the longest estimate was three months. That was five years ago. These have been the five most rewarding years of my life."

Sometimes we need such depth of determination to accomplish our dream. We have to be willing to sit there every day, all day, until we get results. Our will to succeed must be stronger than someone else's will to put us off.

In light of the success, service, and joy that Diane has achieved, her initial efforts seem minor in comparison. If you feel discouraged or put off, remember the bigger picture, and paint it as *you* choose.

I pray to be sufficiently dedicated to my goals that I fulfill my dreams.

I can do anything I set my mind and heart to do.

Christmas Gold

It is in your power to make this season holy,
for it is in your power to make the time of Christ be now.
— A Course in Miracles

There is much more to the Christmas season than meets the eye. This is the time of year when the human race publicly acknowledges the presence of divinity. It is a time when angels are accepted as real, and people sing openly in the streets. It is a time when we are urged to reach beyond self-involvement and bring joy to others. It is a time when we take a respite from our worldly activities to remember the importance of friendship, family, and love.

For many, the Christmas season is a challenging time. The call to love brings forth everything unlike love, and some of us find ourselves feeling stressed or depressed. We face unresolved family issues, and our yearning to be with a special person at a special time is sometimes met with frustration or disappointment. We face unwanted obligations to give to certain people or be present at certain gatherings, and the general level of rush, stress, and conflict does not decrease in the spirit of Christmas, but only escalates in the name of fear.

Consider the Christmas season an invitation to master love, an opportunity to practice the presence of Christ in the face of vast materialism and insanity. To love in a world of love is ideal, but to love in the face of illusion is mastery. Heightened materialism during the season is the ego's response to the increased spiritual energy on the planet. Rather than surrender to love, the ego tries to distract us from Spirit by dangling gold before us. But the real gold is within. You are the gold, and the game is to find the gold in your brothers and sisters.

This year, honor the Christ in you by remaining at peace. If you never send one Christmas card, show up at one party, or give one present, but remain in love, you will give the greatest gift of all. As you go through your Christmas activities, be kind. That is all that Jesus would care about.

Help me to remember the reason for Christmas.
I pray to keep my heart open.

I honor Christ by living His peace.

God Is My Agent

I do not have to worry about what to say or what to do,
for He who sent me will direct me.
— A Course in Miracles

When I self-published *The Dragon Doesn't Live Here Anymore,* I went to New York with $5,000 of borrowed money and made a deal with a printer. As I rose to leave his office, he remarked, "You know, they say you don't make any money until your third book." His words took me by surprise; I felt as if he was trying to dump a load of manure on my dream. Hardly thinking, these words came out of my mouth: "That's what they may say, but what they may not know is that my agent is God."

The printer looked at me, puzzled, and I went on my way. The book became an instant success, my investment was returned, and it went on to be quite profitable even long before my second book was published.

When your work proceeds from Spirit, the universe will take care of you. The laws of right livelihood far supersede the norms and expectations of those who are in business simply to make money. *Don't work for a living; create for a life.* If your idea or product is the result of prayer, intention, and a dedication to true service, you will prosper in miraculous ways. *"The Lord is my Shepherd; I shall not want."*

You do not need to fight to champion your cause; instead, let God open the doors for you. This does not mean that you do nothing and sit around and wait for the money to pour in. If a result is to come through your efforts, Spirit will tell you what to do. You do not need to fret, struggle, scheme, and sweat for your good. The same God that gave you the idea will help it succeed.

I turn my work, my relationships, and my life over to You to guide, knowing that Your love and wisdom will prosper me in wondrous ways.

I take care of God's business, and God takes care of mine.

348

Goods for Guns

The nations shall beat their swords into plowshares.
— Isaiah 2:4

An amazing phenomenon is sweeping the country. In many cities, police departments are offering valuable donated merchandise in exchange for street guns. Many thousands of people have traded in dangerous weapons for tickets to sporting events, stereo equipment, and discount coupons on valued commodities. On a news program, I saw a huge pile of guns that had been voluntarily turned in.

The Goods for Guns program is built on a key principle: Bad habits do not leave unless we have something more positive with which to replace them. If you want to lose weight, it is not enough to just despise your excess weight; it is only when you embrace a vision of yourself at your ideal weight that you gain the leverage to shed the unwanted pounds. If you want to take a dangerous object out of the hand of a child, he will cry if you yank it away. Give him another toy that he enjoys, and he will not miss the first one.

The mind needs something to chew on, and it is just as willing to chew on dog food as fine cuisine. If you are plagued by negative or self-destructive thinking, you will not succeed by trying to simply stop your mind; you must fill it with something more productive. When the mind begins to worry or chatter with self-criticism or doubt, immediately substitute thoughts that will take you where you want to go, such as "Peace, Be still, I walk in love," or "God is the source of all supply." If you are vigilant and diligent, eventually the constructive thinking will take root, and you will automatically think *with* truth, not against it.

I open myself to positive living and feed my mind and heart with healing thoughts and visions.

The word of God is my strength.

Soul Required

It's all about soul.
— from the song, "All About Soul," by Billy Joel

In a parable, Jesus told:

> *The land of a rich man brought forth plentifully; and he thought to himself, "What shall I do, for I have nowhere to store my crops?" And he said, "I will do this: I will pull down my barns, and build larger ones; and there I will store all my grain and my goods. And I will say to my soul, 'Soul, you have ample goods laid up for many years; take your ease, eat, drink, be merry.'" But God said to him, "Fool! This night your soul is required of you; and the things you have prepared, whose will they be?" So is he who lays up treasure for himself, and is not rich toward God.* (Luke 12:17–21)

While a traditional reading of this parable might interpret "your soul is required" as passing from this world, there is a practical lesson here for enrichment of daily living. At any given moment, our soul is required. We must bring forth the riches of our spirit to be fully present and alive in our relationships, career, and spiritual path. If we become preoccupied with material pursuits, worldly worries, or self-protection, we dampen the light of our soul, and miss the true joy of living.

Jesus said, "You are the light of the world. Do not cover your light with a basket." The light is our true nature. The basket is the mountain of distractions we generate when we invest our energy in building a kingdom on earth (the outer world) instead of heaven, the true inner life.

At every moment, our soul is required—not for death, but for greater life.

I want to live in the kingdom today.
Help me remember that my only true joy is in spiritual aliveness.

Clothed in majesty, I walk in the glory of my spiritual identity.

I Forgot

The past is over; it can touch me not.
— A Course in Miracles

An old and sour priest in the Philippines heard of a woman who was reputed to speak to Jesus daily. In an effort to discredit Rosa, he asked her, "Do you really speak to Jesus?"

"I do," she answered in a matter-of-fact way.

"Then the next time you talk to him, would you ask him what was the sin that I committed when I was a young man in the seminary?"

"Come back in one week, and I will have your answer," Rosa told him. The priest left smugly, knowing that Rosa would be unable to answer and be exposed as a fraud.

A week later the priest returned and asked her, "Did you talk to Jesus?"

"I did."

"And did you ask him how I sinned in the seminary?"

"I did."

"And what did he tell you?"

"He said, 'I forgot.'"

Real forgiveness is the complete and utter letting go of past memories that hurt. What the world calls forgiveness is a trick of the mind. We make "sin" real in our mind, and then proclaim to overlook it. But any memory of the act as an offense ensures continued subconscious pain and separation. We bury the hatchet, but then we remember where we buried it.

I know a couple who have been happily married for many years. I asked them, "What is the secret of your successful relationship?" The wife laughed and answered, "Just get over it! We can't afford to hold on to the past. We just keep letting go and coming fully into the present moment with each other."

We are told to "forgive and forget." They are one in the same.

Help me to release the pain I have carried, and to live in the present moment where love abides.

I renounce the past and come fully into the love here now.

Beyond Coincidence

A coincidence is a miracle in which God wishes to remain anonymous.

— Dr. Gerald Jampolsky

"You may have noticed that the airplane didn't land," the pilot announced to the passengers. Of course they did. The plane came within a few feet of touching down on the Chicago runway and lifted off again. "That is because another plane was on the runway and there wasn't room for both of us." Good thinking. "We'll circle around and land again in a few minutes." During that time, my friend Charley struck up a conversation with the couple sitting across the aisle. When John and Bari mentioned that they had just bought land in Hawaii, Charley told them that he and I were about to conduct a seminar there. Charley told them about my book and wished them well. At home in Boulder, John and Bari found my book, signed up for the seminar, discovered they had just enough frequent-flyer miles to make the trip, attended the program, had their lives change immensely, and moved to their property two miles from my home.

How marvelously Spirit orchestrates life! Who put Charley, John, and Bari next to each other on the aircraft? Why did that particular airplane have to abort its landing? How did their frequent-flyer award work out perfectly? How does it all come together? Ah, the sweet mystery of God! If anyone sat down to try to maneuver the miraculous meetings and events in a lifetime, he or she would be boggled in an instant. Meanwhile, every day a billion synchronicities keep the great cogs and wheels of the universe running flawlessly.

Great Spirit, I bow before the mystery of Your wisdom. I quit trying to manipulate life, and trust You to keep me in my right place at the right time, meeting the right people for the right purpose. Thank You for Your exquisite love.

I rejoice in the loving wisdom of God in my life.

Look in My Eyes

The countenance is the portrait of the soul, and the eyes mark its intentions.

— Cicero

While traveling in the West, Cheeah found a community and friends with whom she resonated deeply. After meditating on this feeling, she recognized that she was being guided by Spirit to move there and begin a new life. When Cheeah told her parents, friends, and business clients about her decision, many challenged her. Some told her she was crazy. Rather than argue with her critics, Cheeah simply told them, "Look in my eyes."

The eyes never lie; they are indeed the windows of our soul. Your eyes speak for you in ways that words cannot. People who do not love or believe in themselves have a hard time looking others in the eye because they are afraid to look themselves in the eye. They fear that if they looked upon themselves directly, they would find an ugly, evil, or punishable person. This is not so. If you look at yourself or another long enough, you will pierce through the outer veils of fear and scattered thoughts and arrive at the jewel of the inner being.

Practice connecting with the eyes of others. You do not have to engage in a weighty staring contest; simply give others your full attention and eye contact. In this way, you will invite them to do the same, and your communication will deepen immensely.

We keep enemies by not looking at them, and we make friends by showing others who we are. Let your eyes reveal the riches of your soul.

Help me to see myself clearly and to be unafraid to show others who I really am.

I see clearly through the eyes of God, which are my own.

Traveling Light

To stand up, to leave ***everything*** *behind—to say "Yes!"*
— Dag Hammarskjöld

Peace Pilgrim[21] was a woman of great faith who changed the world in a unique way. At the age of 45, she let go of her history and set out to walk for peace, keeping no possessions except a toothbrush, a pencil and pad, and the clothes she wore, including a blue tunic bearing the large white letters, *Peace Pilgrim.* She vowed that she would not eat unless offered food, she would seek no lodging unless it was given, and she would give love to everyone she met. Peace Pilgrim often slept under bridges and stood in the rain. After a while, she became a legend, and when she entered a city, the media would interview her and she would be asked to speak to school and civic groups.

Peace Pilgrim's message of kindness and compassion was compelling, and without creating any organization or charging any fees for her services, she inspired many thousands of people. Before her death, she walked over 30,000 miles. I saw a video of a television interview with Peace Pilgrim, and her eyes were bright, joyful, and among the clearest I have ever seen. While she had hardly any physical means, she was wealthy beyond measure.

How much stuff do you actually need? Do the things you have make you happy, or are they weights on your soul? If you were promised great peace and freedom by lightening up on your possessions, would you do it?

Our possessions are valuable inasmuch as they bring us joy or serve our spiritual growth. There is nothing wrong with having things, but if the things bring you down, you cannot afford them. Consider the things in your life that bring you closer to God and the things that move you away from Spirit. Then go about the business of blessing what heals you and releasing what binds you.

Teach me how to live in this world.
Give me the strength to travel lightly.

I use what I need and release all else.

Let's Dig Here

And a little child shall lead them.

— Isaiah 11:16

One morning Jeanine's eight-year-old son informed her, "Last night in a dream, I found a whole dinosaur under the earth and we dug it up. I know where it is; will you take me there?"

"Maybe next summer," Mom tried to put him off. But when David kept asking her to take him to the site he described, Jeanine decided this would be a good opportunity to take a family trip, and agreed. David was elated, hoping he might someday meet world-famous paleontologist Mark Thurston. When Jeanine, David, and his younger brother arrived at the state park, David pointed, "It's over there."

The family trekked to the area, and to assuage David's eagerness, they began to dig. Before long, one of them found an unusual bone, then another, then another. Jeanine took the bones to the University of Idaho, where a scientist confirmed that these were indeed the bones of a dinosaur. The professor showed the bones to none other than Mark Thurston, who just happened to be visiting the college, and a team was dispatched to investigate. To everyone's astonishment, they unearthed the skeleton of an entire dinosaur and made history by finding the first fully intact *Albertasaurus*.

After the find, Thurston told David, "You come see me when you're ready for college; I'll put you to work for me." Jeanine sent me several newspaper clippings and told me that Disney Studios had approached her to do a feature on the story.

We must pay attention to our dreams—not just our sleeping dreams, but the visions and insights that touch us in our waking hours. Spirit is always trying to communicate with us, offering us wisdom to bring us the happiness and success we desire. Our role is to keep our antennae up and trust our guidance.

I pray to be an open channel to
receive Your loving messages.

Spirit is using me to do great things.

Well Adjusted

When we allow ourselves to feel our feelings,
what should be intolerable becomes intolerable.
— Kenny Loggins

In an experiment, scientists placed a group of frogs in a tub of water and heated the water. As the water became hot quickly, the frogs jumped out. In another experiment, the scientists put frogs in a similar tub and increased the heat by a few degrees each day. Daily, the frogs adapted and stayed in the pond until they died. Through gradually adjusting to an unnatural environment, they lost their sensitivity to pain and paid a dear price. This phenomenon is called "drift."

We consider it admirable to be well adjusted, but the real question is: "Well adjusted to *what*?" If you are well adjusted to pain, conflict, and poverty thinking, you are not well adjusted at all. If, however, you are well adjusted to listening to your inner voice and acting on it, you are well adjusted, indeed.

We drift spiritually when we accept things that hurt us for so long that we lose our ability to feel pain. While pain is not our natural state or our destiny, and we are certainly not meant to live in pain, pain is the signal that we must make a change. We cannot afford to lose our ability to hear that signal.

To avoid drift, begin to tell the truth about your experience. If you let yourself feel your feelings, you will discover valuable messages that will guide you to be in your right place with the right people at the right time. Many people have told me they had a bad intuition about being in a relationship with someone or entering into a particular business venture, but they overrode their gut feelings and regretted it later. Your body will speak to you. Your gut may say, *"Yes!"* or *"Not for you,"* and it is up to you to hear and act on the voice of love and wisdom within you; it is your best friend.

Show me the way to my good.
Help me hear Your guidance and act on it.

My heart always knows.

Cash Flow

Do what you love and the money will follow.

— Marsha Sinetar[22]

"I had a well-paying job, but I couldn't pay my bills," Cindy told me. "I didn't understand how I could be making so much money and not make ends meet. Then I realized that the only thing I liked about the job was the salary. I did not enjoy going to work, and I daydreamed about all kinds of other things that were more fulfilling to me. Suddenly, I realized that my money problems were tied to my levels of integrity and joy. My internal energy was clogged by being in a place I did not love, and so the external current of abundance and energy, represented by my cash flow, was also obstructed. I decided to follow my heart and trust Spirit to take care of me. I quit my job and immediately became happier. I haven't had a cash-flow problem since I quit."

What is happening in your financial world is a reflection of what is happening in your consciousness. If you are in a state of joy, celebration, and the awareness that you live in an abundant universe, you will manifest those conditions. If you feel internally plugged up, empty, and undersupported, you will see those energies mirrored in your checkbook.

The key to abundance is to get your priorities in order. Prosperity begins with a state of mind, not a bankbook figure. When I began to write, I did so out of joy and delight; making money was not my goal. My readers wanted to tap into that consciousness, and more money flowed to me. Then I generated higher expenses and began to think about what I could do to make more money. Immediately, my creativity jammed up, and the money scene stagnated. Then I remembered how I began; I retraced my steps to my initial motif of writing for fulfillment and service, and the money flow increased. It is a poor idea to make money for money's sake, and a great idea to ask, "What would I love to do?" and "How can I serve?"

Forget about your bankbook balance, and return to balance with the universe; the bankbook will come along well enough.

Help me remember that all the riches of the universe are within me.

I live from love, and the universe responds instantly and abundantly.

Enough of a Reason

To love oneself is the beginning of a lifelong romance.
— Oscar Wilde

My friend Bette was in conflict over turning on her Christmas tree lights. "I usually don't turn on the tree lights unless I have company," Bette told me. "One night I was alone, and I felt like looking at the lights. I thought that it would be foolish and wasteful to turn them all on just for myself. Then I realized that *I* was enough of a reason. I put on the lights and enjoyed one of the most meaningful Christmas-season evenings I can remember."

Do you realize that *you* are enough of a reason to create something beautiful around you? As my friends Jon-Marc and Anastasia were planning their wedding, they learned an important lesson in self-honoring. "When we considered the cost of flowers, our initial reaction was, 'That's beyond our budget,'" they told me. "Then we looked at each other and said, 'We and our wedding are worth the flowers!' The floral arrays turned out to be one of the most meaningful aspects of our celebration."

A bumper sticker affirms, *"I do not need an excuse to experience joy."* We may feel that we need to justify doing something wonderful for ourselves. We declare, "I have worked hard," or "I haven't done anything for myself in a while," or we may create an illness that requires us to rest and play in order to heal. But we have the power to simply say, "I would love to do this, and so I will." We do not need to rationalize, explain, or defend our self-nurturing to anyone. If an activity brings us peace and delight, that is reason enough.

Help me remember that my nature is love, and my birthright is happiness.

Life is my reason for celebration!

H.A.L.T.

Many fears are born of fatigue and loneliness.
— Max Ehrmann, *Desiderata*

Twelve-step recovery programs[23] have a valuable acronym to help during challenging times: *Stop and nourish yourself when you are Hungry, Angry, Lonely, or Tired (H.A.L.T.).* When we start to run on empty, we must heed the internal sensor that reminds us to take care of our needs; indeed, we are ineffective to ourselves and others unless we are fed physically, emotionally, and spiritually.

I went through a period when I would become very irritable around 11 o'clock each morning. Unfortunately, I took out my vexation on my secretary; every day at that time I would become upset with her for a different reason. Finally, I discovered that my upset had nothing to do with her; my blood sugar had plummeted. I was not eating breakfast, and by that time of day, my energy level crashed. I began to eat a proper breakfast, and it was amazing how the quality of her work improved.

If you've been around young children when they're tired, you know that they become cranky about everything. No matter what you say or do, it's not good enough. Finally, the only reasonable response is, "I think you need a nap." Even as adults, we are prone to irrational irritability when we're overtired. At that point, it's wise to step back and say, "I need to rest." You will not be effective until you recharge your batteries.

When we act out of loneliness, we cause more problems than we solve. Loneliness is not a valid reason to have sex or create a relationship. When you feel lonely, instead of trying to find a fix to fill yourself, reach out to a friend and communicate. Acknowledge that you feel lonely, and look the feeling squarely in the eye. As you examine the course of events and feelings that led to the loneliness, you will find healthy ways out of it.

Become a healthy parent to yourself. Give yourself the nurturing you need, and you will be able to be there for others.

Help me to love myself enough to take care of myself.

I feed my spirit.
I give life because I am whole.

Let Your Dreams Come Through

Practical people would be more practical if they would take a little more time for dreaming.

— J.P. McEvoy

In our society, we place a high value on getting things done, but we often overlook where the ideas for things come from. For every great invention, piece of drama, music, art, medical breakthrough, or social innovation, there was a person who dreamed a dream. Descartes, considered the father of modern science, came upon the scientific method in a vision he had under a high fever. President Kennedy envisioned a Peace Corps and established the country's goal to put a man on the moon by the end of the 1960s. The great Egyptian statesman Anwar Sadat declared, "You're not a realist unless you believe in miracles."

Visioning is as important as doing, perhaps more so. Sitting quietly for 20 minutes a day and letting your mind play with possibilities will net you far greater results than 8 hours of work without a vision behind it. While it is fruitless to fantasize without also working to put your dreams into action, the process of fantasizing gives space and breadth for your mind to explore realms that you would not touch if you simply followed the rational thought process. Then when you act, you will be inspired and guided by ideas that proceed from the divine wisdom within you.

Psychologist Patricia Sun suggests that "children should not be punished for daydreaming in school; to the contrary, they would be happier and far more effective students if a period of time was set aside each day specifically for daydreaming."

Give yourself permission to surf on the sea of imagination. Visualize and record your most inspiring and outrageous thoughts. Choose the most exciting ones, and then set about the business of letting your dreams come through.

Show me the value of my dreams.
I pray to follow my visions until they are a reality.

I trust my dreams enough to bring them to life.

The Light Has Come

Christ's eyes are open, and He will look on whatever you see with love if you accept His vision as yours.

— A Course in Miracles

Today is a precious and holy day on Planet Earth. It is a day when the world calls a halt to insanity and acknowledges the presence of divinity. It is a day of joy and appreciation and celebration. It is a day to be happy.

The birth of the Christ as a human being bears tremendous metaphysical import. It means that humanity is ready to accept its own divinity. Jesus brought God to Earth; he discovered his divine identity, he had the courage to live it, and the world has never been the same.

The image of Christ being born in a manger symbolizes that God comes forth in a place of humility. Spirit seeks not fanfare, human riches, or accolades, but the simplicity of an open heart.

The most important message of Christmas is that the Christ is born in you, through you, as you. When interpreting a dream, we must recognize ourselves as all the characters; the same is true for events that occur in the outer dream we call life. The birth of Christ is the emergence of a new consciousness of your own holiness.

Today is your birthday, and every day is Christmas. Thank God that you have remembered your divine nature. Throw off the cloak of smallness, and claim the truth about you: *You are an expression of a perfect God, and everything God is, you are.* You are the holy one. Jesus seeks not our worship, but our equality. He is our elder brother who came to remind us who we really are. We are one with the son of God.

Thank You for bringing Jesus to life, that I may walk the path of divinity with him.

Christ is born in me today.

God Is in Charge

Better to rely on one powerful king than on many little princes.

— Jean de La Fontaine

After my apartment tenant left on short notice, I was not having success in finding a suitable replacement. Several prospective tenants answered my ad, but I did not feel 100 percent good about any of them. When the last day of the month came, I worried that I would have no tenant for the next month. That day, I received a call from an old friend who had moved back into town and wanted a place to live. She moved in the next day, and there was no loss at all, with a perfect continuity of right tenancy and a steady flow of income.

While it appears that we must depend on ourselves and others to make everything turn out right, in the long run God is in charge. The people we deal with are simply agents of the King, and at any moment the King can issue orders to make things turn out in our favor.

For a long time, I believed that I had to manipulate people and influence individuals in positions of power to get what I wanted. Now I recognize that it is not people I need to impress; I just need to remember the presence of God as the Source.

Although the world would have us believe in separation, there is one power behind the scenes. If you are not having success through the human channels, go directly to the Source through prayer, affirmation, positive thinking, speaking, and acting. Your relationship with Spirit is the key factor in any situation.

Source of all good, walk with me today.
Help me to lift my eyes above people and discover
Your hand in all.

I walk forward in trust and confidence.
God is my Source.

Just Show Up

Do whatever comes your way to do as well as you can. Think as little as possible about yourself and as much as possible about other people...put a good deal of thought into the happiness that you are able to give.

— Eleanor Roosevelt

Shortly after my mother passed away, I was invited to present a seminar in Philadelphia. At the time, my fee was 50 percent of the income, with a minimum of $500. Since this was a small group, I quoted a flat rate of $500. When I received a flyer for the event, I saw that the ticket price had been set at $25, rather then the usual $15.

That's too high! I thought. No one will come at that price. As I dialed the sponsor's number, however, an inner voice stopped me, advising, "Don't try to boss the finances; just let it be." When the sponsor later told me that 50 people had signed up for the program, I wondered if I had made a mistake in asking only for the base fee rather than the percentage. A week later, 75 people had registered; now I regretted not negotiating my regular deal. I was tempted to ask the sponsor if she would be willing to go 50-50, but once again the inner voice said, "Let it be. Your job is to show up, offer love and healing to everyone, and let Spirit handle the finances."

The night of the seminar, I watched in awe as 135 people filed into the room. Again, I had to overcome my temptation to regret or renegotiate. When the time came for the sponsor to write me a check, she told me, "Since we had such a good turnout, I think it's only fair that we go 50-50 on the profit," and she wrote me a check for $1,100, the highest income I had earned to that date. The next day, I received my mom's final doctor bill for...$1,100!

In spite of all the meandering of my mind and emotions, Spirit was running that event all the while. Spirit knew how much to charge and who to send. The only voice worth hearing was the one that advised me to just show up and give love.

I pray to remember my true purpose as a giver of peace and healing.

**I am here to be a blessing.
I trust Spirit to handle the details.**

Primed

I fairly sizzle with zeal and enthusiasm and do the things that ought to be done by me.
— Unity co-founder Charles Fillmore, in his 94th year

"You are in remarkably good health for a man of 60," the doctor told Mr. Griggs as he completed his physical. "What, may I ask, did your father die of?"

"My father is alive and well," answered Mr. Griggs. "He's 84, and quite vital."

"That's wonderful," remarked the doctor. "How about your grandfather? What was his cause of death?"

"My grandfather is also alive; he's 106 years old, in fine health, and he just got married."

"Married?" the doctor asked, stunned. "Why would a 106-year-old man want to get married?"

"Did I say he *wanted* to get married?"

Experts from mystical yogis to holistic scientists tell us that a natural human lifespan was intended to be 120. Most human beings do not live that long because we live in unnatural ways—eating tainted foods, breathing polluted air, living under great stress, and thinking small thoughts. Were we to purify our environment, diets, lifestyles, and attitudes, we would nearly double the lifespan we have come to expect.

This means that the ages of 60 to 80 should be our prime. Age is a state of mind, and at any moment you can choose what state you will live in. Satchel Paige asked, "How old would you be if you didn't know how old you are?"

Our culture instills heavy programming about what people at various ages can and cannot do. All of this is but a belief system that is real if you subscribe to it and meaningless if you do not. Live from your spirit, and age means nothing.

I pray to move beyond concepts of years and fears. Help me remember that I am bigger than any concept of time and age.

I am eternally young, free, and whole.

Toxic Thoughts

Only by self-respect will you compel others to respect you.
— Fyodor Dostoevsky

"Hey, Samantha, there's a pig out here!" I called to my office manager.

"Watch for its mother, the dog."

"What?"

"Our neighbors found the pig in a field just after its birth. The only animal role model it had was the dog. The pig thinks the dog is its mother; he follows her around everywhere." As she spoke, a big black dog emerged from the yard. Immediately, the pig nuzzled up to it and followed it home.

Our predicament is not unlike the pig's. We have accepted an identity unlike what we are. We are divine beings, and we think we are limited. We are whole, and we define ourselves by our parts. We are spiritual beings, and we act as if we are bodies.

Toxic relationships are the subject of much discussion. Books, talk shows, and therapy sessions are buzzing with references to toxic parents, toxic children, and toxic partners. The notion is that some people are just unhealthy to be around, and we should avoid them.

Wise, to be sure, but there is more. *A Course in Miracles* reminds us that "I am responsible for what I see" and "I am affected only by my thoughts." Behind all situations in the outer world, our thoughts determine our experience. Our real work is to see through the eyes of love, not fear.

We are not required to stay in abusive situations. The most powerful place to begin extricating ourselves from abuse is in our own mind. Everyone we encounter mirrors something we believe about who we are and what we deserve. Know the good you merit, and you will attract people that honor, not hurt you. If we can learn to love ourselves enough, the thought of blaming anyone else for our pain will be as foreign to us as a pig thinking it is a dog.

Help me to create a world that mirrors the love I deserve.

I am as God created me. I remember who I am. I deserve infinite love.

365

Pushing the Envelope

The darkest hour is just before the dawn.
— Anonymous

The most powerful way to overcome fear is to make friends with it. Instead of labeling fear as your enemy, recognize that it is bringing you a gift. Whenever you feel afraid, you are approaching the edge of your perceived safety zone. But your "safety zone" is just a tiny portion of the world that is available to you. *A Course in Miracles* asks us to remember, "I am in danger nowhere in the universe." If you never tested your limits, you would never grow. The ego, intent on keeping you small, fixed, and miserable, shrieks, "You must not step across this line!" What the ego does not tell you is that on the other side of the line awaits freedom, not death.

The presence of fear means that you are pressing against the invisible membrane that smallness warns you not to pass. Be grateful that you have come to this point and have not stayed bound in the little world of inadequacy.

A time of hardship or darkness is an initiation. You are being tested and strengthened to move ahead to a new level: The blackest night gives way to the brightest day. As I look back on my times of great challenge, I recognize that they were soon followed by significant growth. If you're going through such a time, hang in there. Instead of cursing your situation, bless it as a harbinger of the dawn. You are not being punished; you are really getting somewhere. The world is not unfair; it would be unfair if it let you live in fear. You are not being crushed; you are being squeezed through the birth canal. The flip side of every death is a new life. Claim the presence of good, and your transition will be much easier. Thank God for the opportunity to dump fear and walk in the light you deserve.

Help me to find the gift in my challenges.

All experiences strengthen me as I grow into the light.

The Beginning Is Near

Don't worry about the world coming to an end today.
It's already tomorrow in Australia.
— Charles Schultz

Since the beginning of time, people have worried about the end of the world. Every generation has had its share of gloomy prophets, and every generation has believed its plight was the worst. Yet, we are still here, and somehow humanity keeps surviving and growing in consciousness.

Life on earth is always changing, and it is always improving. Something is always dying, but something is always being born. To fearfully protect yourself today from danger tomorrow is to miss the beauty here now. Live fully today, and you will be taken care of tomorrow.

As we approach the new year, take stock of the last year. What did you set out to do this year? Have you been true to your goals and yourself? What gifts and awakenings did you receive that you did not plan on? How have you been challenged, and have you found a way to turn your challenges into blessings?

Greet the new year with a sense of joyful anticipation. No matter what has happened this year, you have the power to create your next year as you choose. You are not the same person who started this year. You are wiser, deeper, and richer for your experiences. You will take your knowledge and build on it to make a new year unlike any you have lived before.

Devote this new year to gratitude, blessing, and celebration. Write down what you would like to leave behind and what you would like to take with you. Honor those who have loved and supported you this year by thanking them in your heart and with your words. Do you realize how much grace you have received and how loved you are?

Determine that the next year will be the best one ever. It will be what you want it to be, so aim high. You deserve the very best that life has to offer, because you *are* the very best.

Thank you for all the gifts and blessings of this year.
Walk with me into the new year, and help me
find Your love everywhere I go.

I walk in love. My future is blessed by God.

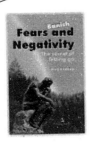

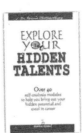